PHILIP'S

MADRID

ARCHITECTURE · HISTORY · ART

PHILIP'S

MADRID

ARCHITECTURE · HISTORY · ART

MICHAEL JACOBS

PHOTOGRAPHY BY JAMES STRACHAN

GEORGE
PHILIP

Author's dedication
To Chata, Pepe and 'Miguelito'

Photographer's dedication
To my Mother, for all her love and support

TITLE PAGE *Madrid seen from the top of the Torre de España, looking towards the church of Las Comendadoras.*

The pictures on the following pages are reproduced by kind permission of the
Bridgeman Art Library: 44, 109, 139 and 170.

Acknowledgement is due to the following for kindly giving permission
to reproduce from copyright material:
Random Century Group: Luis Buñuel, *My Last Breath*, (transl. Abigail Israel),
Jonathan Cape, 1984.

First published by George Philip Limited,
59 Grosvenor Street, London W1X 9DA

British Library Cataloguing in Publication Data

Jacobs, Michael
    Madrid: Architecture, History, Art
    I. Title
    914.64104

ISBN 0-540-01263-7

Maps John Gilkes
Appendices Ian Chilvers
Page design Kathy Gummer
Typeset by Keyspools Limited, Golborne, Lancashire
Printed in Italy

Contents

Preface and
Acknowledgements

....

R ichard Ford, writing in 1845, misled generations of travellers by
saying that the 'more Madrid is known the less it will be liked'. The
intention of this book is to show that the very opposite is true, and
that those who come here with an open mind will encounter one of Europe's
most exhilarating capitals and a wealth of cultural attractions which might
surprise those who think of Madrid essentially in terms of the Museo del
Prado. More than just a guide to the art and architecture of Madrid, this book
is a companion to many aspects of the city's culture, in particular its
fascinating literary associations and its intensive bar and café life.

Author's Acknowledgements

The staff of numerous Madrid institutions have assisted me in the research for
this book, and I would particularly like to thank Lola Baquero of the
Ayuntamiento de Madrid, Enrique Benedito of the Fábrica de Tabaco,
Vicenta Benedito of the Colección Benedito, Maria Condor and Juan
Antonio Juara Colomer of the Alameda de Osuna, Javier Gutiérrez Marcos
of the Comunidad de Madrid, and Santiago Matellano and Alicia Gomez
Navarro of the Residencia de Estudiantes. But a book of this kind has been
dependent above all on the help, suggestions, companionship and hospitality
of my Madrid friends, including Kenny Armstrong, William and Sonia
Chislett, Manuel Fernandez Orgil, Danny Garbade, Ian Gibson, Tito de la
Guardia, Alfonso, Marco and Miguel Ormaetxea, and Alicia Rios. For such
diverse acts of kindness as driving me around the Madrid cemeteries,
providing information on the firm of Capas Seseña, and discussing with me
the Madrid of Pérez Galdós, I must thank respectively Jerónimo Hernández,
Natacha Seseña and Eduardo Naval. Maite Brik and her mother Lola
Matalonga were invaluable accomplices in my investigations of the Madrid
tertulias, while Esperanza Flores, on a visit from Seville, introduced me to

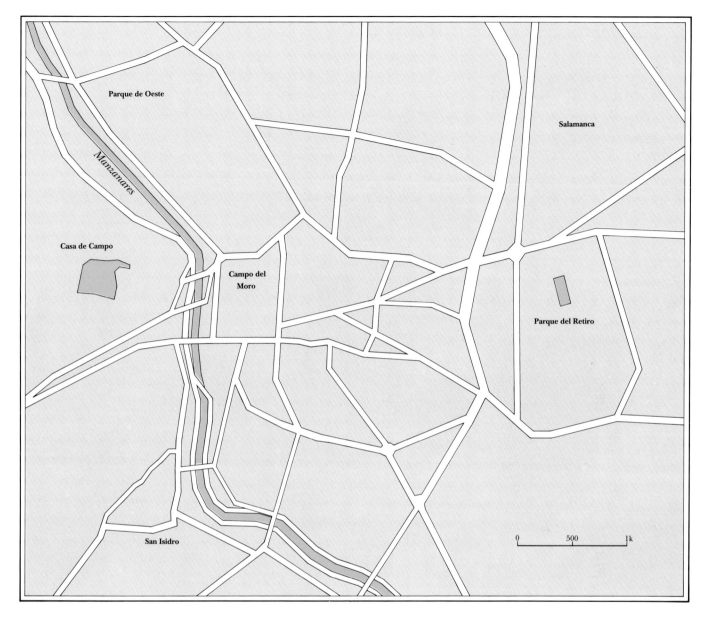

MADRID

such personalities of the Malasaña bars as Maria José, Mario, Miguel, Elia, Paloma, 'El Novillo', and the infamous 'Pollo Colorado'. Annie Bennet's flat above the Sociedad de Autores building has been a second home to me in Madrid, as has that of Carmen de la Guardia and Pepe Llanos in the Barrio de Salamanca. Jackie Rae, with whom I share happy memories of Madrid, has once again kept up my spirits while I was back at my desk in London.

Photographer's Acknowledgements
My thanks, above all, to Julia Cobb, and to Erica Davies, Heather Jones, Sally Gall, Pilar Prado, Alan Lothian, Cathy Lowne, Andrew Sutterby, Vivienne Brar, and both Bruno Anguita and Sixto Lope of the Patronato Municipal de Turismo de Madrid.

Introduction

....

Certain cities such as Venice, Prague or Paris are unfailingly and tiresomely praised. Madrid is not one of these places, and a love for it cannot so easily be explained or acquired. There are few other cities that excite me to the same extent as Madrid, but I have often found myself in the company of first-time visitors who fail to see beyond the grime, traffic and dearth of famous monuments. Hemingway, writing of Madrid in 1932, did not believe that 'anyone likes it much when he first goes there'. Yet he himself became one of the city's greatest enthusiasts, finding it the best of all Spanish cities to live in, and becoming such a ubiquitous presence in its bars and restaurants that one establishment off the Puerta del Sol still makes the lone claim that 'Hemingway never came here'.

'Madrid was until recently the European capital least visited by foreigners', wrote Fernández de los Ríos in his *Guide to Madrid* of 1876, one of the first and most detailed guidebooks ever written on the city. Although Madrid enjoys today an increasing popularity as a tourist destination, the great majority of its visitors see little more than the Museo del Prado or the Palacio Real and spend the rest of their time escaping to surrounding towns and villages. Madrid as a whole remains a remarkably neglected and baffling city, and as yet there are few books other than in Spanish that will guide you beyond the main attractions, and try to define the appeal of a place which was described early this century by its outstanding native writer Gómez de la Serna as 'the most difficult capital in the world to understand'.

Not even those who love Madrid over all other cities would call it a conventionally beautiful place. Hardly anything has survived from its medieval and renaissance periods, while its seventeenth- and eighteenth-century monuments lack on the whole the exuberance of those of other Spanish cities such as Seville and Santiago de Compostela. Its old centre is composed largely of late nineteenth- and early twentieth-century buildings,

OPPOSITE
The monastery and church of the Escorial.

9

but few of these are in the fantastical art nouveau style which makes the architecture of turn-of-the-century Barcelona so popular. Furthermore the people of Madrid have shown almost to the present day an irreverence towards the architecture of the past, and have had little hesitation in pulling down old buildings to make way for the new. By 1895 one English traveller, C. Bogue Luffmann, was writing in *A Vagabond in Spain* that Madrid was 'one of the most modern-looking cities' that he had ever seen, and it is precisely this feature of Madrid which has disappointed so many of its visitors, who have come to Spain with a romantic vision of a country steeped in the past.

Richard Ford, whose *Handbook to Spain* of 1845 did so much to influence foreign attitudes towards this country, disliked Madrid for lacking those qualities that he considered to be typically Spanish, such as Moorish monuments, jasmine-scented patios, and colourful folkloric traditions. To Ernest Hemingway, however, Madrid was 'the most Spanish of all cities', and this is certainly true in terms of its population, which comprises few families of pure Madrilenian origin, but features instead people from every corner of Spain. What is more, in contrast to the traditionally more cosmopolitan Barcelona, Madrid remains one of the most idiosyncratic of Europe's capitals, distinguished by a quite exceptional vitality. George Borrow, the eccentric author of *The Bible in Spain* (1840), was virtually alone among the travellers of the Romantic generation truly to appreciate Madrid. He claimed to have visited 'most of the principal capitals of the world', but found that Madrid fascinated him more than any of these places, above all for its human interest:

> I will not dwell upon its streets, its edifices, its public squares, its fountains, though some of these are remarkable enough . . . But the population! Within a mud wall, scarcely one league and a half in circuit, are contained two hundred thousand human beings, certainly forming the most extraordinary vital mass to be found in the entire world; and be it always remembered that this mass is strictly Spanish!

In terms of its gossip and the ease with which friends and acquaintances meet up in its centre, Madrid has retained some of the endearing qualities of a small town. However, in its vitality, and in the scale of its streets and architecture, Madrid gives a greater impression of being a city than do many other cities that are much larger, such as London. Madrid, like New York, will appeal above all to those who thrive on the excitement of a large metropolis, and begin to feel uncomfortable when exposed too long to the peace of the countryside. In the itineraries that make up the bulk of this book, I have resisted the temptation to take the reader further afield than the former hunting-grounds of El Pardo. I have omitted the impressive peaks of the nearby Sierra de Guadarrama, and such beautiful surrounding towns and villages as Toledo, Segovia, and Chinchón, all of which are worlds in their own right, demanding separate treatment. Although the Madrilenians have developed today a taste for country excursions, this was not always the case, and Antonio Díaz-Cañabate – a passionate recorder of Madrid life in the early years of this century – amusingly described an extreme Madrilenian attitude of old which considered the countryside to be positively dangerous. According to Díaz-Cañabate, there were even those whose discomfort in the face of Nature was such that they went only occasionally to the city park of El Retiro, the large pond of which inspired fears of rheumatism.

I hope that the present book will convince the reader of how much there is to see and do without even leaving the boundaries of the city, and I am sure that many of the places which I have included will be unknown even to Madrilenians. While the Museo del Prado alone might justify a visit to Madrid, there are numerous other excellent but often little-visited art collections that reinforce the city's reputation as one of the great art centres of Europe. Even the architecture of the city, although easily dismissed at first, offers countless surprises, such as perfectly preserved seventeenth-century interiors hidden behind austere brick walls, or massive nineteenth-century buildings enlivened by a wealth of bizarre and colourful detailing. A pleasure very special to Madrid is provided by the remarkable number of old shops, cafés, bars and restaurants that have maintained over the years their traditional appearance, even down to the ceramic advertisements on the exterior, and their often surrealistic window displays. Several of these places have the additional interest of having been the scene of literary gatherings, or *tertulias*, an important feature of this city rich in literary associations.

To all these specific attractions – and to others of a more hedonistic kind to be outlined at the end of this introduction – must be added an elusive element of magic which poets have vaguely attributed to something in Madrid's air, an air which owes its special properties to the city's situation in the middle of the vast Castilian plateau. The climate of Madrid is known for its great extremes, and also for the deceptively gentle winds that creep in unexpectedly from the Sierra, causing sudden drops in temperature even on the sunniest day; these winds, in the words of a much-repeated proverb, 'will not extinguish a candle, but will put out a man's life'. The penetrating air of the Sierra has also the effect of clearing away the hovering pollution and creating intensely blue skies that Salvador Dalí compared to those by the pioneering fifteenth-century landscape painter, Joachim Patinir.

Nina Epton, who had been brought up in Madrid in the 1920s, had to look to the skies to explain a phenomenon which she observed among her fellow passengers when she approached Madrid on the train from Paris:

> ... everybody in the compartment stood up and shouted: 'Madrid!' ... 'Madrid!', Mother echoed with tears in her eyes. People reacted as if there had been a free distribution of champagne. The sight of Madrid in the distance revived the drooping, unruffled the bad-tempered, bestowed the gift of tongues upon the inarticulate. Everybody waved, laughed, cried and shouted.

The staircase of the Society of Authors: a rare and wonderful example of Madrilenian art nouveau.

Sadly, I have yet to experience such a scene myself, but I can none the less vouch for the excitement of arriving at Madrid by train from the north. After crossing the frighteningly monotonous expanses of northern Castile, the train makes its way over the gaunt and often snow-capped granite peaks of the Sierra de Guadarrama. On the southern slopes of the range, near the palace and monastery of the Escorial, you are suddenly offered an extensive view over a flat and scraggy landscape of boulders and scrubland above which hover in the far distance the whitened profiles of apartment blocks. Arriving at Madrid at the height of summer, the city can seem as if it were built right in the middle of a desert, and this impression was at one time strengthened by its modern railway station of Chamartín being situated in a virtual wasteland beyond the city's northern boundary. My favourite point of arrival is the Estación del Norte, the quietest of Madrid's main stations, and a place used mainly by trains coming from Ávila and Salamanca. Lying on the north-eastern side of town, the station obliquely faces the most distinctive element in Madrid's skyline – a long and dramatic cliff supporting the massive bulk of the Palacio Real. It is there, on that cliff-top site projecting high above the modest Manzanares, that the disputed origins of Madrid are to be sought.

When the relatively insignificant township of Madrid was transformed from the late sixteenth century onwards into a major city and the capital of a kingdom, it was perhaps inevitable that historians should try and dignify its history through claiming ancient, and mythical, roots. Thus Madrid became a city of legendary Roman origins, founded by Prince Ocno-Bianor, and named after his mother, the prophetess Manto, a daughter of Hercules. Known as Mantua Carpetana to distinguish it from Mantua in Italy, Madrid was referred to by this bogus Latin name up to the nineteenth century.

The actual, and more prosaic origins of Madrid appear to have been in the small Arab settlement of Magerit, which was built high above the Manzanares in c.856 to guard the important line of communications between Toledo and Aragón. This defensive outpost fell to the Christians shortly after they had captured Toledo in 1085, and lived on subsequently as an agricultural and craft centre with a population made up of Christians, Jews and the Christianized Moors known as *Mudéjars*. During the 200-year occupation of Madrid by the Moors, the arid terrain around the city had apparently been transformed into fertile countryside covered with vines, orchards and kitchen gardens. Under the Christians, however, the Moors' brilliant irrigation schemes came eventually to be neglected, and by the seventeenth century the surroundings of Madrid had been encircled by what one nineteenth-century traveller was to describe as a 'hideous, grassless, treeless, colourless, calcined desert'.

The one feature of the countryside which was to remain unchanged over the centuries – and survives to this day, albeit in a greatly reduced form – was the forest of El Pardo on the north-western outskirts of the city. From Moorish times onwards, this forest enjoyed considerable renown as a hunting-ground, and was indeed the main attraction of Madrid for the Spanish kings who occasionally took up residence here. Philip II was a passionate huntsman, and the presence of a nearby hunting-ground might have been a factor in his eccentric decision of 1561 to establish Madrid as the permanent seat of the hitherto itinerant Spanish court. There were several other reasons for honouring Madrid in this way, including the fact that the city was not ruled by a powerful and potentially independent-minded archbishop as was Spain's ecclesiastical capital, Toledo; neither had the citizens of Madrid ever toyed with heresy, as had those of Valladolid, the Castilian city most favoured by Philip's great-grandparents, Ferdinand and Isabel. But, above all, Madrid had the advantage of being at the very centre of Spain, something which greatly appealed to Philip II's autocratic spirit and led him to overlook Madrid's main drawback as a capital city – its lack of a navigable river.

Madrid's population increased rapidly after 1561, but much of the new urban development was unplanned and architecturally modest. The majority of the new houses were white-washed brick and adobe structures, such as you still find today in some of the poorer Castilian communities; they were rarely built higher than one floor, for the owners of taller houses were forced by law to accommodate members of the court. Philip II gave Madrid scarcely a single monument of note, his principal commission here being the Segovia Bridge, which was erected in 1583 as the first stone bridge to span what Miguel de Cervantes called 'a rivulet with a reputation of a river', the Manzanares. The attention of the monarch was otherwise engaged, for only two years after choosing Madrid as the capital of Spain, he was to neglect the city in favour of the nearby monastery and palace of El Escorial, the construction of which became the overriding obsession of his later years.

Commissioned in 1563 from Juan Bautista de Toledo, the Escorial was completed in 1584 by the architect of the Segovia Bridge, Juan de Herrera, under whom the place became the supreme expression of Philip II's uncompromising architectural tastes. A visit to the Escorial is the usual complement to any tour of Madrid, and is perhaps essential for anyone who wishes to understand the architectural development of the Habsburg city. The prospect of coming here is also a potentially daunting one, and you might well feel certain misgivings when first confronted with this monster of a building, with its unadorned granite surfaces and megalomaniac scale. Guided tours – which in the nineteenth century lasted up to five hours – are fortunately no longer obligatory, and the clear and recent sign-posting have lessened the chances of your being disorientated by the monotonous regularity of the ground-plan, with its two vast and near identical cloisters. The most popular and intimate part of the Escorial is the Habsburg Apartments, where melodramatic notions about the fanatical Philip II are usually fuelled by the sight of the very bed from which the gouty, sore-ridden and rotting monarch could look directly down to the high altar of the monastery church. As for the church itself, this provides a tour of the Escorial with its oppressive high point, especially on a dark day, when the scant detailing of this domed and barrel-vaulted structure is largely lost to the enveloping gloom. The gothick fantasist William Beckford came here on one such day, and was no sooner past the 'cavern-like' porches of the main façade than he was seized by a premonition of entering 'a subterranean temple set apart for the service of some mysterious and terrible religion'. Inside he was immediately overcome by a 'sensation of dread and dreariness', particularly on finding that his sole company here was Pompeo Leoni's gilded but life-like representations of the kneeling families of Philip II and Charles V.

A baroque portal on the Carrera de San Jerónimo, one of the many works of the greatest and most prolific architect of the period, Pedro de Ribera.

No matter how awed or impressed visitors have been by the Escorial, most have been relieved on emerging afterwards into the open air. The French nineteenth-century writer Théophile Gautier even went as far as to suggest that anyone who had ever spent a day in the Escorial would always be able to console themselves with the thought of no longer being there; for him the place was 'the deadliest and most wearisome edifice that a morose and suspicious tyrant could ever conceive for the mortification of his fellow-creatures'. The Escorial is certainly a building of unprecedented austerity, and it also brought to an end a period in Spanish architecture which had been charecterized by joyous exuberance and ornamentation. A more recent travelwriter, Archibald Lyall, wondered if the transition between the two styles could in any way be 'connected with the introduction of syphilis to Europe'; others, more sensibly, have pointed out the links between the so-called 'Herreran style' and totalitarianism, the Spain of the Habsburgs being often described as the first totalitarian state in Europe. The style was at any rate to have an enormous impact on the look of Madrid, as the city finally entered, at the beginning of the seventeenth century, the first important period in its architectural history.

Philip II was succeeded in 1598 by Philip III, whose first minister, the Duke of Lerma, was able to persuade him at the beginning of his reign to transfer the capital to Valladolid. Madrid became the capital again in 1606, and by 1617 had managed in only twenty years to double the size of its population to 150,000. The boom continued under Philip III's successor, Philip IV, during whose rule the city superseded Seville in size and became the fifth largest in Europe. During these years of dramatic expansion, Madrid acquired several of its most salient features, the Plaza Mayor, for instance, becoming transformed after 1610 into a grand and impressive showpiece, and the nearby Puerta del Sol emerging as the bustling, social heart of the city. Curiously, for a European city in an early and critical stage in its development, all this building activity did not include the construction of a cathedral. Madrid remained until 1886 as part of the diocese of Toledo, for which reason the place was referred to in the past not as a city but as a *villa*, or fortified town: work on Madrid's cathedral did not begin until the end of the nineteenth century, and it is still awaiting completion.

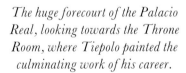

The huge forecourt of the Palacio Real, looking towards the Throne Room, where Tiepolo painted the culminating work of his career.

Religious architecture otherwise flourished in Madrid in the early seventeenth century and accounted for most of the important new building work. Churches, religious hospitals, and, above all, convents, took up much of the city centre, and had proliferated to such an extent that by 1629, one chronicler, Jerónimo de la Quintana, recorded as many as 73 such institutions. As for secular architecture, the most ambitious and controversial new building was unquestionably the royal palace of the Buen Retiro. This was the brain-child of Philip IV's all-powerful minister, the Count Duke Olivares, who was determined that the Madrid court should be the focal point of a brilliant cultural life. The construction of the palace, on the eastern outskirts of Madrid, established the surrounding area as the city's elegant and verdant playground, complete with an animated public promenade or *paseo* known as El Prado. Madrid's adobe defensive walls, which had been extended at the beginning of the century as far east as the Puerta del Sol, were now taken further east to include the Buen Retiro. But from about 1660 onwards, they were to remain unchanged, and up to as late as the mid nineteenth century, the city was not to spread beyond them.

The first century of Madrid's existence as capital of Spain coincided with what is generally known as the Golden Age of Spanish culture. To begin with, it was Seville rather than Madrid which was the undisputed cultural capital of the country, but this situation began to change in the course of the seventeenth century, particularly in the fields of literature and painting. The first major novel in Europe, Cervantes's *Don Quixote*, was published in Madrid from 1604, while the recently founded public theatres of La Cruz and El Príncipe put on plays by such outstanding talents as Lope de Vega, Tirso de Molina and Pedro Calderón de la Barca. Naturally the court played a vital role in this literary life, commissioning plays for its theatres at the Buen Retiro and the nearby summer palace at Aranjuez, and sponsoring respectively the greatest poet and satirist of that generation, Luis de Góngora and Francisco de Quevedo. Under Philip IV the court also became a major centre of painting, thanks principally to having attracted in 1623 a young prodigy from Seville, Diego Velázquez, whose presence here for nearly 40 years provided the main impetus to a local school of painting which came to supersede that of Seville. It is symptomatic of the changing fortunes of Seville and Madrid that Velázquez's former colleague, Francisco de Zurburán, was forced to move to Madrid in 1658 in search of commissions.

The architects working in seventeenth-century Madrid are less known than its painters or writers. The dominant figure was Herrera's pupil, Juan Gómez de Mora, who had a hand in virtually all the principal civic, royal and religious commissions of the early seventeenth century, including the Buen Retiro, the magnificent Convento de la Encarnación, the Plaza Mayor, the Carcel de la Corte and the Palacio de la Villa. While never creating an architecture of such extreme austerity as his master's, he emulated the latter's ornamental restraint, love of rigidly defined geometric compositions, and characteristic high-pitched slate roofs and corner turrets. Herrera's legacy and the sophisticated influence of the court affected the whole course of Madrid's architectural development. They held in check some of the wilder fantasies of the Baroque, and gave to most of the buildings of this period a character far more sober than that to be found elsewhere in Spain. This is particularly evident in the city's churches, which are strikingly similar in their appearance, nearly all being barrel-vaulted, single-naved structures, with shallow transepts, and interiors relieved of their architectural austerity largely by long rows of elaborate consoles supporting richly modelled cornices. Where they differ markedly from the monastery church of the Escorial and other Spanish buildings of the late sixteenth century is in the cheapness of the materials used, brick and plaster being preferred to granite and marble. This feature, common not only to the city's churches, but also to most of its other buildings of this period, highlights one of the main contradictions of Habsburg Madrid. Though a rapidly growing city, so anxious to impress, Madrid seems for much of the century to have been pathetically short of funds. Regular mule trains journeying to Madrid from the Andalusian ports brought to this city much of the fabulous wealth coming in from America, but somehow this was squandered through gross misman-agement, and constant foreign and internal disputes, so that even the royal coffers were seriously depleted.

'Madrid is till as your lordship left it, Prado, coaches, women, dust, executions, comedies, a lot of fruit – and very little money.' These words of Lope de Vega to his patron the Duke of Sessa admirably convey the vitality, confusion, brilliance and squalor of a Madrid which was perhaps not so dissimilar to the city of today. Even at this relatively early stage of its history, Madrid had all the positive and negative qualities of a large city, but to an exaggerated degree. One of the aspects most commented on by travellers of this time was its dirt, which, even by the standards of a seventeenth-century city, was apparently exceptional, with its inhabitants enjoying much notoriety for their habit of throwing all their rubbish out into the streets. The air of Madrid was already becoming polluted by the late seventeenth century, but, in dramatic contrast to the attitudes of today, there were many people who believed that such contamination of the environment was necessary to counteract what was thought to be the excessive and dangerous purity of the Madrid air in its natural state. So widespread was this belief that a local doctor, Doctor Juanini, felt compelled in 1689 to write a book putting forward the rather controversial suggestion that pollution itself might be detrimental to the health.

Madrid was clearly in need of renovation and embellishment by the time that the last of the Spanish Habsburgs, Charles II, died in 1701. The advent of the Bourbons to the Spanish throne following a fourteen-year war of succession was fortuitously timed, leading as it did to a series of major reforms in Madrid that were to bring the place in line with some of the most advanced

A modern example of Madrid's ceramic tradition showing a favourite Castillian dish – suckling pig.

cities in Europe. The Bourbons were eventually to introduce here the latest French and Italian fashions, but the first of their Spanish kings, the Versailles-educated Philip V, made no attempt at first to impose his own tastes on local traditions, and gave the governor of Madrid, the Marquis of Vadillo, a virtual free hand in the latter's ambitious plans for urban renewal. The marquis was fortunately assisted in these plans by one of the most individual and versatile architects ever to have worked in Madrid, Pedro de Ribera.

Ribera's extraordinary achievement must be seen against his provincial training as an architect and the meanness of the funds at his disposal, Madrid still being in a state of near bankruptcy. His early career was almost entirely spent working for the municipality of Madrid, for which he helped solve the difficult problem of access to the city by constructing the Toledo Bridge, a structure combining functionalism, grandeur and exuberant decorative flourishes. Among his many other successes as a town-planner were the turning of the Paseo de la Virgen del Puerto into a handsome, garden-lined thoroughfare, the designing of several gates for the city, and the relaying of the municipal water supply so as to include a number of superbly ornate fountains. As an architect, Ribera was by far the most extreme representative of the baroque style in Madrid, and, to many of the nineteenth-century critics of this style, he was even considered as one of the worst of all Spanish offenders against good taste and classical decorum. However, the baroque elements in his buildings were often limited to his portals, the rest of his structures being remarkably severe. Thus his Hospicio de San Fernando (now the Museo Municipal), his culminating Madrid achievement, has one of the most gloriously elaborate of all Spanish portals, while the church attached to this building is fully in the austere tradition of Herrera and Gómez de Mora.

In later life Ribera was to be active largely as a designer of palaces for the aristocracy, but he was to live to see his work go out of fashion, and be ignored by the Bourbon monarchy. Philip V, under the influence of his second wife Isabella Farnese, recently arrived from Italy, began to tire of the Spanish baroque style and felt that local tastes needed to be tempered by the example of contemporary Italian architecture. The perfect opportunity to put these ideas into practice came after the night of December 24, 1734, when a disastrous fire swept through the *alcázar* (royal palace), destroying the town's main symbol of Habsburg dominance in Madrid. In his desire to create a new palace worthy of the reforming and cosmopolitan spirit of the Bourbon monarchy, Philip V called in from Italy the most renowned exponent of the late Baroque, the aged Sicilian architect Filippo Juvarra. Juvarra died shortly after his arrival in Madrid, a victim to the icy winds of the Guadarrama; but he was succeeded in his task of rebuilding the royal palace by his Piedmontese follower, Giovanni Battista Sacchetti. The vast Palacio Real, built on a scale virtually unrivalled in eighteenth-century Europe, took nearly 30 years to complete, and was to involve the participation of the two leading foreign painters of the day, the German Anton Raffael Mengs, and the last great

A detail of the ceramic decoration of the bull-ring of Las Ventas.

Sabatini's Puerta de Alcalá: a distinguished example of Italianate classicism, commissioned by Charles III.

exponent of the Italian tradition of large-scale decorative painting, Giovanni Battista Tiepolo. The palace initiated a period in Madrid's architectural history which was to be dominated by foreign tastes. The French architect Carlier received the most important commission of the reign of Ferdinand VI, while the Italian Sabatini was the favourite architect of the subsequent ruler, Charles III. Only two Spanish architects were to break this foreign hegemony, Ventura Rodríguez, and Juan de Villanueva, the latter being the creator of that neo-classical masterpiece, the Museo del Prado.

The Museo del Prado was one of the many legacies to Madrid of Charles III, the greatest of Spain's Bourbon rulers, and a man who did even more than Philip V to change the face of this city. The construction of the Museo del Prado, which was intended initially to house a collection of natural history items, was one of a number of Charles's schemes for the instruction and enjoyment of the Madrilenians. Botanical gardens were beautifully laid out alongside it, and the neighbouring Parque del Retiro was opened as one of the earliest public parks in Europe, complete with a neo-classical observatory. The promenade in front of the museum was entirely renovated and adorned with alleys of trees and three superlative fountains, one of which, representing the goddess Cybele, was to become the popular symbol of Madrid. In addition Charles saw that the city was systematically paved, introduced regulations for the collecting of rubbish, initiated Madrid's first sewerage system, and became a figure of the Enlightenment in the literal sense through providing the city with its first street lights. Street lighting helped in turn to reduce the city's notorious crime rate, as did the bringing in at the end of the eighteenth century of night-watchmen or *serenos*, who, with their dangling keys, were a regular feature of Madrilenian night-life right up to the 1950s.

The least popular of the reforms attempted in Charles's reign was also intended to curb the crime rate. This was a law brought in briefly in 1766 by Charles's unpopular Italian minister, the Marquis of Squillace, who, on the grounds that the streets were becoming cleaner, banned the use by men of ground-length capes, and appointed tailors to stand in doorways to cut off the extra cloth of those who defied this decree. These capes supposedly allowed robbers easily to conceal themselves, but they were also symbols of male pride and a typical Spanish fashion. The banning of them not only sparked off a revolt which led to the dismissal of Squillace, but also highlighted the general and growing resentment to what was thought of as Bourbon contamination of the traditional Spanish life-style through the imposition of foreign, and specifically French ways. This resentment led to several attacks on those wearing French clothes and was to provoke a further outcry when a later minister of Charles III proposed the introduction of shoe-cleaners in the streets, an idea which was popularly though to have come from the French pilgrims on the way to Santiago de Compostela.

A wonderful idea of everyday life in eighteenth-century Madrid is provided by the one-act plays or *sainetes* of Ramón de la Cruz, who also played a pioneering role in the history of the musical genre known as *zarzuela*, which combines song, dance and dialogue. In his *Reapers of Vallecas* of 1768, Ramón de la Cruz created the true modern *zarzuela* through breaking away from the classical themes and Italian music of earlier *zarzuelas*, and depicting instead everyday scenes to the accompaniment of popular Spanish airs composed by Antonio Rodríguez de Hita. This new type of *zarzuela* acted as a powerful rival to the Italian opera in Spain, and came to represent what is still one of Madrid's most characteristic and best-loved forms of entertainment.

The world of Madrid's low life, which Ramón de la Cruz so wittily portrayed, found its most famous chronicler in an artist of Aragonese birth, Francisco de Goya. The greatest Spanish painter of the late eighteenth and early nineteenth centuries, Goya began his Madrid career executing cartoons for the royal tapestry factory, which had been founded by Philip V, and is still functioning today, with comparable working conditions. In these cartoons, as in many of his later works, Goya found inspiration from popular customs and entertainments such as the annual *romería* or festive pilgrimage to the hermitage of San Isidro. He also immortalized the working-class dandies known originally as *majos*, a word which probably has its origins in May Day festivities, more specifically with the beautiful, costumed girl chosen as the May Queen. Dressed flamboyantly, sometimes in imitation of the ladies of fashion, the *maja* had a reputation both for brazenness and volubility, her readiness to take up a quarrel being indicated by the sheathed poniard which she carried in the garter of her left stocking. Her equally excitable male equivalent, the *majo*, shared the *maja*'s contempt of the French, and proudly wore the spanish cape instead of the French full-skirted coat, the long hairnet instead of the French wig and the *chambergo*, or large soft-brimmed hat, instead of the three-cornered hat. Madrid may not have boasted the colourful folklore traditions of other Spanish cities and regions, but it had its *majos*, who, as portrayed by Goya, became essential components of the romantic tourist image of the city. Fernández de los Ríos, in his *Guide to Madrid* of 1876, observed how even in his day, there were foreigners whose preconceptions of the city were based to a large extent on popular types and forms of behaviour that had survived after 1800 only in the genre paintings of Goya.

The colourful and essentially pleasure-seeking Madrid of Goya's tapestry cartoons gave way in the artist's later life to a rather darker world, closely inspired by the major political upheavals that Spain experienced from the early nineteenth century onwards. Charles III's son and successor, Charles IV, was a weak and unintelligent man, who let his country be run by his lecherous and devious minister Don Manuel de Godoy, whose rise to power was not entirely unconnected with his having enjoyed the sexual favours of the Spanish queen, María Luisa of Parma. Godoy, who failed in his petition of 1793 to prevent the execution of the French king Louis XVI, compromised with the French revolutionaries and eventually became actively involved in Napoleonic schemes. Such was Godoy's unpopularity that in 1808 an irate mob stormed his house in Aranjuez, an event which was followed immediately by the flight of the Spanish monarchy to France and the occupation of Madrid by French troops led by Marshal Murat. The arrival of the French posed an enormous dilemma to Spanish liberals, who were torn between admiration for the social ideals of revolutionary France and patriotic resentment of the foreign invader. The popular antagonism to the invasion manifested itself most famously in an uprising which broke out on 2 May, 1808 in the Madrid district of Las Maravillas. The date was permanently enshrined in the heroic mythology of Madrid, and the subsequent massacre of the Spanish rebels by the French was the subject of a painting by Goya (now in the Prado) which must be one of the most harrowing in western art.

Napoleon's brother, Joseph Bonaparte, was placed in charge of Spain, and took up residence in the Palacio Real, where, according to an apocryphal remark by Napoleon, he was 'better lodged' than the emperor himself was at the Louvre. Joseph was only in power until 1813, but during the six years of his rule was significantly to alter the look of Madrid and to acquire two nicknames. One of these was 'Pepe Botellas' (roughly equivalent to 'Joe Bottles'), a reference not to any drinking habits but to his having freed alcohol from crippling taxes. The more significant of his reputations was as 'el rey de plazuelas' or 'king of the squares'. Beginning with his demolition of the jumble of buildings in front of the Palacio Real so as to form the Plaza de Oriente, Joseph developed an apparent obsession with creating town squares, and ample opportunity for doing so was provided by his suppression of Spain's convents and monasteries. Many of Madrid's squares of today, such as the Plaza de Santa Ana, were created as a result of the pulling down of the religious institutions that had once congested the city centre.

A fountain in the Parque del Retiro, with mythological figures supporting Madrid's coat of arms.

The Bourbon monarchy was restored to Spain in the form of Charles IV's son, Ferdinand VII, a man generally described as odious by his contemporaries. He had agreed to abide by the famous 1812 constitution drafted by the exiled liberals in Cádiz, but soon repudiated this, and set about introducing the most rigid censorship. In terms of architecture and urban development, his long rule was a period of stagnation in Madrid. The few monuments associated with him in Madrid are largely unmemorable, and it is instructive to compare the richly modelled Puerta de Alcalá, which had been built to commemorate the advent to the throne of his grandfather Charles III, with Ferdinand's dreary and protracted reconstruction of the Puerta de Toledo, through which he had entered the city on his return to Spain in 1814. The only commemorative monument of genuine distinction was the one built by Villanueva's pupil Isidro González Velázquez to honour the victims of 2 May, but even this took over eighteen years to complete. The talents of González Velázquez, like those of all the other architects of this generation, were largely squandered on the designing of minor decorative works or of grand projects that were never realized.

The repressiveness of Ferdinand's regime, however, had at least the beneficial effect of stimulating Madrid's intellectual life, which flourished as a way both of sustaining the spirit under these adverse conditions and of maintaining the underlying political opposition. 1820 saw, significantly, the foundation of what was to become one of the great intellectual institutions of Spain, the Ateneo, a scientific, literary and artistic society which was also to enjoy a reputation right up to the Franco era as a centre of liberal politics. Furthermore, political censorship, combined with an atmosphere of growing revolutionary tension, has always bred the right conditions in which café society can thrive, and it was in these hard years of Ferdinand's rule that Madrid turned into a city of cafés rivalled only by Paris and Vienna.

The origins of Madrid's cafés were in the *botellerías*, shops mainly specializing in wines, but which also sold hot chocolate, sweets and soft drinks. The Spanish love of drinking chocolate, which has existed since the discovery of the New World, came to be replaced at the beginning of the nineteenth century by a taste for coffee. The *botellerías* largely died out at this time, and their premises were frequently taken over by cafés, the greatest concentration of which were in and around the Puerta del Sol. Women who considered themselves as true ladies had never actually entered the *botellerías*, but had insisted on being served while seated in their carriages outside. Similarly, women of high standing were never to be seen in the cafés, which were to preserve up to as late as the 1920s the character of male clubs. Each of these cafés attracted its particular circle of people, who were brought together by a common profession, interest, political standpoint, or region of origin; some of the more intellectual of these groups held regular discussions or *tertulias*, a tradition which goes back to the humanist gatherings in sixteenth-century Seville and was to be a major force in the history of Spanish culture and ideas.

The equestrian monument to Philip III in the Plaza Mayor, designed by Giambologna and executed by Pietro Tacca; the work was placed here in 1847 on the recommendation of the Madrilenian chronicler Mesonero Romanos.

The leading political café during the reign of Ferdinand VII was the Fontana de Oro, which was situated off the Carrera de San Jerónimo, and became the seat of a patriotic society named 'Los Amigos del Orden'. Meanwhile, off the nearby Plaza de Santa Ana, a café of dark and unprepossessing appearance called the Café del Príncipe attracted such a glittering group of artists, writers and architects that it became commonly known as 'El Parnasillo' or 'The Little Parnassus'. The history of Spanish Romanticism can almost be told through the gatherings at El Parnasillo, which drew into its basement room such luminaries of this movement as the landscape artist Pérez de Villaamil, the poet José de Espronceda, and the playwrights Juan Eugenio Hartzenbusch and José Zorrilla, the latter being the author of the Don Juan story which is still the most performed in Spain today. The central figure in this group was Mariano José de Larra, an essayist and satirist of caustic humour, whose much publicized suicide in 1837, at the age of 28, was one of the key moments in the history of Romantic Madrid.

The Parnasillo, like the Fontana de Oro, has long ceased to exist, but the place lives on in a long and vividly detailed description by a friend of Larra's of completely opposed temperament, Ramón de Mesonero Romanos. A bespectacled man of sober and portly appearance, Mesonero Romanos spent much of his life in a meticulously ordered municipal office which has been preserved to this day. Though lacking the charisma of a Larra, the importance of this unassuming man in Madrid's history cannot be underestimated, for he was the first of the true *Madrilenistas*, and devoted his entire literary output to recording obsessively every aspect of his native city. With his characteristic modesty, he defined his literary approach as 'writing for the general public in a plain style without affectation or carelessness, usually describing, rarely arguing, never causing tears, almost always causing laughter . . . and, to sum up, attempting . . . to become a true observer'.

In 1861, almost 30 years after publishing his painstakingly researched *Manual of Madrid*, Mesonero Romanos brought out a work entitled *Old Madrid*, in which the phlegmatic and objective style of the earlier book has become overlaid with a certain nostalgia, a nostalgia which was to intensify in his marvellous autobiography of 1881 entitled *Memories of a Seventy-Year Old, Born and Bred in Madrid*. Not since the first half of the seventeenth century had Madrid expanded in so rapid a fashion as in the years between 1830 and 1868, and in the process much of the character and many of the monuments that Mesonero Romanos had so admired had been lost. The climate of change had set in with the death of Ferdinand VII in 1833, but had become especially pronounced during the reign of his daughter Isabel II, who finally acceded to the throne in 1843 following the first of the Carlist Wars and a long period in which her mother, María Cristina, had acted as regent. By the middle of the nineteenth century, Madrid was bursting at its seams, and in 1860 permission was finally given to pull down the old adobe defensive walls and carry out a plan of expansion which had been drawn up by the engineer Carlos María de

Castro to accommodate a growing population which by the end of the century would reach and then exceed the half-million mark.

Castro's plan, taking the form of a regular grid of streets in keeping with the latest theories of town-planning, earmarked as the main zone of expansion a large area to the north-east of the old walls. The northern continuation of the Paseo del Prado, the Paseo de Recoletos, was extended northwards to form the grand avenue known at first as the Paseo de las Delicias de Isabel II and now simply as the Paseo de la Castellana. To the east of this a wealthy middle-class district was built up which bears today the name of the banker and railway entrepreneur responsible for much of the property speculation here, the Marquis of Salamanca.

And the city was rapidly undergoing a technological transformation. Gas lighting had been introduced here in 1832, and this was followed in the 1850s by a radically improved water supply drawing water from the Sierra de Guadarrama. The city's first public urinal was set up in the newly rebuilt Puerta del Sol in 1863, and eight years later public transport came to Madrid in the form of the mule-drawn tram. The street lights were electrified in 1875, and the trams in 1879.

The changing Madrid of the late nineteenth century was fortunate enough to have a chronicler who, unlike Mesonero Romanos, transcended the role of mere *costumbrista* (an observer of customs and manners) and penetrated the minds of the city's inhabitants. This man, Benito Pérez Galdós, was born in the Canary Islands in 1842, but after settling in Madrid as a law student in 1862, developed such an immediate and consuming obsession with this city that his whole life up to then ceased to hold any importance for him. In old age he was to recall how in his first years at Madrid he would escape whenever possible from the university and spend much of his days 'gliding like a gondola through the streets, squares and alleys, delighting

View from the Casa de Campo featuring three of the earliest skyscrapers in Europe: the Telefónica is seen on the far right and on the left are the Edificio and Torre de España.

A high altarpiece by Luis Velázquez in Ventura Rodriguez's fine late baroque church of San Marcos.

in observing the bustling life of this huge and multi-faceted city'. By night he frequented the cafés and devotedly attended all of the city's theatres, for in his burgeoning literary ambitions he aspired at first to drama. He was to find his true vocation only in 1870, with the publication of his first novel, *La Fontana de Oro*, a work of historical fiction set around the famous political café of that name. As a novelist, Pérez Galdós enjoys today the reputation of being the greatest Spanish writer after Cervantes, and, though still shockingly neglected outside of Spain, deserves to be among the giants of European Realist literature of the late nineteenth century.

Galdós's vast output as a novelist is divided between works chronicling key moments in Spain's recent political history – his so-called *Episodios nacionales* – and novels of contemporary life, which constitute his greatest achievement. Despite being a passionate traveller with a knowledge of most countries in western Europe, Galdós's interests as a writer on the modern world were concentrated almost exclusively on Madrid, which he portrayed with an intimacy which has never been equalled. A timid man who gave little away about his own personal life, he mercilessly exposed the private thoughts of others, and showed a remarkable understanding of schizophrenia and other pathological states. His broadmindedness and fascination with people led to his becoming acquainted with an exceptionally wide range of Madrid society, while his life-long status as a bachelor and belief in free love (but not in promiscuity) gave him access to a variety of close female friendships which was denied to many other men of his time.

Galdós's talents as a novelist and as an observer of Madrid life are shown at their greatest in his epic novel *Fortunata and Jacinta* (1886–7), which deals with a spoiled young man from a wealthy middle-class family, and the love for him of two women of opposed social background, one his mistress, the other his wife. The telling of this tale involves an enormous and motley cast of characters, and much of Galdós's skill and originality as a novelist derives from his constant changes of narrative perspective, so that events are always seen through different eyes, acquiring a particularly grotesque dimension as the reader is taken into the disintegrating mind of the pathetic and deluded man whom the mistress Fortunata, down on her luck, is forced by circumstances to marry. The main part of the action takes place around the Plaza Mayor, but as the novel unfolds a truly panoramic picture of Madrid emerges, with its developing wealthy suburbs to the north, and the scorched slum land to the south. For the traveller to Madrid, part of the fascination of reading Galdós is that the city which he so vividly described is still one which is immediately recognizable today, even down to some of its smallest details.

Much of the present-day appearance of Madrid is the legacy of those years between Galdós's first arrival in the city and the outbreak of the Civil War in 1936. This period began, as it was to end, in political turmoil, and Galdós was an enthusiastic witness of the liberal uprising of 1868 – which resulted in the abdication and flight of Isabel II – and of the subsequent and short-lived First Republic. The restoration of the Bourbon monarchy in 1875 in the form of Isabel's son Alfonso XII, dismayed Galdós and other liberals, but it heralded years of relative tranquillity. Architecturally, the reign of Alfonso XII was characterized in Madrid by a pompous eclecticism which differed from that of other European capitals in comprising a wealth of neo-*mudéjar* monuments and very few neo-gothic ones, the Madrilenians having an apparent aversion to the gothic style. Most of what was put up, although often highly entertaining and splendidly elaborate, lacks architectural genius, but, in compensation, there can be few other places in Europe where even the most modest buildings are enlivened by brilliant ceramic decorations on their exteriors. Madrid's ceramic tradition is not of long standing, but from the 1870s until the end of the 1920s it flourished as an adjunct of architecture, thanks largely to the vision of the architect Ricardo Velázquez Bosco, a man of orientalist leanings who had begun his career restoring the mosque at Córdoba. The ceramics that came to decorate almost all of Velázquez Bosco's buildings were produced in the newly founded Madrid factories of 'La Cerámica Madrileña' and 'La Moncloa', the latter benefiting from the services of one of the greatest ceramicists of the age, Daniel Zuloaga.

Many of the most radical changes to the Madrid skyline were carried out during the reign of Alfonso XII's successor, Alfonso XIII, which had got off to a suitably explosive start with a bomb attack on the occasion of his wedding in 1906 to Victoria Eugenia von Battenberg. The principal urban reform during this period was the construction after 1911 of the Gran Vía, which cut a great swathe through the old centre of Madrid and initiated the growth of the city upwards. The first of the many American-style skyscrapers was built on the Gran Vía to house the Bell Telephone Company, an American company which was later nationalized. Alfonso said on the inauguration of this building that Spain had truly entered the twentieth century, and that the old adage that 'Africa begins at the Pyrenees' was no longer applicable. The building, for all its modernity, has none the less unmistakable borrowings from the Spanish Baroque, as have the works of the most renowned Madrid architect of these years, Antonio Palacios. The latter's masterpiece is the vast and overwhelmingly sumptuous Post Office building of 1904, which is prominently situated at the northern end of the Paseo del Prado, and so dominating and cathedral-like that it amply justifies its sarcastic nickname of 'Our Lady of Communications'.

Spain, during the first 36 years of this century, was the scene of a cultural renaissance comparable to that of the Golden Age. This renaissance was centred principally on Madrid – and not on Barcelona, as many foreigners wrongfully assume – and had as its fathers the so-called 'Generation of 98', a group of writers and philosophers whose works express the need for a spiritual renewal of Spain in the wake of the country's disastrous loss in 1898 of Cuba, Puerto Rico and the Philippines. Miguel de Unamuno, one of the leaders of this movement, had a strong dislike of Madrid, once comparing it to a 'vast caravan of people with nomadic instincts', and adding that 'I shall resist going to it whenever I can.' However, the group's other associates, such as the essayist Azorín, the playwright Ramón María del Valle-Inclán, the novelist Pío Baroja and the poets Antonio and Manuel Machado, were intensely involved in the life of Madrid, and impassioned habitués of its cafés.

The period leading up to the Civil War was the busiest period ever for Madrid's cafés and through these years can be traced the emergence of the brilliant new generation of poets calling themselves the 'Generation of 27' (of whom the best known are the poets Rafael Alberti and García Lorca), as well

The most famous work of Antonio Palacios, this neo-Churriguresque fantasy has the humble function of Madrid's main Post Office.

as more ominous developments of the time, such as the growth of the Fascist movement known as the Falange, the founder of which, José Antonio Primo de Rivera, used to hold regular meetings in the Café Lion. Yet if one place in particular has to be singled out as the cultural centre of pre-Civil-War Madrid, it would not be a café but instead the pioneering educational institution called the Residencia de los Estudiantes. Almost every figure who contributed to the heady cultural life of Madrid during these years was associated at some time with the so-called 'Resi', although today the place is popularly remembered above all for being the scene of the youthful friendship between García Lorca, the painter Salvador Dalí, and the surrealist film director Luis Buñuel.

In surveying Madrid's cultural history during this period, mention must finally be made of Ramón Gómez de la Serna, whose life was inseparable from that of Madrid's, and who indeed was the presiding figure of this period, holding court every Saturday night at the now vanished Café el Pombo. As a *Madrilenista* he is sometimes thought of as the second of the 'Ramones' (the first being, of course, Ramón de Mesonero Romanos), but instead of minutely dissecting the city with cold facts as the latter had done, he did so with dazzling aphorisms and witticisms that manage to make remarkable those features of Madrid that few others would consider worth noting, such as its rooftops or balconies. Gómez de la Serna's capacity for wonder can be as bewildering to foreigners as his near-untranslatable style. But of all the great losses that Madrid was to suffer as a result of the Civil War, it was that of Gómez de la Serna – banished to a disillusioned old age in Buenos Aires – which was to signify the closing of an era.

A most vivid account of what life was like in Madrid during the Civil War is given in the third part of Arturo Barea's powerful autobiographical trilogy, *The Forging of a Rebel* (1944). Those who visit Madrid can also have the evocative experience of descending into the bunker built in the neglected, outlying park of El Capricho. This was used by General José Miaja as the headquarters of the Republican defense of Madrid, and it was here, in November 1939, that the Civil War saw its last ignominious moments, with dissension among the Republican ranks. Madrid had been left devastated and even today you can still see the sad shell of at least one of the many churches that were gutted and pillaged by those whom priests and others continue to refer to as 'the Reds'.

A committee for the reconstruction of Madrid was established at the very end of the Civil War, but the shortage of housing was so desperate that large blocks were to grow up higgledy-piggledy on the outskirts of the city before any official scheme could be implemented. A general plan for the development of the city was finally issued in 1944, and entailed the considerable extension to the north of the Paseo de la Castellana, which was known throughout the Franco period as the Avenida Generalíssimo Franco. The civic architecture of these years immediately following the war was marked by a return to an austere Herrera-style classicism, one of the most impressive if chilling examples of which is the Air Ministry at Moncloa. In other respects, however, Madrid continued to develop the look of an American – and specifically South American – city, and by the early 1950s acquired two of the highest skyscrapers in Europe. The Bloomsbury writer and Hispanicist Gerald Brenan, visiting Madrid in 1949 after a thirteen-year absence, was amazed to find here more American cars than he had seen in any other European city. The irony, though, was that this same place – which through new waves of immigration in the 1960s had a population of 3,000,000 by 1970 – kept until very recently two centrally placed stones marking the ancient sheep trail along which transhumatory shepherds would cross the harsh Castilian plateau to and from summer grazing lands.

The Estacion del Norte: one of the best-preserved of Madrid's old stations, but now scarcely used.

One of the saddest and most significant changes to Madrid after the Civil War was the disappearance of most of its famous cafés, replaced either by the premises of large banks, or, more humiliating still, by American style cafeterias. The ever-sentimental Antonio Díaz-Cañabate, a chronicler of the literary cafés of old, rhetorically asked if a *tertulia* could ever be held in a cafeteria, and answered himself immediately: 'A *tertulia* in a cafeteria! Don't even think of it!'. However, despite the great reduction in the number of cafés, the literary café enjoyed in the post-War years a last but intensive revival, nourished by similarly repressive political conditions to those under Ferdinand VII. Gómez de la Serna may have gone, but new *Madrilenistas* had taken his place, most notably César González Ruano, whom the present-day writer Francisco Umbral remembered as the only person he had known actually to 'dress up as a writer'. The main venue for this new generation was the Café Gijón, which in its heyday in the 1940s and 1950s swarmed with artists, writers and politicians, among whom was the novelist and future Nobel-Prize winner Camilo José Cela. A café life of this intellectual intensity did not outlive the Franco era, and though the great literary figures of old can still be seen in the little-changed Café Gijón, most of these would agree that the *tertulia* has finally had its day, killed off by a combination of greater political freedom and television.

The social revolution which Spain experienced in the wake of Franco's death in 1975 turned Madrid into what it had never been during the years of his rule – a city of fashion. The leaders of fashionable Madrid in the late 1970s and early 1980s were those who allied themselves to the so-called *Movida*, or Movement: a group of young artists, writers, designers and others, who used the elusive term *posmodernismo* to celebrate the tacky and ephemeral. Their reputations as cultural figures will probably prove as ephemeral as their interests, with the possible exception of that of the film-maker Pedro Almodóvar, whose witty films of Madrid life provide if nothing else a refreshing antidote to the earnestness of much earlier Spanish cinema. The *Movida* is now defunct, but Madrid has survived as a city highly concerned with image, modernity and design, reflected in the exceptional stylishness and originality of recent architecture, and in the current vogue for creating cultural institutions, which have mushroomed in the last years in the same way that convents did in previous centuries.

The Madrid of today is promoting itself not only as a leader of cultural fashions, but also as a place where the visitor can whole-heartedly indulge a love of eating, drinking and night-life. The French novelist Stendhal considered that the best way to understand a place was to see how its people enjoyed themselves, and there is no question that one of the principal pleasures of the Madrilenians is going out to restaurants and bars, on which they spend – according to a recent survey published in the newspaper *El Independiente* – more than five times as much money as they do on culture. It is appropriate that I should have left the subject of food and drink to the end of this introduction, for it is the one which perhaps best sums up both the charms and idiosyncrasies of Madrid.

Of all the attractions of Madrid, that of eating is the one most difficult to convey to foreigners, many of whom come to Spain with prejudices about Spanish food in general which date back to the time of Romantic travellers such as Richard Ford. The virtual phobia which Ford and others had towards the use of garlic and olive-oil in Spanish cooking has fortunately been superseded by a widespread recognition of the healthy properties of these ingredients, but even so there are those who critically assume that all Spanish food is 'greasy' and saturated with garlic to an unpleasant degree. What is more you will still come across certain guidebooks that repeat Ford's comments that Spaniards eat to live rather than live to eat. How untrue this last statement is of the Spaniards of today is evident even in Spanish attitudes

The La Bola restaurant on the Calle de la Bola – a traditional Madrilenian establishment which has retained intact its turn-of-the-century appearance.

towards 'fast food': McDonald's and other hamburger chains have spread around Madrid, but they cater largely for foreigners, and have been counteracted recently by a Spanish chain called the 'Museo de Jamón' ('the Museum of Ham'), where you can eat snacks of the finest hams and cheeses to the accompaniment of an equally wide range of wines.

Spanish food is one of the exceptional regional variety, and there are few better places to acquire a love for it than in Madrid, where you will find restaurants from every Spanish region, as well as from almost every former Spanish colony, such as Cuba. The traditional cuisine of Madrid itself is that of the region of La Mancha, and is a cuisine of great simplicity which was maintained in the modest inns and households of Madrid at a time when the Bourbons were introducing French tastes to the country. Its strengths derive from the quality and freshness of the raw materials used. Lentil stew (*lentejas a la Manchega*) or soup made with bread and garlic (*sopa de ajo*) are popular starters, while characteristic main courses might comprise a thick sirloin steak (*solomillo*) or a succulent breaded hake (*merluza rebozada*): the Spanish love of seafood is as strong here as it is in the country's coastal regions, as is apparent in the bewilderingly rich displays of fish and crustaceans to be found outside many of Madrid's restaurants. One of the most typical of Madrid dishes is *callos a la Madrileña*, which is tripe stewed with wine, black pudding, and spiced sausage. The most famous of all local specialities is the meat and vegetable stew known as *cocido Madrileño*, which is a meal in itself and rarely eaten other than at lunch, the principal meal of the Spanish day. The broth of the *cocido* is served first, followed by the meats (usually chicken, salt pork, beef and spiced sausage), and lastly by the vegetables: cabbage, chickpeas and potatoes. Puddings, if eaten at all, are also simple, and although commercially made flan and *crème caramel* have become depressingly ubiquitous features of Spanish restaurants, the traditional Madrid sweets are flavoured custards (*natillas*) or the unappealingly named *leche frita* ('fried milk'), a custard-like mixture which has been fried in batter. To find this traditional Madrid fare you would do best to avoid the smarter and very expensive modern restaurants and go instead to the *mesones* (inns) or *tascas* (a humbler form of *mesón*), both of which function equally as eating and drinking establishments, and often have intimate ceramic interiors often dating back to the last century. The preference of most foreigners for eating earlier than Spaniards forces many to go to hotel restaurants or other such tourist establishments, but the unappetizing dishes served in these places will only confirm foreign prejudices about Spanish food.

Foreigners, if they are to get the most out of Madrid, have to a certain extent to adapt to the peculiarities of the Spanish life style, which, in relation to food, means having to enjoy sharing (it is common for Spaniards who go out to a restaurant to order as a starter a selection of dishes to share around). But above all it means having to respect as much as possible the Madrilenian time-table, which is more idiosyncratic than that of any other European capital, and – unlike that of Barcelona – has resisted all attempts at outside interference. The Madrilenians get to work as early as other Europeans, but between 10.30 and 11.30 are usually out of the office having breakfast. *Tapas* (snacks) taken in bars from about 1.30 onwards provide the necessary sustenance to keep going until lunchtime, which tends to be after 3.00, at the end of many a Spaniard's working day. Apart from the bars and restaurants, most of Madrid is closed until at least 5.00, and there is something slightly absurd about those groups of foreigners who have lunched early and continue sightseeing when virtually nothing is open and the heat is at its worst. The late afternoon is traditionally the time for the stroll or *paseo*, and, in the summer months, this is the ideal moment to try that popular Madrid drink known as *horchata*, a cool and milky concoction made from tiger-nuts. Supper is at 10, which is perhaps the aspect of the time-table which most infuriates tourists, particularly those tired out by a day's sightseeing. 'And I, wrote H. V. Morton in the appropriately named *A Stranger in Spain* (1954), 'who regard it as one of life's greatest pleasures to be in bed at ten, groaned inwardly'.

The Spaniards have not always kept such late hours, for Richard Ford makes no mention of this peculiarity, and Galdós, writing in 1867, said that Madrid was asleep by 12.00. The change seems to have set in by around 1900, and shortly afterwards Ramón Gómez de la Serna was reporting that the streets of Madrid were crowded with people until the early hours of the morning. Today the animation of a Madrid night can be almost unbearable, and there are many lovers of the nocturnal life style who make a point of never going out on Fridays or Saturdays, when the crush is at its worst. The choice of bars to try after supper is as wide as the choice of districts, each one of which has its own particular nocturnal atmosphere. In the summer months the places to go to are the *terrazas* or open-air bars, the most animated of which where once those that lined the Paseo de Recoletos, a district which in 1990 was superseded in popularity by that of Rosas. As befitting its new image as a city of fashion many of the Madrilenian young spend their nights searching out the latest in fashionable bars, places where the music is exceptionally loud, the design chic, the clientele made up largely of *yuppís*, and the door policy restrictive. Fortunately Madrid has bars to suit all tastes, and the streets at night are filled not just with the fashionable young but with all types and ages.

Their nocturnal habits have earned the Madrilenians the nickname of *los Gatos* ('the cats'), and the true night-lovers will be prowling the streets until dawn, making as a possible last gesture a visit to a *churrería* for a sustaining dose of doughnut fritters (*churros*) and hot chocolate. At least one such night is necessary to complete the full Madrid experience, but your mood the next day may not be entirely conducive to carrying out one of the itineraries outlined in the following chapters.

1
The Habsburg City

....

THE PUERTA DEL SOL *to* THE HERMITAGE OF SAN ISIDRO

The novelist Benito Pérez Galdós, discovering Madrid as a young man, was as much absorbed by the main architectural monuments of the city as he was by the cafés, the shops, the theatres and the humblest of its streets. In the routes that I have chosen to guide the reader around Madrid I have aimed above all to show a variety of attractions, so that 'the huge and multi-faceted city' which Galdós described comes fully to life. However, not wishing to lose the reader in the back-streets of Madrid's history and culture, I have ordered the chapters of the book in such a way that a roughly chronological portrait of the city will also unfold. Thus the first route, dealing with the area to the south-west of the Puerta del Sol, covers the few monuments that survive from medieval and renaissance Madrid, and has among its main attractions three outstanding squares that illustrate different moments in the city's development from the medieval period up to the late seventeenth century – the Plaza de la Paja, the Plaza de la Villa and the Plaza Mayor. Much of what remains of the secular architecture of the seventeenth century is also featured here, and includes a number of inns that have maintained their traditions of hostelry up to the present day.

There are few more appropriate places to begin a tour of Madrid, or indeed of Spain, than the PUERTA DEL SOL, which is the very hub of the city, on which converge ten streets and from where the distances to all other Spanish towns are calculated. 'La Puerta del Sol!', wrote Mesonero Romanos in 1861, 'what Madrilenian, or should we say what Spaniard, were he to be in one of the furthest corners of the kingdom, or in one of the most remote parts of the world, is not stirred by the mention of this name, and does not take pleasure in the thought of going one day to this celebrated place ... this vital centre of Spain's monarchy, this emporium of its modern history, of its civilization, of its poetry?' The very name of this elliptical square – 'the Gate of the Sun' – seems befitting of the splendour evoked in Mesonero Romanos's description,

OPPOSITE *The recently restored Plaza Mayor, with its central statue of Philip III.*

35

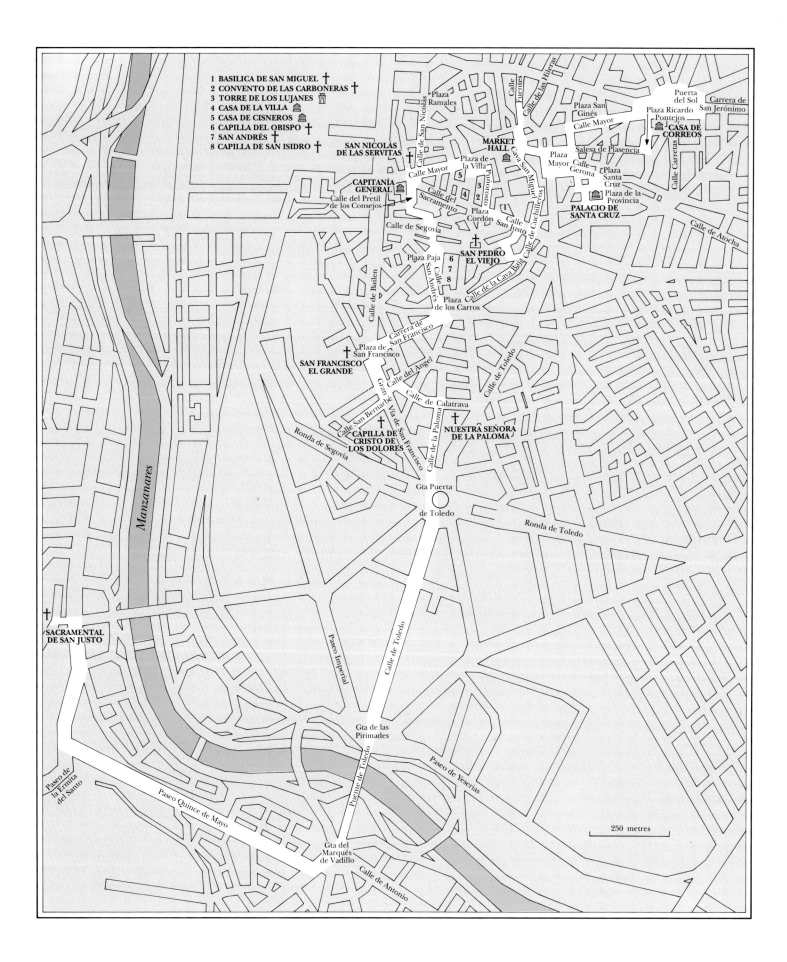

1 BASILICA DE SAN MIGUEL †
2 CONVENTO DE LAS CARBONERAS †
3 TORRE DE LOS LUJANES 🏛
4 CASA DE LA VILLA 🏛
5 CASA DE CISNEROS 🏛
6 CAPILLA DEL OBISPO †
7 SAN ANDRÉS †
8 CAPILLA DE SAN ISIDRO †

Plaza Ramales

Puerta del Sol

Carrera de San Jerónimo

Plaza San Ginés

Calle de las Hileras

Calle Fuentes

Calle de San Nicolás

SAN NICOLÁS DE LAS SERVITAS †

MARKET HALL

Plaza Ricardo Pontejos

CASA DE CORREOS 🏛

Plaza San Cruz

Plaza Mayor

Calle Mayor

Calle Mayor

Salesa de Plasencia

Calle Carretas

CAPITANÍA GENERAL 🏛

Plaza de la Villa

5

3

Calle del Pretil de los Consejos

Calle del Sacramento

4

2

Puñorosto

1

Cava San Miguel

Plaza Cordón

Calle San Justo

Calle de Cuchilleros

Calle Gerona

Plaza Santa Cruz

PALACIO DE SANTA CRUZ

Plaza de la Provincia

Calle de Segovia

Plaza Paja

SAN PEDRO EL VIEJO †

Calle de Atocha

6
7
8

Calle San Andrés

Calle de la Cava Baja

Calle de Bailén

Plaza de los Carros

Carrera de San Francisco

Calle de Toledo

Calle del Ángel

SAN FRANCISCO EL GRANDE †

Plaza de San Francisco †

Gran Vía de San Francisco

Calle de San Bernabé

CAPILLA DE CRISTO DE LOS DOLORES †

Ronda de Segovia

Calle de Calatrava

Calle de la Paloma

NUESTRA SEÑORA DE LA PALOMA †

Manzanares

Gta Puerta de Toledo

Ronda de Toledo

SACRAMENTAL DE SAN JUSTO †

Paseo Imperial

Calle de Toledo

Paseo de Yeserías

Gta de las Pirimades

Paseo de la Ermita del Santo

Puente de Toledo

Paseo Quince de Mayo

Gta del Marqués de Vadillo

Calle de Antonio

250 metres

though in fact its origins are relatively prosaic, and are to be found in a medieval castle which was built at the time of the revolt of the Comuneros and apparently bore a decorative motif of the sun. Situated alongside what was once the eastern gate of the city, the castle was pulled down shortly after the suppression of the revolt in 1522. During the reign of Philip II, the gate itself disappeared as the city's walls were extended to the east, and the surrounding area took on the form of a square, which came to be lined by three important religious foundations – the Hospital del Buen Suceso (founded apparently at the time of a great plague), and the convents of Nuestra Señora de las Victorias, and San Felipe el Real. The last of these no longer surviving institutions was situated between what are now the calles Correo and Esparteros, and rose up above the square on a terrace which became such a popular meeting-place that it acquired the name of the *Mentidero* or 'gossip centre' of the city. All of Spain's Golden-Age writers mention the *Mentidero*, which was the focal point of a square already bursting with shops and market stalls by the seventeenth century, and alive to the cries of hundreds of street vendors. In the early eighteenth century the architect Pedro de Ribera provided the square with another popular attraction in the form of the fountain known as the Mariblanca, the waters of which served both as a convenient place in which to duck the occasional drunkard, and as the main supply for the city's numerous water-sellers.

The Mariblanca, together with the two convents, was removed in the course of the nineteenth-century reforms to the Puerta del Sol. The process of enlarging the square to double its previous size was initiated at the beginning of the nineteenth century by Joseph Bonaparte, but it was not until 1858 that the rebuilding work was completed. The architecture of the square has changed remarkably little since then, the main difference being that the Hospital del Buen Suceso was replaced at the turn of the century with the imposing Hotel Paris. However, the character of the square as a meeting-place was lost irredeemably with the disappearance after 1939 of its market stalls and, above all, its cafés. The numerous cafés that grew up in the course of the nineteenth century took over the rôle which had once been played by the *Mentidero* of San Felipe el Real, and contributed more than anything else to the square's extraordinary animation. This animation made a profound impression on many of the foreign visitors to Madrid in the nineteenth century, including an Englishman called Dr Granville, who characterized the square in 1808 in terms of a 'perpetual revel'. George Borrow, with his fascination with people, was another of the square's enormous enthusiasts, although the greatest foreign tribute ever paid to it was made in 1870 by the gushing Italian novelist De Amicis, who found himself unable to leave the square, defining the place as a 'mingling of salon, promenade, theatre, academy, garden, a parade-ground, and a market'.

As well as being a great playground, the Puerta del Sol was also the scene of most of the great disturbances to have troubled the capital from the mid

KEY TO MAP SYMBOLS

🏛 Monuments

✝ Churches.

Ⅱ Columns and statues

🏛 Houses, palaces and museums

⌂ Parks and gardens

OPPOSITE
THE HABSBURG CITY

37

eighteenth century onwards, beginning with the rebellion of 1766 which deposed Charles III's unpopular minister the Marquis of Squillace. The square's 'baptism of blood' – to use the words of Mesonero Romanos – was received on 2 May 1808 when Napoleon's troops under Marshal Murat, aided by the infamous Egyptian Mameluke cavalry group, viciously attacked a rioting crowd with their sabres, an event which was to be glamorously portrayed in a famous canvas by Goya as well as in the third novel of Galdós's *Episodios nacionales*. Some 28 years later George Borrow witnessed here the failed 'revolution of la Granja', while in 1865 the suppression of another uprising in the square was to give the young Galdós his first taste of political violence and lead him to run home and try and 'find relief in my dear books'. The writer and republican Ramón Sender, describing anarchist disturbances in the square three years before the outbreak of the Civil War, compared the place 'to a bay of the sea, always in agitation'. Not only did the square reflect the political history of Madrid up to the Civil War, but also its technological transformation up to that time. It was here, in 1830, that gas lighting was used in Spain for the first time, and it was also here, in 1906, that the country's first arc lamps were put up, to celebrate Alfonso XIII's wedding; when the city's tram-lines were laid out after 1870, the square also became the terminus of the new transport system, as also happened after 1919 with the inauguration of Madrid's new metro.

The most recent improvements to the Puerta del Sol were carried out after 1986 and included the laying out of a large pedestrian area and the repainting of the elegant mid nineteenth-century buildings on the square's curved, northern side. For all this face-lift, however, the place remains as Mesonero Romanos found it in one of his more sober moments, 'more renowned for its crowds and central position than for the beauty of its architecture'. The crowds today are probably as numerous as they were in the past, but the idlers and potential revolutionaries of old have given way to shoppers and office-workers rushing to the underground station. From being the social heart of Madrid, the square is now the Madrilenian equivalent of London's Oxford Circus, and the nostalgic traveller, mentally trying to recreate the brilliant café life of former days, might experience a particular feeling of poignancy on discovering what has happened to one of the most famous and long-lived of its cafés. This café, the Universal, was to be found up to as late as 1955 on the north-eastern corner of the square, at what is now number 14. Covered in a lavish decoration of gilded mirrors, the Universal was a famous liberal centre from the early nineteenth century onwards, and in the 1860s was a popular haunt of Galdós, who met up here with many of his fellow Canary-Islanders. In 1955 it was converted into an American-style cafeteria by the name of Quick, and remains under the same management today, complete with a bland interior of formica and light polished wood. Ramón Gomez de la Serna – whose enthusiasm for the square in its pre-Civil-War days had been so great that he had written a whole book devoted to it – made a sad return visit to

Madrid in 1949. Recalling the occasion in his autobiography, he referred to the fate of the famous café, and could only utter the words, '*Sic Transit!*'.

Another monument testifying to the transience of earthly glory is the HOTEL PARIS, which was built in 1894 on the narrow eastern side of the square, in between the Calle de Alcalá and the Carrera de San Jerónimo. At the time of its construction it was Madrid's most luxurious hotel, and as such was chosen in 1906 as the place to lodge the numerous dignitaries who had been invited to Madrid from all over the world to attend the ill-fated wedding of Alfonso XIII to Victoria Eugenia von Battenberg. The stuccoed, neo-baroque exterior of the hotel still retains much of its former grandeur, but the gloomy interior, tackily transformed in the 1950s, will appeal largely to those with a love of kitsch, and features such high points of bad taste as a ceramic corgi dog pathetically tied by a chain to a table on the staircase landing.

Continuing this clockwise tour of the Puerta del Sol, you will come, on its south-eastern side, to one of the square's few shops to have survived the Civil War, the Librería de San Martín. Situated at number 6, next to the Calle Carretas, this small and crammed bookshop has specialized for many years in military books, and was itself the scene of a famous terrorist event when on 12 November 1912, the radical Liberal Prime Minister of Spain, José Canalejas, was assassinated while browsing at its shop-window. As you cross the Calle Carretas, you will pass to your left, at what was once number 4 of this street, the site of one of Madrid's most famous literary cafés, El Pombo. Its fame is due principally to Ramón Gómez de la Serna, who organized here in the 1920s the best attended of the city's literary *tertulias*. These were held every Saturday night in the café's basement, and became such a revered institution of Madrid that the basement came to be dubbed 'the Sacred Crypt of the Pombo'. Gómez de la Serna dedicated to the Pombo what must be the longest book ever written on a café, but a pithier description of the place is to be found in the spirited autobiography of Luis Buñuel, *My Last Breath* (1982):

> At the Café Pombo . . . we used to arrive, greet each other, and order a drink – usually coffee, and a lot of water – until a meandering conversation began about the latest literary publications or political upheavals. We loaned one another books and foreign journals, and gossiped about our absent brothers. Sometimes an author would read one of his poems or articles aloud, and Ramón would offer his opinion, which was always respected and sometimes disputed.

The café did not survive Gómez de la Serna's exile to Argentina in 1936, and in 1963 Archibald Lyall wrote that 'to add insult to injury, the same building now houses a cafeteria called Tío Sam, decorated with pictures of Uncle Sam'. Later even this cafeteria was closed down, and in its stead a shop selling leather goods was opened. Today, the café's ignominious decline has gone one stage further, the walls of the sacred crypt having been cleared to form a large building site directly behind the former CASA DE CORREOS.

This former Post Office, the most important building on the Puerta del Sol, occupies most of southern side of the square, and was built for Charles III in the 1760s. Designed by the French architect Jacques Marquet, it served as the city's post office up to 1847, after which it became the seat of the Ministry of the Interior. In 1867 the pedimented frontispiece of this neo-classical brick structure was crowned with what is today the building's most popular feature, a clock tower which has the same symbolic and practical importance as London's Big Ben: it tells the time for the Spanish nation, and its chimes are daily heard on Spanish radio. The life story of the man who designed the clock's original mechanism, Ramón Losada, is in itself of interest. A shepherd from the Astorga region of north-western Castile, Losada fled to Madrid after having been beaten up by the owner of his flock. In Madrid he became involved in politics, and soon was persecuted for his beliefs by Ferdinand VII. Fortunately he was able to obtain a safe conduct to France after having bribed Madrid's mayor at this time, José Zorrilla, a man whom he had caught out having an affair. Losada went from France to London, where he married and made his way up from being an apprentice clocksmith to the owner of a highly successful shop manufacturing clocks. Although still illiterate at the time of his arrival in London, he soon achieved a reputation as an intellectual, and he organized in his London shop a special *tertulia* for Spain's many distinguished literary and political exiles then resident in this city. Ironically, among these figures was José Zorrilla's son, the famous romantic poet also called José, who dedicated a poem to Losada. While in London, Losada designed two clocks for Spain, one for his native village, and the other for the Puerta del Sol, the latter clock distinguished by a large metal sphere which is regularly lowered at the chiming of twelve.

A plaque to the victims of 2 May 1808 is placed on the façade of the Casa de Correos, while inside the main door is the stone slab denoting 'Kilometric Zero', from where all the distances in Spain are measured. No longer the Ministry of the Interior, the building is now shared by the main offices of the local government of Madrid (the Comunidad) and the city's police headquarters. A certain amount of ingenuity and bravado is needed to persuade your way past the armed police in the entrance hall, and visit the interior. The elegant neo-rococo Assembly Rooms on the main floor include a room which is named after Canalejas and leads out on to the balcony from where in 1931 the advent of Spain's Second Republic was proclaimed to the waiting crowds in the Puerta del Sol below. A rather less glamorous event in Spain's recent political history took place in the glazed courtyard belonging to the part of the building which is run by the police. This was an incident which still arouses strong feelings, and the friend whom I was with lowered her voice as she indicated the window from which the Communist militant Grimau was supposedly thrown in 1963. Grimau did not die immediately and had to be finished off shortly afterwards by firing squad, an execution which led to a large international outcry.

The plaque on the former central Post Office commemorates the popular uprising of 1808 against the French.

On the western side of the Casa de Correos the short Calle Correo heads south to the small and dignified square named after Ricardo, Marquis of Pontejos, an urban reformer who died in 1840. This is a detour which should be undertaken by readers of Galdós, for it was around this square that he set much of the action of his greatest work, *Fortunata and Jacinta*. Juanito de Santa Cruz, the spoilt male protagonist of this novel, and the cause of the eponymous heroines' misfortunes, lived with his wife Jacinta in an immense first-floor apartment overlooking the square from the Calle Pontejos (the house, with its twelve balconies, can still be identified). The simple fountain in the middle of the square – erected in 1849 and graced with a bust of Pontejos – is mentioned in the novel, as is the jumble of narrow commercial streets that extend between here and the nearby Plaza Mayor. The best known of these streets is the Calle de Postas, so-called because the house at number 32 was the site of Madrid's first post office, which dates back to the sixteenth century. The mother of Juanito de Santa Cruz, Barbarita Arnáiz, was born and brought up at a house on the corner of the Calle de Postas and the Calle San Cristobal, 'in one of those dreary terraced houses that look more like shoe boxes because of their miniature scale'. Her family was associated with the manufacture of manila shawls, a recent fashion of oriental inspiration which gave to her childhood memories a strong exotic flavour, 'redolent of sandalwood and oriental fragrances'. Manila shawls can no longer be bought on this street, but a comparably exotic textile shop is to be found at number 14, a musty institution from another era: it specializes in textiles used in the making of religious garments.

The principal street leading west from the Puerta del Sol is the Calle Mayor, a street of medieval origin which was widened for carriages in the seventeenth century, and became thereafter the main artery through the city. Favoured as a processional route used by royalty and visiting dignitaries to Madrid, the Calle Mayor came also to attract from the seventeenth century onwards many of the city's important commercial enterprises and administrative institutions. Although rich in seventeenth-century associations, and with much of the character of this period, this dark and animated street is lined today mainly with buildings from the turn of the century. At the entrance to the street from the Puerta del Sol once stood the Palacio de Oñate, in front of which the homosexual poet and courtier, the Conde de Villamediana, was murdered by means of a cross-bow on the night of 21 August 1622. The pavement outside this building also served as a place where seventeenth-century painters exhibited their works, and it was here that the Sevillian artist, Bartolomé Esteban Murillo, attracted the notice of Charles II with a picture of the Immaculate Conception. The site of this palace is now occupied by a grand commercial building designed by Antonio Palacios in 1919, and featuring inside a lively elliptical patio glazed with colourful stained glass (the entrance to the building is at number 4). At number 3, on the opposite side of the street, a door next to a flamboyant turn-of-the-century

The curious interior of a commercial building on the Calle Mayor, designed by the prolific Antonio Palacios.

structure by José López Sallaberry marks the entrance to a building housing one of Madrid's more traditional photographic studios, Bariego. The approach to these studios, up a dirty staircase with peeling paint and crumbling plaster, is distinctly seedy, and once inside you will find yourself in a world which seems scarcely to have changed from the 1920s, complete with old and dusty studio props and a white-bearded Mr Bariego himself. Continuing west along the Calle Mayor, you will pass, at the junction of the Calle Felipe III another of the many relics of Madrid's commercial past, a jewellery shop adorned on the outside with amusing figurative reliefs of men at work. Before turning left here into the Plaza Mayor, those who enjoy

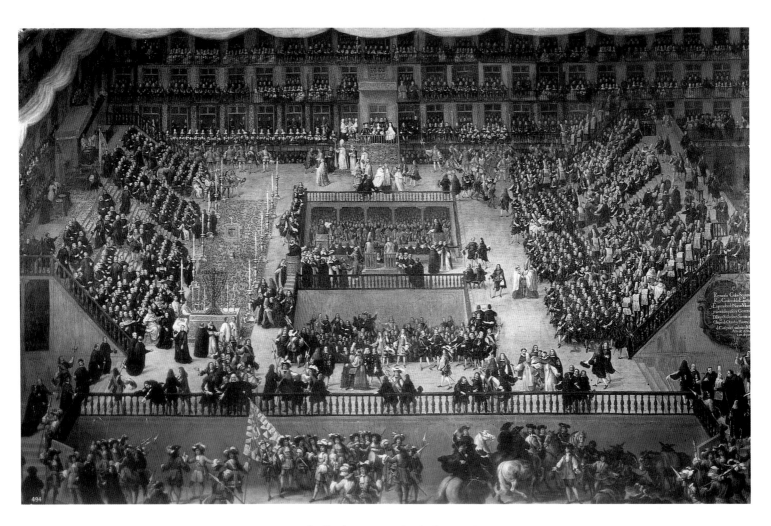

An Auto de Fe held in the Plaza Mayor on 30 June 1680, painted by Francisco Rizi. One of the heretics on trial is wearing the tall hat later featured in Goya's scenes of the Inquisition.

assimilating esoteric information should direct a passing glance at the apartment block on the other side of the street, at number 28. A long-time inhabitant of this block, until his death here in 1923, was Alfred Löwy, who had a distinguished career as a director of Spanish railways but is remembered today – if at all – as the uncle of Franz Kafka. This life-long bachelor, known always to Kafka as 'the uncle from Madrid', made frequent return visits to his native Prague, where he inspired in his young nephew a yearning to go to Madrid. The Spanish capital appeared to offer the future writer an exotic means of escaping from the claustrophobic influence of family life at home. Much to Kafka's disappointment, the uncle was not able to find a job for him in Madrid, but Löwy was none the less to play a significant role in his nephew's life by persuading him to work with an insurance company. The uncle lies today buried and forgotten in the ugly Madrid suburb of Carabanchel, but this story of Kafka and Madrid deserves – like that of Hitler and Liverpool – to be revived in the form of an imaginative novel.

The vast, pedestrian square of the Plaza Mayor was by far the most formidable example of town-planning left by the Habsburgs to Madrid, and rivals in its beauty the greatest squares of Europe. This bold and dramatic conception had humble beginnings, for its predecessor was an irregular square surrounded by tiny, slum-like houses and situated until the sixteenth century outside the city gates. The architect of the Escorial, Juan de Herrera, was commissioned in the late sixteenth century to transform and dignify this chaotic space, but it was not until the time of Philip III that the definitive plans for a new square were drawn up. The architect eventually chosen for the task was Herrera's pupil, Juan Gómez de Mora, who carried out the work with remarkable speed, beginning it in 1617 and completing it two years later. The end result could be described as an especially grand, tidy and homogenous version of the arcaded town centres traditional to Castile. A specific source of inspiration for so formal a work might have been the square which had been rebuilt in Valladolid by Philip II, but no other previous Spanish square had been conceived on such an ambitious scale. The surrounding buildings were able to house up to 3000 people, while, on festive occasions, no less than 50,000 could be crammed inside the square itself. The architecture and scale of the Plaza Mayor were to be emulated in many later Spanish squares, but perhaps only that in the town of Salamanca was to achieve a comparable grandeur.

In its layout and overall austerity, and in such details as the slate spires and steeply pitched roofs with dormer windows, the Plaza Mayor of today reflects Gómez de Mora's original concept, and in turn the architectural legacy of Herrera. However, due to severe fires, the square has been subject to several rebuilding campaigns, the last major one being that begun in 1795 by Juan de Villanueva. It was not until 1847 that the square received – thanks to the initiative of Mesonero Romanos – one of its finest features, an equestrian bronze statue of Philip III, designed by the mannerist sculptor Giambologna and his pupil Pietro Tacca. The most recent developments in the square's history have included the building of a large car park underneath it, and a thorough restoration of its balconied houses to create what are now among the more fashionable addresses in central Madrid.

In common with the Puerta del Sol, the Plaza Mayor was once filled with shops and market stalls, and the names Panadería (bakery) and Carnicería (meat market) are still given to its two most prominent buildings, on the northern and southern sides respectively. But it has also been regularly converted into a stage for grand and sometimes chilling spectacles, the action being watched by the king and other dignitaries from the balconies above the municipal bakery. The Plaza Mayor was officially inaugurated in 1622 with festivities marking the canonization of St Isidro, and since then the square has been used for such diverse events as public executions, trials by the Inquisition, bullfights, jousts, coronations, and performances of plays by Lope de Vega and others. Ballets and theatrical performances are still put on

A typical example of the tightly packed nineteenth-century streets surrounding the Plaza Mayor.

in the square during the summer months, but the last major festivities to be seen here were those celebrating the wedding of Isabel II in 1846. The square today is very different to and more sedate than it used to be, and its commercial establishments have virtually all given way to expensive and unfriendly cafés catering almost exclusively for tourists, who – completely contrary to local habits – have a tendency to sit outside in the blinding sun. Few Madrilenians would ever think of coming to the square, other than to visit the stamp market which is held under its arcades every Sunday morning.

Another of the major civic monuments of Habsburg Madrid, the former Cárcel de Corte (Court Prison), now called the PALACIO DE SANTA CRUZ, lies off the south-eastern corner of the Plaza Mayor. Its main entrance is on the small Plaza de la Provincia, which in its earlier days was animated by the noisy commercial life which overflowed from the larger, adjacent square. A prison had been built here by Philip II in 1563, and had had as one of its most distinguished inmates Lope de Vega, accused in 1587 of writing scurrilous poems against the family of the actress with whom he had been conducting an illicit, adulterous affair. Stricter security regulations issued by Philip IV led to the old building being replaced after 1629 by the Cárcel de Corte, the new structure being intended both as a prison for persons of high rank as well as offices for justices of peace of the royal household. The main architect was Gómez de Mora, who created a symmetrical block in the style of the Escorial, but departed significantly from Herrera's austere influence in the richly modelled frontispiece and in the delicate carvings on the central staircase inside. Among the last people to be imprisoned here was the writer and adventurer George Borrow, who was arrested in 1838 for his evangelizing activities on behalf of the Bible Society. Prone to wild exaggeration and great flights of imagination, he was later to evoke the prison as if it were a dungeon of Piranesi-like proportions, 'so irregular and rambling' as to defy too close a description. To him the building did no 'credit to the capital of the Spain', and he seriously doubted if a place with such vile conditions had ever been intended as a prison in the first place. Typically for Borrow, however, he appears to have been far less concerned about his own well-being here than were his friends in England, and indeed he made use of his prison stay to study the dialect of thieves. Later in the nineteenth century the building was put to a variety of different municipal uses before finally becoming, in 1901, the seat of the Ministry of Foreign Affairs. The large annexe at the back dates from the Franco period and clearly indicates the way in which Fascist architects appropriated the principles of the Herrera school.

Leaving the Plaza Mayor by its north-western corner you will soon emerge at the junction of the Calle Mayor and the Plaza de San Miguel, the latter dominated by a fanciful ironwork MARKET HALL dating from 1916, and the only building of its kind still left in Madrid; the site was originally occupied by the church of San Miguel de los Octoes, one of the many religious institutions pulled down by Joseph Bonaparte. A short detour to the north of the square, crossing the Calle Mayor, can be made to see the former boarding house – at number 3 Calle Fuentes – where Galdós stayed from 1862 to 1863, shortly after he had moved to Madrid from the Canary Islands. The future novelist had a room on the second floor, which was reached in his time by way of a poorly lit staircase badly in need of a coat of paint. This elegantly classical building of the early nineteenth century, recently given a vivid ochre face-lift, is of great interest for being virtually the only one of Galdos's many Madrid dwellings to have survived.

South of the Plaza de San Miguel descends the picturesque Cava San Miguel, hugging the curved walls of the tall seventeenth-century houses comprising the western side of the Plaza Mayor. These houses all feature ground-floor cellars, as do those on the Cava San Miguel's continuation, the Calle de Cuchilleros, a street named after the knife-makers who until comparatively recently had their shops here. Many of the cellars on the two streets have hostelry traditions of long standing, and at number 17 Calle de Cuchilleros is to be found what the *Guinness Book of Records* calls the oldest restaurant in the world, the CASA BOTÍN. Dating back to 1725, it even gets a mention in Galdós's *Fortunata and Jacinta*, as a plaque on the outside records. Inside is a series of intimate wooden beamed dining rooms, where you can eat roast meats cooked in an old oak-fuelled oven. Hemingway described the place not simply as the oldest but also the best restaurant in the world, and this exaggerated assessment, combined with the Casa Botín's proximity to the Plaza Mayor, have ensured that the place is packed daily with tourists. A number of other famous old restaurants can be seen by continuing south from Botín, the first of which – at number 11 Plaza de la Puerta Cerrada – is Casa Paco, a small, ceramic-tiled establishment well known for its hams and steaks. Below the Plaza de la Puerta Cerrada runs the Calle de la Cava Baja, one of the Madrid streets which, for all its nineteenth-century buildings and recent changes, best conveys the domestic character of sixteenth- and seventeenth-century Madrid. Several traditional craftsmen still have their workshops here, but the fame of the street lies principally in its numerous *mesones* or inns, of which the most celebrated is the POSADA DE SAN PEDRO at number 30. Better known as the Mesón del Segoviano, this establishment was founded in 1740 and is the only Madrid inn to have preserved its traditional vestibule and quaintly irregular, balconied patio, above which the inn's guests would sleep. The place functioned until this century as a staging post for *dilgences* serving the provinces of Toledo, Segovia and Guadalajara, and it was not so long ago that a mule drawn cart from the Toledan town of Illescas – the so-called *Ordinario de Illescas* – could be seen drawing up here every Friday, sometimes sharing the patio with the expensive cars of foreign visitors. The inn's restaurant has been popular both with tourists and writers, and in 1927 a famous literary banquet was put on here for the Burgos writer Francisco Gramontagne, in whose honour such prominent members of the Generation of 98 as Azorín and Antonio Machado gave speeches.

Whereas the character of old Madrid is well evoked by the Calle de la Cava Baja, the actual look of the city before being drastically changed in the nineteenth century can be wonderfully appreciated in the small area of quiet squares and narrow ascending streets which extends north-west of the Plaza de la Puerta Cerrada. Leaving the square on the Calle San Justo, you will come almost immediately to one of the few churches in Madrid that architectural purists would define as truly baroque, the BASILICA DE SAN MIGUEL. Most of Spain's so-called 'baroque' churches are 'baroque' only by virtue of their ornamentation, and are relatively simple structures, lacking the dynamic ground-plans characteristic of the works of the great Italian or

A modern ceramic plaque marking the street where knife-makers once had their shops.

Central European architects of the seventeenth and eighteenth centuries. San Miguel, in contrast, has an exciting convex façade and an interior of undulating bays and diagonally projecting piers. It comes as no surprise that the architect was an Italian, Santiago Bonavia, and one very much inspired by the great Piedmontese architect, Guarino Guarini: the latter's influence is clearly apparent in Bonavia's combination of a baroque ground-plan with cross-vaulting and tall proportions of gothic derivation. The building was designed at the very end of the seventeenth century, but was heavily embellished in later years.

Immediately beyond the church of San Miguel, the Calle San Justo widens into the tiny Plaza Cordón, which is bordered on its southern side by an eighteenth-century palace of Herreran simplicity. Adjacent to the north-western corner of the square, at number 2 Calle del Sacramento, is an exquisitely carved renaissance portal belonging to the Casa de Cisneros, the

One of the best-known of Madrid's surviving old restaurants.

main entrance to which is on the Plaza de la Villa. The latter square can be reached from here by climbing north up the narrow Calle Cordón, but a more interesting route is to follow the alley called Puñorostro, which begins its short ascent alongside the church of San Miguel, and passes next to the CONVENT OF LAS CARBONERAS. This Jeronymite convent, founded in 1607, has an exceedingly plain brick exterior, the austerity of which is relieved purely by the relief carving above the church portal. The interest of this institution, however, is less an architectural than a gastronomic one, for this is one of the last remaining convents in Madrid to make and sell its own cakes and pastries. Ever since the time that St Teresa of Ávila distributed sweetened egg yolks to the poor of her native Ávila, the making of sweets has been one of the great specialities of Spanish convents, and an important source of their income. Las Carboneras is a closed-order convent, and buying from these nuns has its own exotic ritual, the negotiations being carried out through a rotating drum on which both the goods and your money are placed. The traditional way of addressing a nun is with the words '*Ave Maria Purissima*', to which she will reply '*Sin pecado recibido*' (without inherited sin). This formality over you then put in your request from a list of specialities pinned to the wall, one of the sweets on offer in this particular convent being a long, dry biscuit with the appropriate name of *Huesos de Fray Escoba* (Bones of Father Escoba). After leaving the convent you only have to carry your bones a few more metres uphill before coming out at the Plaza de la Villa, noting just as you turn the final corner the *mudéjar* horseshoe arch of the Torre de los Lujanes.

The Plaza de la Villa, although backed on its northern side by the Calle Mayor, is a quiet and dignified square, which in 1980 was thankfully cleared of traffic, a car park, and a central landscaped reservation. In its stone-paved centre stands a statue – by the leading turn-of-the-century sculptor Mariano Benlliure – of Don Alvaro de Bazán, an admiral of Philip II who had distinguished himself at the Battle of Lepanto in 1571. A suitably splendid backcloth to this great admiral is provided by the surrounding buildings, which constitute Madrid's oldest architectural ensemble. The TORRE and adjoining PALACIO DE LOS LUJANES, although heavily restored, date back to the early fifteenth century, and, together with the neighbouring palace at number 3, are virtually the sole survivals of Madrid's civil architecture of this period. The Madrilenian nobility, led by the magistrate Vargas, defended themselves in the Palacio de los Lujanes at one point during the revolt of the Comuneros of 1521–22, and it is also said that the French king François I was imprisoned here after his defeat at the Battle of Pavia in 1525. The palace's boldly carved stone portal is particularly impressive, as is the large *mudéjar* arch through which you enter the smaller palace at number 3. The latter building has been adapted as municipal offices, but is worth visiting for its fragments from the destroyed fifteenth-century hospital of La Latina, notably a gothic balustrade and the finely carved plateresque tombs of Beatriz Galindo ('La Latina') and her husband, Francisco Mirez ('El Artillero').

Allegorical relief above the main portal of Santiago Bonavia's basilica of San Miguel.

The façade of Madrid's Town Hall, showing baroque ornamental additions to the austere Herreran conception.

A palace slightly later in date and more sophisticated in appearance is the CASA DE CISNEROS, which takes up the southern side of the square, and is a typical example of the so-called plateresque, a term derived from the use by Spain's renaissance architects and sculptors of filigree detailing imitative of the work of *plateros* or silversmiths. The building dates back to 1537 but was almost entirely remodelled in the early years of the present century, when the 'plateresque' was taken up as the Spanish national style. A gallery now connects the palace with the adjacent CASA DE LA VILLA (Town Hall), the largest and most important of the square's buildings. It is indicative of the absolutist spirit of Habsburg Spain that the mayor of one of the most rapidly growing capitals of Europe should be merely an employee of the court, and that he and his city council should not have a building of their own until the construction of the Casa de la Villa in the middle of the seventeenth century. The initial plans were drawn up in 1640 by the then aged Gómez de Mora, but the building was not completed until the end of the seventeenth century, by which time the typically Herreran structure had acquired baroque portals and other fanciful details. In 1771 the façade overlooking the Plaza Mayor was modified by Juan de Villanueva so as to incorporate a balcony from which royal parties could watch the city's Corpus Christi processions. The building can be visited by guided tour on Monday afternoons, but this is not an experience which can be whole-heartedly recommended, especially as it entails listening to an interminable talk about the origins of Madrid's coat of arms. The interior has for the most part a drab municipal character of the early years of this century, and the original patio, damaged during the Civil War, has been closed in with stained glass. Most of the treasures that were once displayed here have now been removed to the city's Municipal Museum, including a late sixteenth-century *custodia*, and a famous allegorical work by Goya (p. 150). For lovers of nineteenth-century academic art there is at least the consolation of V. Palmaroli's huge canvas of 1871 depicting the *3rd of May*, the subject of Goya fame being interpreted here with hysterical women set against a dawn panorama of Madrid. But the best reason to visit the Casa de la Villa is to see the remarkable Sala de Actos, which, with its public gallery and facing benches, has been compared to a miniature version of Britain's House of Commons. The sumptuously gilded heavy decoration, however, is wholly Spanish, and features the main survival of the original interior – a late baroque illusionistic ceiling painting by Antonio Palomino.

On the northern side of the Plaza de la Villa, rising above the present Calle Mayor, once stood the seventeenth-century church which gave the square its original name of Plaza de Salvador. The church of San Salvador had fallen to ruin by the nineteenth century, and was pulled down in 1842, its memory being preserved today in a stone inscription attached to number 70 of the Calle Mayor. A more recent plaque on the same building records that the tower of the church was used as the main setting for a highly popular novel of 1641 by the Andalusian-born satirist Luis Vélez de Guevara: this work, *El Diablo Cojuelo* (The Lame Devil) deals with a student who releases a devil from an astrologer's phial and is taken by him on a tour of Madrid and Andalusia. Just to the east of here, at number 48 Calle Mayor, a modern building marks the house where Lope de Vega was born in 1562. His father had come to Madrid to move in with a Greek girl called Helen, but the wife whom he had abandoned in Valladolid soon caught up with him and managed to separate the pair. By great coincidence, Lope's main rival as Spain's leading dramatist of the Golden Age, Calderón de la Barca, died in 1681 on the opposite side of the street, in a house just to the west of the Plaza de la Villa, at number 61. This house, though heavily restored and remodelled, retains much of its original appearance. Calderón spent the last years of his life here, during which time he served as a chaplain to the church of San Salvador. On the day following his death his body was carried from here by priests to the church, and buried temporarily in a chapel while awaiting transference to a splendid black marble mausoleum planned for the right transept. The mausoleum was completed shortly afterwards, but for some reason the body remained where it was, and was only moved when the church was finally destroyed. From that moment onwards the body made up for its previous inactivity by a series of constant transferences from one part of Madrid to another, each occasion marked by a solemn procession. The church where it eventually ended up, on the Calle de San Bernado, was gutted during the Civil War, and the mortal remains of Calderón – as with those of many other Golden-Age writers – remain missing to this day. As Miguel de Unamuno ruefully commented, the dead in Spain are never allowed to rest.

Continuing to head along the Calle Mayor from Calderón's house, you will pass to your right the Calle de San Nicolás, where you will find the charming small church of SAN NICOLÁS DE LAS SERVITAS, the exterior of which is distinguished by a brick tower decorated with blind arcades of horse-shoe arches. The tower is thought by some to have been originally the minaret of a mosque, in which case it would be virtually the sole relic of Moorish Magerit; more probably a *mudéjar* work of the twelfth century, it is in any case one of Madrid's oldest surviving structures. The light and cheerful interior of the building has been heavily altered over the centuries, but still retains *mudéjar* elements as well as a fine late fifteenth-century apse. On the other side of the Calle de San Nicolás is a curious temporary-looking structure completely dwarfed by its surroundings. It is in fact a Basque club known as a Cloxto, the members of which take it in turns to cook for each other.

Near the westernmost end of the Calle Mayor, at number 84, is a well-known old tavern and restaurant called Casa Ciriaco, which was founded in 1917 by Ciriaco Muñoz. Among the many literary, artistic and other celebrities to have been regulars at this place were the bullfighter Juan Belmonte, the ubiquitous frequenter of *tertulias* Díaz-Cañabate, and the humorist and gastronome Julio Camba, in whose honour a regular monthly dinner is held in the modern dining room at the back of the bar. The attractively tiled bar displays numerous cuttings relating to the establishment's history, and there is also a plaque placed above the marble table where on October 25, 1945, the painter Ignacio Zuloaga enjoyed the last meal of his life. The building in which Casa Ciriaco is housed carries further mortal associations, for it was from one of its second floor balconies that on 31 May 1906 one Mateo Morral threw a bomb at the nuptial processional carriage carrying Alfonso XIII and Victoria Eugenia von Battenberg. The explosion killed several passersby and even the horses of the royal carriage, but the young couple themselves escaped without injury. Morral committed suicide to avoid being captured; his body was identified by the writer Valle-Inclán.

A bronze angel commemorating this assassination attempt and its victims is to be found on the opposite side of the street, in front of the late seventeenth-century church and convent of EL SACRAMENTO. From here you should descend down the Calle del Pretil de los Consejos, noting to your right the

Glazed turn-of-the-century balconies on the Calle Mayor.

impressively sober palace (now the CAPITANÍA GENERAL) built between 1609 and 1611 by Juan Gómez de Mora to plans supplied by his father Francisco. Below the palace you have a good view of the bridge known as the SEGOVIA VIADUCT, which connects the hill of the Palacio Real with that of las Vistillas. The deep hollow which the viaduct spans effectively divided in two Habsburg Madrid, and the search for a way of joining the two areas was one which had long preoccupied the city's architects. The Italian architect Sacchetti proposed a solution to this problem in the early eighteenth century and another one was put forward by Silvestre Pérez during the rule of Joseph Bonaparte. However, it was not until 1868 that a plan for a bridge – a metal structure based on a design of 1859 by Eugenio Barón – was finally approved, the structure being inaugurated six years later with a procession carrying Calderón's remains from the church of San Francisco el Grande to the cemetery of San Nicolás de las Servitas. In the 1930s the original bridge was replaced by the present one, a concrete functionalist work comprising great parabolic arches. The Segovia Viaduct is much admired by some as an architectural and engineering achievement, but most Madrilenians tend to think of it simply as 'The Bridge of Suicides'. The last of Madrid's *costumbristas*, Emilio Carrere, popularized this nickname in a newspaper article which apparently led to far more people throwing themselves off the viaduct than ever before. On this morbid note, it might be worth mentioning the ironic but hitherto unremarked fact that one of the most famous suicides in Spanish history, the Romantic poet Mariano José de Larra, was born in 1809 in a house directly overlooking the site of the future viaduct. His birthplace, long since gone, is marked today by a plaque on the modern apartment building at number 11 Calle del Pretil de los Consejos.

At the bottom of the street you will find yourself on the Calle de Segovia, which runs along the furrow between the two hills, and has several old taverns and ceramic shops. From the Plaza de la Cruz Verde you should head south on the gradually ascending Costa San Andrés, which – at the point where it widens into the Plaza de la Paja – passes immediately on the left the Calle de Príncipe Anglona. The latter street beautifully frames another of the rare survivals of *mudéjar* Madrid, a brick tower of 1354 attached to the church of SAN PEDRO EL VIEJO. The church itself, founded probably on the site of a mosque, was largely rebuilt in the seventeenth century, but has kept a renaissance west portal of 1525, and – on the south portal – the only royal coats of arms in Madrid which predate Ferdinand and Isabel.

The sloping and irregularly shaped Plaza de la Paja is one of the most enchanting but also neglected corners of old Madrid, and you might find it difficult to believe that this slightly run-down place enlivened today only by the shrieks of playing children was the largest and most important square of the medieval city. In contrast to the squalid predecessor of the Plaza Mayor it was an aristocratic square and lined on all sides with imposing palaces, one of which was known as the Palacio de Isabel la Católica for having lodged on one occasion the Castilian queen. Although all these palaces had been taken down by the end of the nineteenth century, the city's greatest renaissance jewel is still to be seen here, dominating the narrow, upper end of the square. The story of this monument, the so-called CAPILLA DEL OBISPO (Bishop's Chapel), is connected with that of the most powerful family to have lived on the square, the Vargas. The Palacio Vargas occupied a site marked today by a 1920s building imitating the adjacent sixteenth-century façade which gives access to the chapel. From the time of Iván de Vargas, in the thirteenth century, the family had in its possession the relics of Madrid's patron saint, St Isidro, and it was to house these in a suitably dignified fashion that Don Francisco de Vargas – councillor to Ferdinand and Isabel as well as to the Emperor Charles V – commissioned in 1520 the present chapel. The chapel was originally connected to the neighbouring parish church of San Andrés, but when a long dispute led in 1544 to the transference of the relics to the church itself, Don Francisco's son, the Bishop of Plasencia, decided to convert the chapel into a family pantheon. The surrounding area was consequently rebuilt and firmly separated from the church, and it was thanks to this that the chapel was able to survive the fire which gutted San Andrés in 1936.

Disgracefully and quite inexcusably, the chapel has been closed to the public for many years, and special permission to go inside is required from the Archbishopric of Madrid, which has owned the monument since 1980. It is well worth persevering in your efforts to get in, for the dusty interior, reached through a ruinous cloister, forms a surprisingly unspoilt sixteenth-century survival, complete with flamboyant late gothic vaulting, as well as superlatively intricate furnishings that are amongst the finest expressions of the Spanish plateresque. Virtuoso relief carvings in wood of Old Testament subjects decorate the doors of the west portal, while on the south wall of the nave is the alabaster wall tomb of the Bishop of Plasencia, a work exquisitely adorned with renaissance detailing, and with a group of musical angels recalling those of Luca della Robbia from the choir of Florence Cathedral. Finally, flanked by the tombs of Don Francisco and his wife, comes the high altar, a dazzling structure in gilded wood rising in true Spanish fashion up to the ceiling. As with all the other works in the chapel, the high altar is by an unknown artist, but it is generally attributed today to Francisco Giralte, a pupil of Spain's sculptural genius of the Renaissance, Alonso Berruguete. The abbot Antonio Ponz, the eighteenth-century author of an eighteen-volume account of Spain's artistic treasures, considered it as 'one of the most elaborately worked pieces of sculpture that Spain possesses, and amongst the best produced in this country at the beginning of the sixteenth century'.

Leaving the Plaza de la Paja by its southern corner, make your way round to the back of the complex containing the Capilla del Obispo. All that survives of the original church of San Andrés is its bell-tower, but rising up next to this is a most eloquent domed chapel which was added to the church in the mid seventeenth century to commemorate the canonization of St Isidro in

The baroque skyline of Madrid from the Hotel Emperador looking towards the church of San Francisco el Grande in the far distance.

1622. Gómez de Mora drew up the initial plans, but in the end the work was carried out by later architects, who conceived a sumptuously coloured and richly modelled interior, with a lower level of gilding and dark marble which was directly inspired by the early baroque Pantheon of the Kings in the Escorial. Terribly damaged by the same anarchist attack of 1936 which ruined for ever the adjoining church, the chapel has recently been excellently restored, and although missing its flamboyant baldacchino, and surrounding altars by Claudio Coello, Francisco Rizi and others, still retains much of its original decorative splendour.

The CHAPEL OF SAN ISIDRO looks out over an untidy series of interconnecting squares stretching in a south-easterly direction all the way to the Calle de Toledo. To the south-west meanwhile descends the broad Carrera de San Francisco, which will land you directly in front of the massive church of that name, the largest in Madrid, and the one which most forcefully dominates the city's skyline. The origins of the BASILICA DE SAN FRANCISCO EL GRANDE are in a

Franciscan hermitage, founded, according to tradition, by St Francis himself in the early thirteenth century. Originally it occupied a peaceful site outside Madrid, but later acted as a powerful magnet to the growing city. In exchange for their spiritual services, the monks extracted an annual tax both from the court and from the citizens of Madrid, and in so doing soon acquired enormous wealth. A vast new monastery was begun in 1762 by the Franciscan lay brother Francisco Cabezas, and completed in 1784 under the supervision of the royal architect Francesco Sabatini. Early the following century Joseph Bonaparte considered turning the church into a parliament building, but the place remained in the hands of the Franciscans until the confiscation by the state of monastic properties in 1836, after which the monastery buildings were taken over for use as an army barracks. In 1869 the church was converted into a national pantheon, and the much-moved bones of Calderón, together with the bodies of such illustrious Spaniards as the poet Garcilaso de la Vega, Quevedo, Ventura Rodríguez, and Juan de Villanueva, were brought here, only to be taken away several years later following protests from the churches from where they had come. In 1878, following the funeral obsequies that were held here for Queen Mercedes, the Minister proposed that the church be made into a National Church where grand state ceremonies could be celebrated on solemn occasions. With this in mind, the whole church was extensively restored and redecorated and its huge dome covered with an ambitious cycle of paintings by Carlos Rivera.

Since 1926 San Francisco el Grande has belonged once again to the Franciscans, and the few visitors to this lugubrious place are obliged to follow a guided tour. The church, entered from an austerely classical portico, comprises an oppressively heavy rotunda surrounded by chapels, and so gloomy in its lighting that you might find yourself tripping up over the stalls. An early painting by Goya of St Bernardino of Siena is to be found in one of the chapels, and is interesting for being virtually the only religious work by him in the same colourful vein as his tapestry cartoons; the podgy-faced artist himself is depicted on the right-hand side of the canvas, clearly rather bored with St Bernardino's sermon. Baroque choir stalls taken from the Segovian monastery of El Parral line the walls of the presbytery, and set the tone for the cavernous sacristy and chapter house, which are filled with similarly elaborate stalls of earlier date, these ones originating from the monastery of El Paular, near Rascafría. Over-exposure to so much wood, combined with the mustiness and greyish-green colouring of these back rooms, begins to induce a certain feeling of nausea, and, by the time you are led around the suitably grand cloister, you might have difficulty in appreciating the many fine pictures to be seen here, in particular a late canvas, by Zurburán, of St Bonaventura. The immediate reaction on coming back to the entrance portico might be to rush out as quickly as possible into the open air, but you should walk through the side door to your left to visit the quite separate CHAPEL OF CRISTO DE LOS DOLORES. Built in the 1660s, this well preserved and very heterogeneous building is a model of church architecture during the reign of Philip IV, its lavish furnishings and elaborate ornamentation being offset by its structural simplicity and sobriety.

The religious order responsible for the building of the Chapel of Cristo de los Dolores, the Trinitarians, founded shortly afterwards a hospital and church just to the south of San Francisco el Grande, at the junction of the Calle San Bernabé and the Gran Vía de San Francisco. Behind a most decrepit façade the hospital continues to function today, and is worth a short visit to see the grand staircase, where you will find two canvases by Velázquez's follower Juan Carreño de Miranda as well as a religious work by Van Dyck originating from the Escorial. Leaving the busy and unappealing Gran Vía de San Francisco, you should head east on the more homely Calle de Calatrava until you reach the Calle de la Paloma. Around August these two streets become the scene of one of the liveliest of Madrid's local festivals, held in honour of the Virgin of la Paloma (or the Dove). The story goes that a dove belonging to a local convent attached itself to a procession carrying a statue of the Virgin of las Maravillas. Later a painting of the Virgin was discovered in the walls of the same convent, and it soon attracted such widespread devotion that an oratory was built to house it in 1791. The fame of this Virgin spread well beyond the neighbourhood, and in the following century such distinguished people as María Luisa of Parma and Isabel II came to pay their respects to her. In the course of this century the population of the whole district grew enormously, and by 1896, plans were made to replace the oratory with the present, much larger church. The church, at the southern end of the Calle de la Paloma, was built by Lorenzo Alvarez Capra, and is a light and cheerful example of the so-called neo-*mudéjar* style. Higher up on the street, at number 5, is a candlemaker's shop, a delightful old establishment which was founded here in response to this massive popular devotion to the local Virgin.

The church of NUESTRA SEÑORA DE LA PALOMA stands on high ground, and from the open space besides it you can look down to the drearily neo-classical PUERTA DE TOLEDO, which was completed in 1817; the inscription honouring Ferdinand VII was desecrated at various times in the nineteenth century, but has recently been restored, for purely historical reasons. The gate, isolated by dense surrounding traffic, marks the southern boundary of old Madrid, and below it stretches the ugly modern development which makes up most of the southern half of the city. A tour on foot becomes undesirable from this point, but dedicated sight-seers might wish at least to see the TOLEDO BRIDGE, which can be reached by heading south down the broad southern end of the Calle de Toledo. This outstanding bridge, designed by Pedro de Ribera in 1719, is a nine-arched construction featuring approach ramps, turreted bridge-heads, and two delightfully elaborate road-side shrines housing statues of saints María de la Cabeza and Isidro. At one time it must have made a most beautiful entrance into Madrid, but today the surroundings could scarcely be

OPPOSITE *Details of the apse in San Francisco el Grande. The paintings are by Alejandro Ferrant and Manuel Domínguez.*

One of the lively baroque tabernacles decorating Pedro de Ribera's Toledo Bridge.

less appealing, with blackened apartment blocks, factories, and a great spaghetti junction. The urban landscape becomes even worse to the south of the Manzanares, for this is traditionally the poor area of the city, and much of what has been put up here was completely unplanned. A sort of climax of desolation is reached in the normous suburb of Carabanchel, but to those tourists hardy enough to make it as far as here, there is the consolation of the cemetery church of SANTA MARIÁ LA ANTIGUA, a relic of the *mudéjar* past within earshot of the loudspeakers from Madrid's largest prison.

The most practicable and attractive excursion to be made from the Toledo Bridge is to the HERMITAGE OF SAN ISIDRO, which lies a short distance to the west of the bridge, along the Paseo Quince de Mayo. This engagingly simple eighteenth-century structure occupies a quiet and shaded hill-top position with extensive views down to the Manzanares and across to San Francisco el Grande and the more distant Palacio Real. Every year, on St Isidro's day, a festive pilgrimage or *romería* is made to the hermitage, an occasion which was vividly portrayed by Goya, an enormous bust of whom towers over the neighbouring park. Next to the hermitage can also be found the most pleasant of southern Madrid's many cemeteries, this one containing a superb art nouveau tomb at the end of its overgrown central alley. Sculpted by Agustín Querol to house the mortal remains of one Doña Luisa Sancho Mata, this dynamic, multi-figured work is at present in a most ruinous condition, and, when I was last here I found that the arm of a kneeling mourner had fallen off, and was lying by the ground beside it. The neglect of the San Isidro cemetery, however, is as nothing in comparison to that of the adjoining SACRAMENTAL DE SAN JUSTO, where many of Spain's distinguished literary figures of the nineteenth and twentieth centuries lie buried, including Ramón Gómez de la Serna and most of the protagonists of the Romantic era such as Larra, Espronceda, Ramón de Campoamor and Hartzenbusch (the poet José Zorilla's tomb is also here, but the body itself has been transferred to his native Valladolid). The future film director Luis Buñuel had a particular fondness for this cemetery, which was as run-down in his day as it is now, but he loved it for harbouring 'our great romantic poet Larra' and for having 'a hundred of the most beautiful cypress trees' that he had ever seen. One evening, in the company of some of his literary friends, he paid the cemetery a midnight visit, and, in the haunting silence of this deserted place, was excited by stumbling across an open tomb. Underneath, lit up by the beam of moonlight was a coffin with its top ajar, from which protruded the dry, dirty hair of a woman.

> Nervous and excited, I called out, and the others immediately rushed down. That dead hair in the moonlight was one of the most striking images I've ever encountered.

Many years later he was to use this image in his film *The Phantom of Liberty*.

2
The Barrio de los Literatos

....

THE CARRERA DE SAN JERÓNIMO *to* EL AVAPIÉS

A s Madrid rapidly grew beyond its medieval walls after 1560, a district rose up to the east of the Puerta del Sol where virtually all the leading writers of Spain's Golden Age lived and worked. This triangular district bordered to the south by the Carrera de San Jerónimo and to the north by the Calle de Alcalá, is known to this day as the 'Barrio de los Literatos', and sometimes even as 'las Musas' or 'Parnasso'. Printers had their workshops here, and bookshops were later to proliferate, but the area's literary character was consolidated above all by its theatres, which in turn gave the inhabitants of the place a reputation for being Bohemian, loose-living and pleasure-seeking. Already in 1635 the dramatist Castillo Solórzano was reporting that this was the Madrid district 'most frequented by the young and unattached, owing to the presence here of the city's two main theatres, as well as for being the home of many ladies of the profession'. Intensive rebuilding campaigns in the nineteenth and early twentieth centuries rid the district almost entirely of its Golden-Age monuments, but its literary character was maintained in later years by its theatres and wealth of literary cafés, and the place remains to this day the entertainment heart of Madrid. This district, richer in literary associations and night life than in architectural or artistic treasures, forms the main part of this chapter, but I have also taken the reader slightly to the south, into an area of Madrid which has given enormous inspiration to writers, owing to its celebrated flea market, the coarse vitality of its street-life, and to the legendary world of its *majos*.

The Barrio de los Literatos begins as soon as you leave the Puerta del Sol by its south-eastern corner and enter the Carrera de San Jerónimo. The early growth of the district was initiated by this street, which has its origins in a carriageway built in 1538 to join the Puerta del Sol with the fifteenth-century monastery of San Jerónimo, at that time the sole monument of note on the eastern outskirts of the city. The importance of the street increased

OPPOSITE *The façade of the historic restaurant and confectioner's, Lhardy, unchanged since the late nineteenth century.*

63

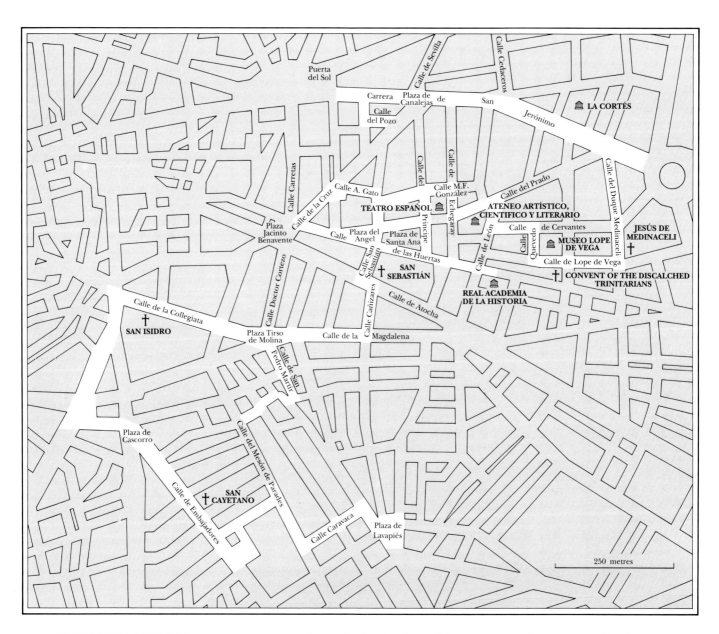

THE BARRIO DE LOS
LITERATOS

enormously at the beginning of the seventeenth century with the construc-tion, alongside the monastery, of the royal palace of the Buen Retiro. The street, at one time bordered by the modest houses of artisans, came now to be dominated by palaces and convents, and became also the scene of spectacular royal processions. Furthermore it served as the main route to the ever more popular recreational district of the Prado, to where all of fashionable Madrid would be drawn in their carriages for the evening *paseo*, in particular from the late eighteenth century onwards. The nineteenth century was the lively heyday of the Carrera de San Jerónimo, but the character of the street was to change in the course of this century, with the establishment here of the Spanish Parliament, the demolition of the convents, and the replacement of the aristocratic palaces with apartment blocks for the middle classes. Today the street has been altered more than almost any other part of the Barrio de los Literatos, having lost its residential function and nearly all of its cafés, and being lined instead with the headquarters of banks and multi-nationals.

At the beginning of the Carrera de San Jerónimo stood the late sixteenth-century convent of La Victoria, the church of which was a popular meeting-place in seventeenth-century Madrid, and as such features in numerous plays of the Golden Age. The pulling down of the convent in the late 1830s allowed the construction, behind the street, of the Pasaje Matheu, a shopping arcade which was considered at the time to be one of the smartest in Europe; it survives today as a curious pedestrian precinct, lacking both its roof and entrance arches. Nearby, at the junction of the Carrera de San Jerónimo with the Calle de la Victoria, a plaque records the site of the Fontana de Oro, the celebrated political café of the 1820s which was to give Galdós the title and subject of his first novel. The opening chapter of this historical work imaginatively recreates what the Carrera de San Jerónimo must have been like in 1821, no less busy than in Galdós's time, but dark and narrow, and, as dusk fell, filling up with animated, argumentative groups who had lingered earlier at the Puerta del Sol and now made their way to the cafés, above all to the Fontana de Oro, 'the magnet for the city's ardent and clamorous youth, troubled by both impatience and inspiration, anxious to stir the passions of the people, and to hear the people's spontaneous applause'.

Of the places on the Carrera de San Jerónimo frequented by Galdós himself there remains today one solitary survival, but what a magnificent survival this is. The LHARDY restaurant and confectioner's, situated at number 8, almost next door to the site of the Fontana de Oro, has been running since 1839, and still retains its striking nineteenth-century interior. Its founder was a Frenchman from near the Swiss border who styled himself Emilio Lhardy, and opened this establishment on the advice of his friend Prosper Mérimée. Functioning to begin with primarily as a confectioner's, but with lunches and dinners prepared on request, it popularized in Madrid such French delicacies as éclairs, *millefeuilles* and *petits-choux*. The culinary repertory of Lhardy's increased in tandem with the place's growing reputation, and soon the establishment became the most fashionable gastronomic institution in Madrid, mentioned in all the books about the city, and visited by most of the foreigners who came here. Among these was Alexandre Dumas, Père, who for some reason was under the impression that the owner was Italian, a delusion which gave him an opportunity to voice his prejudices against all food cooked outside of France: 'In Italy, where one eats badly,' he wrote shortly after visiting Lhardy's in October, 1846, 'the good restaurants are French; in Spain, where one does not eat at all, the good restaurants are Italian.' Dumas's was a lone dissenting voice, for right up to the present day the place has inspired paeans of praise from a list of distinguished patrons which includes almost every notable Spanish political and cultural figure of the last one and half centuries, and even the monarchy

The ground-floor of Lhardy with, on the right-hand side, the famous silver tureen in which consommé is always kept.

itself. The writer Azorín was not exaggerating too greatly when he wrote early this century that 'if the shop-window of Lhardy's were a film projector, the whole of modern Spanish history would be seen in it'.

Galdós was one of the place's most regular customers. Interestingly, the establishment of today is virtually unchanged in its decoration and furnishings from the one known to him, even down to the splendid silver used. At street-level is the actual confectioner's, a tiny, crowded room of mirrors and dark wood, where you can enjoy an aperitif of vermouth while standing at the counter. A custom peculiar to Lhardy's, and dating back to Galdos's time, is helping yourself to a cup of consommé served from a majestic silver samovar which forms the centrepiece of a glistening display of glasses, decanters and silverware at the back of the shop. Squeezed between this and the kitchen is a staircase leading up to a series of small dining-rooms, one of which has walls adorned with Japanese inlay. The principal dining-room, overlooking the street, has diminutive wooden columns, dark panelling, and candelabra, and features several paintings by the founder's son, Agustín Lhardy, a trained landscapist who took over his father's business in 1887. The menu today still comprises a mixture of French and Madrilenian dishes, and this is the Madrid restaurant with the greatest tradition for tripe and *cocido*.

Gastronomic temptations are a major feature of the Barrio de los Literatos, and you will find immediately behind Lhardy's – at number 8 Calle del Pozo – one of Madrid's finest and oldest cake shops, the ANTIGUA PASTELERÍA DEL POZO, which was founded by Julian Leal in 1830 and preserves a dignified, turn-of-the-century appearance. Continuing, if you still can, east down the Carrera de San Jerónimo, you will soon cross a round and noisy intersection, featuring, on its north-western side, the oppresively grand Banco Hispano Americano of 1902–5. Beyond this, the street widens as it begins its slow descent towards the Paseo del Prado. At the corner with the Calle Echegaray was once to be found the Cervezería Inglesa, a favourite haunt of late nineteenth-century writers, including the literary critic and novelist known as 'Clarín' (his real name was Leopoldo Alas), who referred to the place as 'The Spleen Club'. There are many surviving old bars to the south of here, but for the moment you should try and remain on the Carrera de San Jerónimo, allowing as the only further gastronomic stop a visit to Casa Miura at number 30, another well-preserved turn-of-the-century institution, this one enjoying a reputation as Madrid's leading specialist in *turrones*, a soft, Spanish version of nougat. Just beyond the shop, at the corner of the Calle de Ventura de la Vega, a marble plaque records the building where on St Isidro's day, 1896, the films of the pioneering French film-makers the Lumière brothers, were projected in Spain for the first time: admission was one peseta, and, by the end of the first month, it was reported that 'all of Madrid', from the royal family downwards, had been to see them.

On the opposite, northern side of the Carrera de San Jerónimo, an imposing baroque portal at number 19 distinguishes the street's only surviving palace, a building by Pedro de Ribera which was heightened in the 1920s. In the middle of the quiet and very smart area which extends to the east of here is the TEATRO DE LA ZARZUELA, a well-restored classical building of the 1850s specializing in light operas, most notably *zarzuelas*. Adjacent to this, and with its main, pedimented façade overlooking the Carrera de San Jerónimo, is the Spanish Parliament building or CORTES, which was begun in 1842, twenty years after the Parliament's foundation by a group of radical patriots exiled in Cádiz. The interior of the building became known the world over when on 23 February, 1981 Colonel Antonio Tejero of the Guardia Civil, in full view of television cameras, held the whole Parliament at gunpoint, and threatened for a few tense hours Spain's newly found democracy. The architecture itself is not so exciting, although perhaps Théophile Gautier went too far in 1845 when he described this rigidly symmetrical, neo-classical building as being in such 'abominable taste' that he doubted whether any serious constitutions could possibly be drafted inside it.

Gautier was equally unenthusiastic about the bronze statue of Cervantes which stands in the small garden directly in front of the main façade, although at least he was generous enough to acknowledge that the 'immortal author of Don Quixote' deserved some form of commemoration. The part of Madrid most closely associated with Cervantes and other Golden-Age writers is a short walk to the south of here, and you should head towards it along the Calle del Duque de Medinaceli. As with the Carrera de San Jerónimo, this street has been radically altered by turn-of-the-century development, the principal change being the demolition in 1910 of the baroque palace originally belonging to the dukes of Lerma to make way for the suitably palatial PALACE HOTEL, a grand hotel in the style of those on the Côte d'Azur, complete with a sumptuous oval saloon covered in coloured glass. In ironic juxtaposition to this monument to materialistic decadence is the ugly modern church containing the miraculous image of Jesús of Medinaceli, one of Madrid's most venerated votive images, and one which attracts on the first Friday of every month a long queue of worshippers spilling out into the adjoining streets. The church which it replaced formed part of an early seventeenth-century monastery founded by the dukes of Lerma for the Discalced Trinitarians. Greatly favoured by the many people of the area involved in the theatrical profession, this church acquired considerable notoriety for its 11 o'clock Sunday masses. These occasions were regularly attended by the most famous actresses of the Golden Age, and came to be known as 'the Masses of the Marías' on account of the glamorous threesome comprising María Calderón, María Riquelme, and María de Córdoba, the last of these being the mistress of Lope de Vega whom the playwright had dubbed Amarillis. Dressed in their most ostentatious finery, they attracted far more attention than the services, and helped fuel the wrath of the clergy, who were shocked by the way the church had been turned into a mixture of a cat-walk and a gossip parlour.

The literary and theatrical heart of Golden-Age Madrid lies immediately to the west of the Jesús of Medinaceli, its entrance marked by the Taberna de Dolores, a lively bar serving excellent sandwiches and canapés, and decorated on the outside with an attractive ceramic decoration of 1928. From here ascends the Calle de Lope de Vega, one of a grid of dark and narrow streets that can still be imagined in their Golden-Age state despite having been almost entirely rebuilt in later periods. Much of the upper part of the street is taken over by the austere, brick walls of the CONVENT OF THE DISCALCED TRINITARIANS, which was founded in 1612 and rebuilt between 1668 and 1673. Cervantes's daughter Isabel was a nun here, as was one of Lope de Vega's, who, under the name of Sor Marcela de San Félix, rose to become prioress of the convent, and the author of a codex of poetry which the place still possesses. But the literary renown of the convent is due largely to it being the burial-place in 1616 of Cervantes, an association which led the Spanish Academy to rescue the building from ruin in the mid nineteenth century. Every year, on the anniversary of Cervantes's death, the Academy holds a commemorative

The pedimented neoclassical façade of Spain's Parliament Building.

mass here for him and other great names of Spanish literature. However, as is the way with the famous dead in this country, the exact whereabouts of Cervantes's tomb are no longer known.

Directly across the street from the convent begins the short Calle de Quevedo, at the entrance to which, on the right-hand side, is the site of a house associated not only with the seventeenth-century writer Francisco de Quevedo – who made his cruel and brilliant mark both in verse and prose – but also with the greatest poet of the Golden Age, Luis de Góngora. Both these men were the subjects in their maturity of powerful portraits by Velázquez, Góngora being shown with the sober, stoic features befitting a native of Seneca's Córdoba, Quevedo portrayed behind a pair of heavy spectacles that accentuate the venomous smirk of a satirist whose view of life had been warped through physical deformity and a hatred of his mother. Their respective works represented the two rival strands in seventeenth-century Spanish writing, the former's being associated with the exceedingly learned and artificial style known pejoratively by its detractors as *culteranismo*, the latter's with the at times equally impenetrable *conceptismo*, the complexity of which stems less from density of descriptive vocabulary or recourse to obscure classical allusions, than from the use of literary conceits, paradox, wit, ambiguity, and difficult images and metaphors. The rivalry between the two men, however, was not simply a professional one, but was fired by personal animosity of the most vicious kind. Góngora, who had managed to hold his own in an exchange of angry satirical verses with Lope de Vega, found himself defeated in his poetic outbursts against Quevedo, the greater and unrivalled master of vindictive. *Be ashamed, go purple, Don Luis*, is a characteristic title of one of Quevedo's sonnets directed against Góngora, and an aptly cruel one, for Góngora suffered from premature arteriosclerosis and was to die of apoplexy in 1627. No wonder that Góngora's time in Madrid was an unhappy one, and that he took refuge in pastoral verse, eventually retiring to a farm on the outskirts of Córdoba. Quevedo's triumph over Góngora, combined with the offhand manner with which the latter was treated generally while staying in Madrid, seems to have had lasting consequences for Góngora's future reputation here. Thus, when in 1848 the Madrid municipality decided to rename the street in the Barrio de los Literatos where the two men lived, Quevedo was honoured and not Góngora, and, to compound this insult, the plaque marking the site here of the former's house makes no mention of the previous tenancy of Góngora. Góngora hired the house in 1619, writing afterwards to a friend that the place 'had the size of a finger and the price of silver.' In the winter of 1625, which was a particularly harsh one for Góngora, Quevedo bought the property, and had no hesitation in throwing his rival out into the street. Quevedo stayed here until 1634.

Further up the Calle de Quevedo, at number 5, is the birthplace of José Echegaray, a man who would be largely forgotten today were it not for the popular, bar-lined street in the Barrio named after him. This versatile man,

French opulence in the central hall of Madrid's Palace Hotel.

born in 1832, managed in his life to work as an engineer, become Minister of Finance and founder of the Bank of Spain, and to write melodramatic plays which were to earn him in 1904 the Nobel Prize for Literature, thus making him the first of the two recipients of this prize from this small district of Madrid (the other was the playwright Jacinto Benavente). The obvious Spanish candidate for the prize in 1904 was Pérez Galdós, but in honouring the mediocre Echegaray instead, the Nobel committee in Stockholm displayed once again its uncanny knack of making the wrong choice.

At the top of the street, you enter the Calle de Cervantes, and are plunged once again into the world of Golden-Age literature. Almost directly in front of you, at number 11, you will find the Barrio's most eloquent survival of this era, the brick-fronted, two-storeyed house which Lope de Vega bought after deciding to settle permanently in Madrid in 1610. He lived here until his death in 1635, writing in the house the plays by which he is best remembered today such as *Peribáñez*, *Fuenteovejuna*, *El caballero de Olmedo* and *El castigo sin venganza*. Known to Cervantes as 'the monster of Nature', Lope de Vega was always a prolific writer, but his work rate increased enormously after moving in to this house, the relative peace of which allowed him to work undisturbed from early in the morning until late at night. By 1613 Lope claimed to have written 230 plays, but by 1618 this number had risen to 800, and to 1500 by 1632. Even more remarkable was the way in which he managed to maintain both his work rate and peace of mind while continuing to lead a personal life of a complexity which few other writers can rival. After a series of scandalous affairs in his youth, and a first marriage which had ended with the death of his wife during childbirth, Lope had married again in 1598, but more for money than for love, according to his jealous rivals. At the same time he had kept up an affair with the actress Micaela de Luján, by whom he had five children, as opposed to only three by his second wife, Juana. The long-suffering Juana had come with him in 1610 to Madrid, but died here three years later, after which Lope brought into the house two of his illegitimate children by Micaela, Lope Félix, and the future prioress Marcela. In 1614, Lope prepared for ordination as a priest, although this did not in any way prevent him from having other furtive liaisons, the most passionate of which was the married woman called Marta de Nevares Santoyo, by whom he had another illegitimate daughter, Antonia Clara. An increasing and perhaps inevitable element of tragedy entered Lope's life from this point onwards. Marta, who had come to live with Lope after the death of her husband, went gradually blind and died insane in 1632; the playwright's son, Lope Félix, drowned on a pearl-diving expedition to South America; and the seventeen-year old Antonia Clara was seduced by one Cristóbal Tenorio, an incident which caused the playwright enormous, and, some would say, deserved grief. Despite the many, well-publicized scandals of his life, Lope de Vega acquired in later years a saintly aura, and, on his forays into the street became one of the sights of the city, gathering around him crowds who kissed his hand and pleaded for his blessing.

Lope's house was in a ruinous condition by the 1960s, when it was turned into a museum to the writer, and lovingly restored to its original state. The delightful small garden which nourished Lope's verse was reconstructed, and the writer's rooms were furnished with items of his that had been kept over the centuries in the convent of the Discalched Trinitarians. The decoration of the house is remarkably sparse and simple, for although Lope de Vega was the best paid of Spain's Golden-Age dramatists, he was always very careful with his money, either out of meanness, or because he had to pay dearly both for his complex personal life and for the upkeep of this large building.

Mysteriously, the Museo Lope de Vega – one of Madrid's greatest attractions – has been closed for many years, supposedly for further restoration, although the cobwebs on the front door would appear to indicate that very little is happening inside. At least, however, the building remains, which is more than can be said for the house in which Cervantes spent the last years of his life. Situated formerly at the western end of the Calle de Cervantes, at what is now number 2, it was pulled down in 1833, despite the protests of Mesonero Romanos, who succeeded only in recording the site with the present plaque. Cervantes had moved from Valladolid to Madrid in 1606, following in the footsteps of the court, which supplied him with minor administrative posts. His Madrid years, as with those of Lope de Vega, were to be the most productive in his literary career, though they were also beset by financial problems and tainted by an unhappy marriage. In 1613 he published here his highly successful *Exemplary Novels*, and two years later brought out the second and greater part of *Don Quixote*. In the moving, final pages of this last work the dying and repentant knight is finally cured of his fantastical delusions, and of his obsession with the courtly romances that Cervantes had so brilliantly parodied. It is therefore particularly ironic that the final year of Cervantes's own life was to be spent writing such a romance himself, *The Travails of Persiles and Sigismunda*, a work which appears to have been created in a spirit of pure escapism, the real world being now too hard for the ill, aged and near destitute writer to bear. For many years he had suffered from a disease which could either have been diabetes or cirrhosis of the liver, and on Wednesday, 20 April, 1616, dictated, as the preface to his final work, what were his last words to have come down to us: 'My life is ending. It will finish its course this Sunday at the latest; and I shall finish the race of life … Farewell, witticisms; farewell jests; farewell cheerful friends; for I am dying, and anxious to see you again soon, happy in the next life.'

The main entrance to Cervantes's house stood on the Calle de León, one block to the north of the former *Mentidero de Representantes*, a small square (now gone) were everyone involved in Madrid's theatrical world of the sixteenth and seventeenth centuries would come and gossip and exchange opinions about the latest plays. The city's main theatres were then, as they are now, just to the west of here, but before heading in this direction, you should walk north along the Calle de León towards Madrid's great literary and political

The late nineteenth-century entrance to the Ateneo – a famous centre of literature and liberal politics founded in 1820.

institution of recent times, the Ateneo. The ATENEO ARTISTICO, CIENTIFICO Y LITERARIO, to use its full name, was founded in 1820 as a patriotic society devoted – like Britain's Royal Society – to the furtherment of the arts and sciences. The original institution was situated on the Calle de Montera, but, as a result of its Liberal politics, was soon closed down by Ferdinand VII. On the initiative of Mesonero Romanos and other members of his intellectual circle, it was reopened in 1835 on the Calle del Prado, the street where most of the writers' cafés of the district were once concentrated. The present building, at number 21, dates back to the 1880s and is far more impressive inside than its modest exterior suggests. Past the main entrance you ascend a grand flight of steps and enter a world darkened and impregnated with the smoke of over a century of Spanish intellectual life. Long rows of portraits of those who have contributed to this life run down the walls of a narrow gallery which disappears into the gloom, while, on the floor above, one of Spain's finest libraries spreads out from two fine turn-of-the-century halls into the surrounding, greying corridors. With luck you might persuade the porter to let you in to the vast, oval lecture theatre, where, in a setting of faded splendour, so many of Spain's writers have made their literary début.

West of the Ateneo you will soon find yourself drawn in into the labyrinth of bars and restaurants which radiates from the Plaza de Santa Ana. The second street to your right as you walk up the Calle del Prado is the southern part of the dark, narrow but nocturnally animated Calle Echegaray, the name of which was given to a novel of 1950 by Marcial Suárez, who claimed in the preface to this that the numerous incidental characters featured in his episodic story were largely based on people whom he had met here. At number 7 is one of the more popular of this street's bars, the Venencia, a cramped Andalusian establishment unchanged in its decor since the 1920s, with walls layered with grease and torn bullfight posters, and large oak barrels from which sherry is served, accompanied always by olives. A much smarter but less friendly bar, at the corner of the calles Echegaray and Manuel Fernández y González, is the recently restored Los Grabieles, which is worth entering purely to see the superlative ceramic decorations inside, among which is an enormous reproduction of Velázquez's painting, *The Topers*. Walking west down the Calle Manuel Fernández y González you will pass further ceramic scenes of the 1920s decorating both the exterior and interior of Viva Madrid, a bar which has now been taken over almost entirely by young tourists. Eventually you will emerge at the middle of the Calle del Príncipe, a street especially rich in literary associations, many of these being linked to its numerous, luxuriously appointed shops of the turn of the century. The famous wine shop of Pecastaing was frequented by both Hemingway and the Nobel-Prize-winning dramatist Jacinto Benavente, while the elegant optician's shop known as Villasante was the scene early this century of literary *tertulias* presided over by the novelist Pío Baroja. The now vanished café of El

Ceramic decorations in Los Grabieles a detail from Velázquez's The Topers *appears on the right.*

Gato Negro – where Benavente held court, and where the renowned Catalan painter Santiago Rusiñol could frequently be seen – was also on this street, and was an especially lively cultural haunt, deriving much of its popularity from its position next to the Teatro de la Comedia. Many of Benavente's plays were premièred at this latter theatre, a grand if rather decayed structure of the 1870s where Pérez Galdós tried in later life to establish himself as a dramatist, enjoying several popular triumphs but no lasting successes.

The name of the Calle del Príncipe is taken from the most important of Madrid's Golden-Age theatres, the Corral del Príncipe, which was situated at the lower end of the street, on the site now occupied by the Teatro Español. Until the late sixteenth century the performances of plays in Madrid had largely taken place in improvised, open-air settings in the yards or *corrales* of houses, the more distinguished spectators watching the action from the windows or balconies. The Corral del Príncipe, which was founded in 1583, was one of the first theatres built especially for the purpose, and, while emulating the layout of the original *corrales*, was probably roofed, and came in later years to acquire such attributes of a court theatre as a proscenium arch, drop curtains and painted scenery. The passion for drama during this period was quite remarkable, and foreign visitors to Madrid were struck by the fact that plays were put on during the daytime, with people rushing in to reserve the best places as soon as the theatres opened their doors at 12 o'clock. A court official, aided by bailiffs, was responsible for maintaining order and deciding when the plays should begin, but chaos and long delays seemed to proceed each performance, with fights invariably breaking out, caused either by impatient members of the audience, rivalries between dramatists, people trying to get in without paying, or men being prevented from making their way to the actresses' dressing-rooms, which were strictly out of bounds. The spectators who were most feared by performers and playwrights alike were the so-called 'musketeers', a motley crowd, made up largely of craftsmen and tradesmen, who stood in between the rows of seats at the front of the auditorium and the women's gallery at the back. Known also as 'the people's jury', they determined the success or failure of a particular production, and came to the theatre armed with rattles, whistles and bells. The author most pilloried was the hunch-backed, pigeon-chested, Mexican-born Juan Ruiz de Alarcón, whose misanthropy and physical deformities earned him widespread ridicule, and some of the most brutal satires in seventeenth-century literature. Lope de Vega, a man much-loved by the Madrid public, paid friends among the musketeers to whistle during Alarcón's plays.

The Corral del Príncipe was demolished in the early eigthteenth century to make way for the rather more sedate Teatro del Príncipe, which saw performances of several of the charming one-act comedies or *sainetes* of Ramón de la Cruz, Spain's answer to Goldoni or Marivaux. In 1802 the building was replaced by the present Teatro Español, which, despite remodelling inside following a recent fire, retains a neo-classical facade by Juan de Villaneuva,

featuring a large pediment and a giant order of pilasters. Many of the great classics of modern Spanish drama have had their premières here, including García Lorca's controversial study of a childless woman, *Yerma*, at the first performance of which, in 1934, right-wing hecklers taunted the author and principle actress with shouts of 'queer!' and 'lesbian!'. The theatre first came to prominence during the Romantic era, supporting the brilliant generation of writers who had been nurtured at the adjoining CAFÉ DEL PRÍNCIPE.

Juan de Villanueva's distinguished façade for the Teatro Español, which marks the site of the Corral del Príncipe.

This celebrated café, known generally as El Parnasillo, or Little Parnassus, was situated in the basement of a house attached to the northern side of the theatre, a site at present awaiting redevelopment. Mesonero Romanos described the place as dark and poky, without any fancy decoration or even comfort, its principal furnishings beng a dozen pine tables painted a dark chocolate colour. Before being taken up by Madrid's Bohemians, the establishment was always half empty, patronized largely by a group of retired diplomats, who came here every night out of habit and inertia, oblivious apparently to the surrounding dinginess and even to the poorly washed glasses and cups in which their coffee or chocolate was served. According to Mesonero Romanos, it was precisely these 'negative conditions' that were to make the café so appealing to young artists and intellectuals, all of whom felt far more at home here than at more luxurious establishments. But no-one perhaps would have predicted what an enormous impact the place was to have on the cultural and intellectual development of Spain in the early nineteenth century. 'From here', wrote Mesonero Romanos, 'from this miserable little room, the renaissance of our modern theatre was initiated; from here emerged the *Ateneo*; from here the brilliant *Liceo Arístico*, the *Instituto* and various other literary societies; from here the renewal of the universities and the daily press; from here the parliamentary orators of the fiery tribunes who brought about a complete transformation of our society.'

The TEATRO ESPAÑOL faces the Plaza de Santa Ana, the verdant space created by Joseph Bonaparte's demolition of the Carmelite convent of Santa Ana. Despite its trees and nineteenth-century statue to Calderón de la Barca, it has about as much beauty as does London's Leicester Square, to which it can also be compared in being at the centre of Madrid's entertainment world. In the harsh light of day it is the visual equivalent of a hang-over, a confused medley of architectural styles, with the odd, painfully discordant note, and a general air of seediness. By night, however, the selective lighting, together with the ceaseless vitality of its nocturnal crowds, help you to forget the square's uglier aspects, particularly if you have had a few drinks yourself. The oldest and best known of its bars is the Cervezería Alemana, a beautifully preserved establishment founded in 1904 on the southern side of the square. Its spacious main room, with its wooden tables and panelling, was popular with many Spanish writers in the early years of this century, including members of the Generation of 98 such as the dramatist Valle-Inclán. However, to the numerous foreigners who come here today, this is essentially Hemingway's bar, and indeed there is a story of two young American women who were trying to imagine what the place was like in Hemingway's day when, to their considerable surprise, they were approached by none other than the bearded old writer himself. The various paintings and photographs of bullfights that line the bar's walls are an indication of what particularly attracted Hemingway to this place. It was a favourite haunt of bullfighters, among whom were such luminaries of the art as Bienvenida, Manolete and Luis Miguel Dominguín. This is traditionally the bullfighters' area of Madrid, and most of those who come to fight here continue to be put up at the Hotel Victoria. A plaque to Manolete has recently been placed by the entrance to this tall and splendid hotel of the second decade of this century, the architecture of which, with its rows of glazed balconies, would seem more suited to a seaside town in northern Spain than to the centre of Madrid.

At the north-western corner of the square, ceramic decorations of particular lushness cover the exterior of the now closed Villa Rosa, a place once known for its flamenco shows or *tablaos*. From here you should head west down the tiny Calle de Alvarez Gato, where there is a bar displaying on the outside two distorting mirrors of concave and convex shape. They were

OPPOSITE *Cervezería Alemana, a favourite haunt of bullfighters, which achieved international fame for being mentioned once by Hemingway.*

mentioned by Valle-Inclán, who referred to them in his definition of the *esperpento*, the word he used to define his grotesque tragi-comic vision of life: 'The *esperpento* is reality reflected in the mirrors of the Alley of the Cat.' The ugly bar itself, called las Bravas, is in itself of interest, for it gave birth to one of Spain's most popular bar-snacks of today, the so-called *patatas a las bravas*, a patented dish of cubed, deep-fried potatoes covered in a spicy tomato sauce. Should you wish to try out these potatoes at their source, I strongly recommend you not to observe the culinary proceedings too closely, for you might well be repelled by the sight of the dark pink sauce oozing out from a metallic hose like a flow of lava. Diced pigs' ears, or *orejas*, are also served here in this way, but this is perhaps an experience only for the very brave.

The 'Alley of the Cat' will lead you out on to the Calle de la Cruz, at a point where once was situated the first of Madrid's permanent theatres, the Corral de la Cruz. Although it never enjoyed quite the same popularity as its main rival, the Corral del Príncipe, it was greatly favoured by Philip II, whose affair with one of its star actresses, María Calderón (La Calderona), resulted in his illegitimate son, John of Austria. The attraction of this long and narrow street today lies mainly in its traditional shops, the most interesting of which is Seseña, at number 23. Founded as a tailor's shop in 1902 by Santos Seseña Rojas, it was later transformed by Santos's son Tomás into an establishment specializing exclusively in Spanish capes. Tomás was one of the great personalities of Madrid, and it was probably he who thought up the witty, promotional ruse of placing, one cold winter's day, a cape on the shoulders of the city's scantily clad statue of the goddess Cybele. He earned for the shop the reputation of being the leading place in Spain for capes, but was a poor businessman owing to his habit of presenting these capes as gifts to his many famous friends. The interior of the shop is filled with photographs of caped celebrities, many of whose signatures and comments are inscribed in a series of bound books recording the names of all the customers. Among these names are such diverse personalities as Luis Buñuel, Andrés Segovia, Gary Cooper, Liberace, and Paloma Picasso, the last of these opining that capes make her feel so Spanish. Spain, and Madrid in particular, is the last bastion in Europe of this age-old fashion, but these garments today are rarely worn in an everyday context, and are used instead mainly by those who wish to make a dramatic effect when going to the opera or to some glittering social occasion. Perhaps the cape will enjoy a revival in popularity, for it is not just an elegant but also a practical fashion.

South of the Calle de la Cruz is the Calle de las Huertas, which runs east all the way down to the Paseo del Prado, forming an almost indigestible succession of bars and restaurants. A short architectural detour down the street reveals two fine buildings representing the stylistic extremes of the Spanish eighteenth century. The first of these, at number 13, is a palace of 1734 by Pedro de Ribera, containing on its eastern façade an excellent example of one of this architect's characteristically elaborate portals;

The recently repainted corner-tower of the Hotel Victoria where Manolete and other famous bullfighters have stayed.

meanwhile, further down the street, at number 28, is Juan de Villanueva's impressively austere block of the REAL ACADEMIA DE LA HISTORIA, a brick and granite structure dating from the time of Charles III. Return to the western end of the street, where, on the Plaza del Angel, you will find one of Madrid's leading jazz venues, the Café Central. Immediately to the south of here, on the short Calle de San Sebastián, a plaque marks the building which housed during Charles III's reign the Fonda de San Sebastián. This inn had been a great meeting-place for Spanish intellectuals of the Enlightenment such as Gaspar de Jovellanos and José de Cadalso, and as such had given Madrid a foretaste of the literary cafés of the following century. As an appropriate farewell to the Barrio de los Literatos, you should pay a brief and purely sentimental visit to the church of SAN SEBASTIÁN, on the opposite side of the street. The building itself, brutally restored after 1936, is grimly neo-classical, but the list of writers associated with the place is quite formidable, as a glance at the memorial plaques displayed in the south transept will show. Lope de Vega, Ramón de la Cruz, Echegaray and Benavente were among those who were baptized in the church, while Larra, Gustavo Bécquer, Zorilla, and Valle-Inclán all had their weddings here. As for the deaths recorded in the parish register, these include Cervantes, Ruiz de Alarcón, Vélez de Guevara, and Espronceda, in addition to the architects José de Churriguera, Ventura Rodríguez and Juan de Villanueva. And this is where Lope de Vega was buried, though it goes without saying that his remains have since been lost.

Pérez Galdós wrote that the church of San Sebastián had two distinct faces, one of which looked up to the elegant, commercial district of the Plaza del Angel, the other down to the poorer quarters which lay below the Calle de Cañizares. The descent south from the church is both a social and literal one, and some idea of the different and traditionally less sophisticated world which you are now entering will be had the moment you cross the busy and ugly Calle de Atocha. The first part of *Don Quixote* was printed in 1605 at a building situated at number 87, but a more telling reflection of the street today is the presence at number 24 of an establishment claiming to be the larget sex shop in the world. The Calle de Cañizares leads south to the Calle de la Magdalena, beyond which, at the beginning of the Calle del Olivar, is a basement bar of extreme tackiness called Candela, which only begins to liven up in the early hours of the morning, when its largely gypsy clientele bursts suddenly into flamenco song and dance. Heading west along the Calle de la Magdalena you will pass another outstanding portal by Pedro de Ribera (at number 10) before emerging at the Plaza Tirso de Molina, a noisy, triangular square marking the site of a Mercederian monastery which was demolished after 1836. A statue of the minister who confiscated this and other Church properties in that year, Juan Mendizábal, once adorned the square's unkempt, verdant centre, but it was replaced after the Civil War by the present monument to the former monastery's most distinguished son, Fray Gabriel Téllez, who is better known under his theatrical pseudonym of Tirso de Molina. Tirso de Molina entered the Mercedarian order in 1600, when he was seventeen, and remained with it until his death in 1648, his activities as a playwright being combined with more worthy tasks such as writing up the official chronicle of his order. A romantic and recent tradition believes Tirso to have been the illegitimate son of the Duke of Osuna, but his life seems to have been disappointingly free of scandal or gossip. The one major set-back in an otherwise smooth and successful career occurred in 1625 when the Council of Castile admonished him for depicting vice too vividly on the stage, and threatened him with excommunication if he were to write secular plays again. As a playwright his ouput was very modest in comparison to that of Lope de Vega, being a mere four hundred works. Of these only *The Trickster of Seville* is widely known internationally, not so much because of the play itself, but because of its protagonist, Don Juan Tenorio, whose cynical seductions became an integral part of the Romantic image of Spain.

One of the many dark, narrow streets running south of the Plaza Tirso de Molina is the Calle de San Pedro Martír, where the young Pablo Picasso stayed at number 5 in 1897 and 1898, the house of this rather short-lived association with Madrid being marked today with a ludicrous series of ceramic reproductions of some of his more famous works. Three blocks to the west, at number 13 of the parallel Calle de Mesón de Paredes, is the delightful Taberna de Antonio Sánchez, another of Madrid's historic taverns, this one dating back to 1830. It owes its name to a famous bullfighter, who bought the establishment in 1920, following his retirement from fighting. Sánchez was also a painter of some talent, and the dark-panelled walls of this cosy tavern – which has been virtually unchanged since his day – feature a number of his portraits of matadors, set alongside other bullfighting souvenirs, including a large trophy of a bull's head. The artist who taught Sánchez was Ignacio Zuloaga, an enormously successful painter who had been a close and influential friend of Picasso in the 1890s, but later became associated with the academic art of the Franco period. The back room of the tavern was where Zuloaga's last exhibition was held, and a plaque recording this has been placed above the marble table where the artist always used to sit, surrounded by his friends and admirers. A vivid picture of the tavern in Zuloaga's day can be had from reading Díaz-Cañabate's highly entertaining *Historia de una Taberna* (1947), which can still be bought here. Among the aspects of tavern life that he described were the bread fritters or *torrijas* that were at one time common to most of the city's wine bars, and were supposedly the only sweet food which hardened drinkers could tolerate. Sánchez's wife was renowned for her fritters, and in deference to her this dying gastronomic tradition has been maintained here.

A short walk west of the Plaza Tirso de Molina will take you to the large and depressing church of SAN ISIDRO, which has served provisionally as Madrid's cathedral since 1886, when the city was finally given its own diocese. The building has its origins in a Jesuit college of the early seventeenth

OPPOSITE *The interior of the Taberna Antonio Sanchez features a portrait sketch by the founder and a bull which he killed.*

century, but was remodelled by Ventura Rodríguez in the late eighteenth century, following Charles III's expulsion of the Jesuits and the subsequent transference to this church of the relics of St Isidro. The building's sole architectural distinction is its stately twin-towered façade, which was conceived so as to make an impression even when seen sideways from the once narrow street which it faces, the Calle de Toledo.

The façade of San Isidro is today the sole monument of interest along the northern half of a street which the well-travelled Pérez Galdós considered to be one of the most beautiful in the world. When this part of the street was widened at the end of the nineteenth century, it lost the magnificent late fifteenth-century monastery of 'La Latina', which stood just to the south of San Isidro. Below this, on the Plaza de la Cebada, there was also an outstanding mid nineteenth-century market-hall, but this pioneering ironwork structure was pulled down in the 1960s to make way for the present concrete building housing Madrid's largest food market. Before becoming a market square the Plaza de la Cebada had taken over from the Plaza Mayor as a place of public executions, and Larra could not pass here without thinking of the 'blood which has stained this square and will stain it again'. In Galdós's time the whole street was red, although not, as the novelist hastened to add, 'on account of the slaughter-house or of the blood from revolutionaries, but rather as a result of the painted signs of the 'eighty taverns which can be found here'. To Galdós the beauty of the Calle de Toledo lay essentially in its bustling life, which is also the main attraction of the streets lying to the east.

At the Plaza de Cascorro, which lies to the south of San Isidro, begins the celebrated Sunday flea market of the RASTRO, its stalls running all the way south down the sloping Calle de Curtidores and spilling over into the adjoining streets. All those who have written on Madrid since the last century have attempted to evoke the life and character of the Rastro, and Ramón Gómez de la Serna, with his characteristic effusiveness, felt obliged to dedicate a whole book to the market. Among the more successful descriptions was that of Arturo Barea, who came here frequently as a child in the years before World War I, and remembered the whole district when it was

Nineteenth-century apartment blocks on the street much loved by Galdós and Gómez de la Serna—the Calle de Toledo.

pervaded by 'an acrid smell of rotting flesh' emanating from the tanners' workshops that gave the Calle de Curtidores its name. On that street, Barea wrote, you could buy everything 'except what you set out to buy', and then listed the diverse goods on sale, which ranged from 'river crayfish wriggling in dripping mud' to 'stuffed cats' and 'outworn files with iron dust choking their ridges'. All of Madrid walked about the Rastro on Sunday mornings, and it still remains a popular Sunday activity, in particular between 12 and 2 o'clock. None the less it is going the way of London's Portobello Road, and the bargains are fewer and the overall character much smarter.

Unless you are visiting this area on a Sunday, you should descend south from the Plaza de Cascorro not on the Calle de Curtidores but on the yet narrower and more attractive Calle de Embajadores. One of the finest of the city's baroque churches, SAN CAYETANO, stands near the top of this street, its twin-towered brick façade distinguished by the wealth of its sculpture and ornamentation. José de Churriguera, whose family name is frequently invoked to describe the decorative excesses of the Spanish baroque, was involved in the design of this church, though the actual façade is more likely to have been the work of Pedro de Ribera, an architect who was more genuinely 'Churrigueresque' than Churriguera himself. Badly gutted during the Civil War, the relatively simple interior has now been almost entirely rebuilt. On the opposite side of the street, at number 26, is a well-preserved old bar and wine shop, its interior lined with tiles, and its wooden frontage displaying a collection of bottles of venerable antiquity. Further down, at number 31, you will pass another engaging survival of the past in the form of a barber's shop with a ceramic decoration outside of a man having his hair cut. Craftsmen's shops, a lively food market, and cramped and decayed nineteenth-century buildings on the point of demolition are among the features that you will notice as you continue your descent. At the very bottom of the hill you might well mistake the large neo-classical building to your left as a neo-classical palace, but in fact it was constructed in 1790 as a distillery. In 1809 it was converted into a tobacco factory, and continues to function as such today, making it the oldest such factory still working in Europe. This building has a fascinating history, principally on account of its large female work force, which in the late nineteenth century made up almost a fifth of Madrid's population. The so-called *cigarreras*, whose job was often proudly inherited over generations, enjoying a reputation for their solidarity as a group, strength of character, relative freedom from the social constraints of the time, and their genius for organizing themselves. They were responsible for such social reforms as special schools and crèches, and it is even said that the trade unionist Pablo Iglesias formulated the idea of a workers' union after attending one of their strike meetings. Their flamboyant behaviour and refusal to be bullied by the authorities were a cause of both admiration and scandal. A large veterinary college was once situated opposite, but it had to be removed because of the explosive combination of students and *cigarreras*.

The back of the tobacco factory overlooks the southern end of the long Calle de Mesón de Paredes, where you will find, one block to the north, a large and dilapidated square featuring on one side the overgrown ruins of an eighteenth-century church and college destroyed during the Civil War. Facing the ruins is 'LA CORRALA', a tall and lone survival of a traditional Spanish tenement building of the early nineteenth century. Its balconies, supported by both wooden and metal pillars, would originally have looked out over a yard, but in their restored state of today, are now exposed to the square, together with their long and colourful lines of washing. A plaque now placed in front of the building records that it was in a crowded dwelling such as this, subjected to all the gossip of neighbours chatting to each other from the balconies, that Spain's popular singer of the turn of the century, 'La Revoltosa', was born and brought up. The Calle Sombrerete leads from here to the Plaza de Lavapiés, but you could take instead the parallel street to the north, the Calle de Caravaca, where, at number 10, a wall with cheerful painted decorations marks the entrance of a well-known pastry and liquor shop known as Los Madroños. The owner of this simple and modestly furnished establishment, Cruz Palomo, managed in 1941 to create a tasty liquor out of the insipid orange-red fruit from the Arbutus or strawberry tree, a tree which is normally grown purely for decorative purposes. He called this liquor 'the true liquor of Madrid', for the Arbutus is the tree which features in the city's coat of arms, together with a contented bear licking it as if it were a giant ice-cream cone. A quick visit to this shop will thus give you a taste of the real Madrid, and more than just a literal one if you are lucky enough to meet the aged Palomo himself, a legend of his *barrio*.

Entering the Plaza de Lavapiés, you reach the heart of the district known traditionally as 'El Avapiés', a district which has preserved a very human scale, and evokes so many memories of old Madrid that its name has been given to a publishing house which deals exclusively with the history of this city. The square itself, from which radiate tightly packed rows of nineteenth-century residential blocks, has little of specific interest to attract the visitor, but has always had sentimental associations for those who have come to Madrid in search of the colourful types who inhabit Goya's world. This was the main haunt of the low-class dandies referred to in Madrid as *manolos*. The word *manolo* derives from the habit of converted Jews of calling their eldest son Manuel. Until 1492 the Plaza de Lavapiés formed the nucleus of Madrid's Jewish ghetto, the synagogue of which was on the southern side of the square, on a site now occupied by the Teatro Olimpia.

The world of the so-called *Manolería* belongs today to an ever more distant past, and one which was always tinged by legend. In contrast a remarkably life-like and still recognizable picture of El Avapiés emerges from the pages of Arturo Barea's wonderful autobiographical trilogy, *The Forging of a Rebel* (1941–4). This great work, which appeared in English translation before it came out in Spanish, was written in exile in England, to where Barea had

La Corrala. The one remaining example of a type of tenement which is constantly featured in popular Spanish songs and plays.

taken refuge on account of his political affiliations during the Civil War. The knowledge that he would probably never return to Spain seems to have lent an added intensity to his vision of Madrid, in particular of El Avapiés, which was the domain of his childhood. Brought up in a garret by a poor widowed mother who supported her four children through washing clothes in the Manzanares, Barea certainly had an early taste of life in the raw. He came to think of Madrid as a social ladder of which the highest rung was represented by the Palacio Real 'with its gates open to plumed helmets and diamond-spangled *décolletés*'. El Avapiés, however, was by no means at the bottom of this ladder, for below it, near the Manzanares, lay a semi-wasteland where gypsies lived surrounded by rubbish and 'evil-smelling trickles', an area 'where the city cast its ash and spume' and which was known by the ironic name of 'the New World'. To Barea, El Avapiés was a frontier district between poverty and wealth, populated both by those on the way down the social ladder and those on their way up: it was 'the pointer of the scales, the crucial point between existence and non-existence.' As a child he found himself constantly ascending and descending the hill which led between the Palacio Real down to the New World, and so developed an acute social conscience. El Avapiés, that delicate balance between these two extremes of Madrid society, was to be a formative influence of a most lasting kind:

> 'There I learned all I know, the good and the bad, to pray to God and to curse Him, to hate and to love, to see life crude and bare as it is, and to feel an infinite longing to scale the next step upwards and to help all others to scale it.'

3
The Royal Core

THE DESCALZAS REALES *to* THE ENCARNACIÓN

A fter having made the descent down to El Avapiés, it is perhaps only fair now to take the reader up to the highest rung of Arturo Barea's social ladder and enter the Palacio Real where, 'from the marble galleries guarded by halberdiers', the young writer watched 'the pageant of the royalty, the princes and grandees of Spain'. To include the palace at this stage of the book is also to take the reader beyond the dirty, chaotically developed Madrid left by the Habsburgs, and witness the beginnings of the elegant transformation wrought by the first of the Bourbons. The royal palace is a world in its own right, and in the course of this chapter I have not strayed far from its sight, concentrating on a small but exclusive area of Madrid which counts as its other main attractions, two convents of royal foundation.

Once again, and not for the last time, I propose that you commence your walk at the Puerta del Sol, more specifically at its north-western corner, at the beginning of the busy commercial avenue of the Calle del Arenal. This gently descending street marks the site of a fast-flowing stream which in the Middle Ages ran outside the city walls, and, in times of drought, dried up to form the area of sandy ground which gave the street its name. Already a lively thoroughfare in Habsburg times, it acquired an added importance under the Bourbons, becoming in the nineteenth century a direct link between the Puerta del Sol and the newly created Plaza de Oriente and Teatro Real.

The great bulk of the Teatro Real looms in the distance as soon as you enter the street, but, long before coming to it, you will pass on your left the former TEATRO ESLAVA, which was founded in 1872 as a lightweight, popular alternative to the aristocratic opera house at the other end of the Calle de Arenal. Specializing at first in light operas and *zarzuelas*, it experienced a change of artistic direction after 1916, when it became a home to the theatre company of Martínez Sierra. Martínez Sierra, who was both a playwright and director, managed in the course of three years to turn the Eslava into the

OPPOSITE *The sober brick and stone façade of the seventeenth-century royal convents of Las Descalzas Reales, incorporating on the left the rubble-work of an earlier palace.*

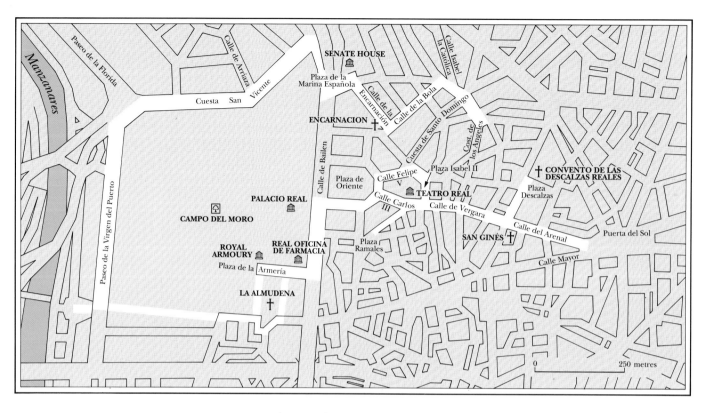

THE ROYAL CORE

most innovative theatre in Madrid, despite its small stage and inadequate equipment. In 1919, always on the lookout for new and exciting talent, Martínez Sierra commissioned for his theatre a work from the young García Lorca, a budding poet but as yet untried as a playwright. Lorca responded with a play on the unpromising theme of the amorous misfortunes of cockroaches, *The Butterfly's Evil Spell*, and this was premiered here on 22 March, 1920. The result was a cat-calling, foot-stamping fiasco, and one member of the audience even brought the whole house down with laughter by suggesting loudly that one of the insect protagonists should be put down with Zotal, a well known brand of insecticide. Later in the decade Martínez Sierra's directorship of the Eslava was to come to an end following a real-life drama in the foyer, when two authors got into an argument which culminated in one of them being shot dead. The Eslava is now a discothèque.

Just beyond the Eslava, past a tiny alley blocked by a well-known second-hand book-stall, is the porticoed main entrance to the church of SAN GINÉS. Although dating back to shortly after the Christian conquest of Madrid, and as such one of the first churches to be founded in Madrid, this sober structure in stone and brick was entirely rebuilt in 1643 and restored in the following century. Quevedo was baptized in the church, Lope de Vega was married here, and the celebrated polyphonist Tomás Luís de Victoria – who lived in the neighbouring street now named after him – was buried somewhere in the parish. All this information can be gleaned from a plaque underneath the portico, to the right of which – and completely separate to the main body of the church – is a chapel containing a fine painting by El Greco of the *Expulsion from the Temple*, another version of which is in London's National Gallery.

Further art treasures await you in the nearby CONVENT OF THE DESCALZAS REALES (Discalced Royal Sisters), which can be reached from San Ginés by crossing the Calle del Arenal and walking north up the short Calle de San Martín. The convent's austere walls of brick and rubblework conceal an interior of fabulous wealth and even a large orchard, incongruously situated within sight of the ugly modern department stores that make up the crowded shopping district just to the north of the Puerta del Sol. The building occupies the site of a medieval palace, which belonged originally to the kings of Castile, but later came into the hands of Alonso Gutierrez, treasurer to the emperor, Charles V. Charles V's younger daughter, Joan of Austria, had been born in this palace, and it was she who later decided to have the building transformed into a convent for nuns of royal blood, entrusting the work in 1556 to the first architect of the Escorial, Juan Bautista de Toldeo. The whole complex, which was thoroughly restored in the late eighteenth century by Diego de Villanueva, was magnificently endowed as a result of numerous donations by the distinguished women who have resided here, among whom were the empress Isabel Clara Eugenia and her sister María of Austria. In recent times the Franciscan nuns who now occupy the convent turned part of the building

The nuns' chapels surrounding the upper cloister of the Descalzas Reales.

into an evocative museum, which in 1988 received the Council of Europe award for the best European Museum of the Year. The resulting publicity had the effect of making this hitherto little-visited place one of the main tourist attractions of the capital, but having achieved this, the nuns then decided to claim back a section of the museum for their own purposes. The reduced museum of today has none the less a sufficient amount on show to satisfy most people, particularly those who do not relish long and enforced guided tours: here tours are led by the elegantly jacketed and officious-looking staff of the Patrimonio Nacional, the body responsible for the upkeep of Spain's royal monuments.

The tour of the Descalzas Reales begins with a magnificent staircase hall, the walls and ceiling of which were decorated in the mid seventeenth century with illusionistic frescoes attributed to Claudio Coello and Ximenez Donoso, and featuring a delightful scene of Philip IV and his family staring down at the spectator from a fictive balcony. The staircase leads eventually to the upper cloister, around which are a series of small chapels founded by the royal nuns of the seventeenth and eighteenth centuries on being received into the order. Every detail of the sumptuous decoration of these baroque chapels will be outlined for you by your guide, but your lasting impression will probably be of the numerous sculpted images of the baby Jesus resting on a skull, an iconographic motif peculiar to Spanish art of this period and symbolizing the triumph of life over death. One of the chapels originally boasted a painting of the Annunciation by the Tuscan artist Fra Angelico, but this was later removed to the Prado and replaced by a crude nineteenth-century version of the subject. It is not until you reach the nuns' former dormitory, which lies off the upper cloister, that you will come to the most outstanding of the convent's treasures – a series of Rubens tapestries presented by Isabel Clara Eugenia in 1627. Representing the Triumph of the Eucharist, and based on vivid oil sketches that can be seen today in the Prado, these are compositions of extraordinary energy framed by massive *salamonicas* or twisted columns comparable to those in Raphael's famous tapestry of *The Judgement of Solomon* in the Vatican. The remaining part of the convent includes the cell of Marguerite of Austria (complete with her sandals, crucifix and other of her belongings), and a charming nuns' choir decorated with quaintly unsophisticated wall paintings of scenes from the life of St Francis. Numerous portraits (mainly school works) of members of the Habsburg family give the guide an opportunity to bore you with involved genealogical accounts, and there is also an inordinate number of polychromed devotional images of the Virgin of Sorrows by seventeenth-century artists such as Pedro de Mena and Luisa Roldán. The overall atmosphere of the convent ends up by being more interesting than the specific detail, and the religious images drift through your consciousness as if they were the distant sounds of polyphonic music. At the very end of the tour is a small picture gallery, filled mainly with dubious attributions, but with a curious Bosch-inspired *Ship of Fools*, and a fascinating seventeenth-century Flemish work depicting the empress María of Austria travelling with members of her court from Prague to Madrid.

Back on the Calle del Arenal, and continuing to head west, you will soon come out on to the verdant square named after Isabel II, a statue of whom stands under the shadow of the pompous neo-classical bulk of the TEATRO REAL or Opera House. The latter, begun during the reign of Ferdinand VII by a pupil of Juan de Villanueva, was not opened until 1850, the inaugural production being of Donizetti's opera, *La Favorita*. The Teatro Real subsequently played an important role in popularizing Verdi's works in Madrid, introduced this city in the 1870s to the music of Wagner, and brought over here early this century Diaghilev, Nijinsky and Stravinsky. The building itself, at present closed for extensive renovation, is a singularly top-heavy structure when seen from the Plaza Isabel II, but has a more elegant western façade, which was designed by Isidro González Velázquez to harmonize with the grand Plaza de Oriente.

If you choose to approach the latter square along the northern side of the Teatro Real, you will pass to your right, at number 6 Calle de Felipe V, the Taberna del Alabardero, which was the first of one of several wine bars and restaurants founded by Fray Luis Lezama, a well-known Madrid personality of today who manages to combine the life of a priest with that of a highly successful entrepreneur. This particular establishment, originally a sculptor's studio, was converted by Lezama into a cosy imitation of a turn-of-the-century tavern, comprising numerous authentic furnishings of this period, together with photographs of Lezama himself, and newspaper cuttings outlining his triumphs in America. Those walking instead along the southern side of the Teatro Real, might wish to lengthen slightly their journey to the Plaza de Oriente by turning off on to the Calle de Vergara. This is strictly a detour for devotees of the Romantic writer Larra, for you will pass almost immediately to your left the Calle de Santa Clara, on which stands – at number 3 – the corner house where the 28-year-old essayist and poet put an end to his life on 13 February, 1837. His satirical articles, written under the pseudonym 'Figaro', reveal a mordant wit, misanthropy and linguistic brilliance worthy of Quevedo, and were directed against the Spanish way of life, which he had hoped to reform. Social and political disillusionment might have underlain his much-publicized suicide, but the more obvious motive was connected with his unhappy personal life. In 1829, to use his own words, he had married 'young and badly', and had later entered a stormy relationship with one Dolores Montijo, who, in the company of a woman friend, had been to see him at his house on the day of his death. The reasons for her unexpected visit were to demand a final end to their scandalous affair and to be given back her letters to him. At 8.30 that evening, shortly after Dolores had left, Larra shot himself with one of the guns that now occupy a special show-case in Madrid's Museo Romántico. His body was taken to the neighbouring church of Santiago, and laid out briefly in the crypt, where a plaque has recently been

Elegant late eighteenth-century shops in the vicinity of the Teatro Real.

placed to his memory. His shocked friends from El Parnasillo including Mesonero Romanos – who had spoken to him on the morning of that fateful day – rushed in disbelief to the church, and saw the body before it was removed for burial in the Sacramental de San Justo. The enormous sense of loss occasioned by Larra's early death was to be felt acutely by later Spanish writers, including the Generation of 98, who on 13 February 1901, strewed violets on his grave and read out a speech referring to him as 'the guiding light of today's youth'. An empty seat was always kept for Larra at the celebrated *tertulias* organized by Gómez de la Serna in the 'sacred crypt' of El Pombo.

The elegant gardens which make up the Plaza de Oriente were created to provide a full and dramatic view of the immensely long Palacio Real, which, until the early nineteenth century, was obscured on its eastern side by a collection of medieval houses, one of which had belonged to the painter Diego Velázquez. The demolition of the houses was ordered by Joseph Bonaparte, but work on the square was only begun under Ferdinand VII, and, not completed until 1842, the final plan featuring the Teatro Real as the apex of two diagonally placed residential blocks, which today contain smart shops and cafés patronized mainly by coachloads of tourists. Among the statues which decorate the square is a series of larger-than-life-size figures of kings, who appear, in their present weathered and marooned state, to be distinctly unhappy at not occupying the commanding position which had been planned for them on the parapet of the Palacio Real. In contrast, a magnificent addition to the gardens is the bronze equestrian statue of Philip IV which rears up at the very centre of the square as if trying to make a leap towards the Teatro Real. The Count Duke Olivares, as part of his ambitious promotional activities on behalf of Philip IV, had commissioned the work in 1636 from the Florentine baroque artist, Pietro Tacca, who in 1616 had executed the statue of Philip III which is now in the Plaza Mayor. To begin with Tacca planned an equestrian statue similar to that of Philip III, but Olivares was not satisfied with the preparatory model, and insisted that the horse should be rearing rather than walking. The technical problems of such a composition were enormous, and it has even been said that Tacca was forced to call on Galileo to help him solve them. The monument, finally completed by 1639, had the distinction of being the first of a rearing horse ever to be realized in bronze.

The time has finally come to gather all your strength and prepare for your assault on the PALACIO REAL itself, a daunting prospect. A mere glance at this inhumanly proportioned structure is exhausting enough, and you might find it difficult to believe that the plan which the Italian architect Juvarra had drawn up for it in 1735 was far larger in scale. To have carried out Juvarra's plan would in fact have necessitated relocating the building, and Philip V refused to allow this, insisting that the new palace should rise phoenix-like above the ashes of the old one, which in turn had evolved out of the foundations of the original Moorish *alcázar*. The cliff-top site was a difficult and restricted one, and even the more modest plan eventually carried out by Sacchetti – who replaced Juvarra after the latter's timely death in 1736 – involved the construction of massive basements on the northern and western sides of the building. The palace was completed in 1764, the first monarch to move in here being Charles III. In the following century the life within the palace was to inspire an outstanding novel by Pérez Galdós, *La de Bringas* (translated in English as *The Spendthrifts*), which deals with the months leading up to the flight of Isabel II and her court in 1868. Ideally this should be read by anyone who comes here, for it manages to give a human dimension to what would otherwise be a monstrous pile of statistics. Characteristically for Galdós, the novel focuses not on the protagonists of the court but on its minor functionaries, specifically on the spendthrift wife of a miserly worthy, Bringas. These are among numerous people hidden in modest apartments on the palace's upper floor, people whose petty preoccupations form an ironic contrast to the splendour of the setting below. Even the dreary rooms of the couple's apartment are named by their academically-minded son after those of the famous apartments underneath them, the drawing room being called the Ambassadors Room, the matrimonial bedroom the *Sala de Gasparini*, the little inside room where they did their ironing the *Furriela*, and so on. The sharpness of Galdós's social satire, and his exposure of the hollowness and

Pietro Tacca's statue of Philip IV, looking towards the Teatro Real.

grotesque farce of court life, becomes particularly acute in a description of a charitable banquet put on by Isabel II for a carefully chosen group of beggars. The terrified expressions of the beggars as they are magnanimously served their food becomes a great spectacle to the bejewelled members of the court, but this scene acquires an awfulness by being described through the eyes of the Bringas's epileptic daughter, who deliriously observes the proceedings from a second-floor balcony: 'In the courtyard below the halberdiers were going round and round with their coachmen and lackeys: it was like a great casserole in which many-coloured human limbs were turning round and round in the heat.'

The public entrance to the palace is alongside the southern gates of that vast forecourt known as the Plaza de la Armería, a bare, paved space which manages even to reduce the daily throngs of tourists to the size of scurrying ants. On a hot, sunny day the glare from all the surrounding stone can be quite merciless, forcing you to shield your eyes as you walk across the desert-like forecourt towards the palace's south and principal façade. Behind this lie the main state rooms of the palace, and it is a sobering thought that the windows to the central Throne Room – where the Italian artist Giovanni Tiepolo Battista painted one of the largest frescoes in his career – occupy a proportionally small area of the enormous façade. The exterior, comprising a rusticated basement supporting a giant order of columns and pilasters, impresses through its repetition of architectural elements than through any specific detail, although you should note at main floor level two statues portraying Atahualpa of Peru and Montezuma of Mexico. They form part of the series of statues representing kings of Spain and Spanish possessions intended mainly for the parapet of the palace. Not only were they among the few works in this series actually placed on the building, but they were also two of the earliest sculptures of Americans to have been executed in Europe.

Although Spain's royal family no longer live at the palace, they use it frequently for official functions, and I have often arrived here to find the building unexpectedly closed. Furthermore the palace is at present being extensively restored, and many of the rooms that were once open to the public might be taken over after their restoration for the exclusive use of the royal family. A more appealing recent development is that you are no longer obliged to follow a guided tour, but can wander around at your own pace, directed solely by the occasional arrow. The layout of the palace is straightforward, Sacchetti having rejected the many courtyards that had been planned by Juvarra in favour of a single, central courtyard, the northern side of which is dominated by the royal chapel. From the moment you ascend the monumental main staircase in the southern wing, the overall impression of the interior is of a great sea of different coloured marbles, highlighted by gilding and a wealth of frescoes. The general style is late baroque with incipient neo-classical elements, but there is also the occasional foray into the Rococo, as in the magnificent *Sala de Gasparini*, where all the available space is covered with chinoiserie stucco-work, chinese porcelains, and lush, oriental silks. The setting of the palace is almost too rich to be able to give too much attention to the many paintings on display here, although it must be said that the majority of these are minor or school works. The outstanding exception is a late fifteenth-century polyptych by Juan de Flandes, a Flemish artist who was invited to Spain by Isabel la Católica. This particular work comprises fifteen small, exquisitely painted panels of the life of Christ, some with landscape backgrounds that combine minute detailing with atmospheric depth.

From the miniature vision of Juan de Flandes, it is a great step to the world of gods, angels and mythological heroes who fly around the palace's numerous and splendid ceiling frescoes. Among the main artists responsible for these were the German-born court painter Anton Raffael Mengs, Goya's teacher Francisco Bayeu, and the Neapolitan Corrado Giaquinto, who painted the luminous, Correggio-inspired ceilings in the royal chapel. But the most renowned of the decorators at work here was Giovanni Battista Tiepolo, who had arrived in Madrid in June 1762, after a tiring journey from his native Venice and an apparent reluctance to come here in the first place. The by now 66-year-old artist was accompanied by his two artist sons, Giandomenico and Lorenzo, but had left his wife and remaining family back in Italy. Early biographers of Tiepolo, in a desperate attempt to give some spice to a life which is almost entirely free of anecdote, have absurdly speculated that the artist had come to Spain with a gondolier's young and beautiful daughter. There is slightly more basis to the stories that Tiepolo's stay in Spain was beset by a ferocious rivalry with Mengs, although it is highly unlikely that the German painter – together with a group of henchmen – had one day laid in wait for the Italian in the branches of a tree. What can be said, however, is that Tiepolo's years in Spain were not quite the spectacular conclusion to a glorious career that they might have been. The Throne Room ceiling, which he completed in 1764, portrays the grandiose theme of *The Triumph of the Spanish Monarchy*, but, for all its splendour and colour, lacks the painterly conviction of his earlier apotheoses, largely due to an increased reliance on studio hands, but also perhaps because the values that it represented were becoming increasingly difficult to sustain in a world already touched by the Enlightenment. The artist undertook two further ceilings for the palace (in the guard-room and so-called *Saleta*), and then, instead of returning home to Venice, asked Charles III if he could stay on in the country. He was subsequently commissioned to paint some canvases for the royal chapel at Aranjuez, but the finished works did not apparently appeal to the church authorities, much to the consternation of the artist, who died suddenly in Madrid on 27 March. His tomb in San Martín was later demolished.

If you are still capable of standing once you have left the palace, you might wish to visit two other places on the Plaza de la Armería. One of these, on the eastern side of the forecourt, is the REAL OFICINA DE FARMACIA, which incorporates the contents of a pharmacy founded by Philip II in 1594, as well

A decorative lamp on the main façade of the Palacio Real.

as numerous elegant furnishings and furniture from the eighteenth and nineteenth centuries. Opposite this, suspended above the Casa de Campo, is the ARMERÍA which is said to be the finest of its kind in the world. Collections of armour generally make for rather heavy viewing, and this particular one could well have benefited from the eccentric atmosphere, say, of Madrid's Museo del Ejército. None the less, the sheer historical importance of the objects here – which range from el Cid's sword to Philip IV's coat of armour – amply make up for the general coldness and dreariness of the display. Of special interest to art historians, and as a valuable prelude to a visit to the Prado, is the coat of armour which was both worn by Charles V at the Battle of Mühlberg, and painted by Titian in his famous equestrian portrait of the emperor, which now hangs in that museum.

Immediately on leaving the Plaza de la Armería, you will find yourself facing the future CATHEDRAL OF LA ALMUDENA, work on which has been almost continuous since 1879. The west façade, which is directly opposite the palace gates, is in a classical style in keeping with that of the palace, but the building had originally been intended as a neo-medieval monument. The first architect, the Marquis of Cubas, had managed by the time of his death to build the present neo-romanesque crypt, and also to start work above this on an east end with radiating chapels inspired by that of Rheims Cathedral. From the back of the cathedral you can descend towards the Casa de Campo on the Cuesta de la Vega, passing to your right, a large fragment of the city's medieval walls. At the bottom of the hill, on the other side of the modern Paseo de la Virgen del Puerto, you will come to the quiet, shaded promenade laid out by Pedro de Ribera while working for the Marquis of Vadillo. Vadillo was later buried in the delightful hermitage which Ribera built in 1718 at the promenade's southern end, a brick structure of engaging simplicity crowned by an extraordinary tent-shaped roof. At the northern end of the Paseo de la Virgen del Puerto is the entrance to the Campo del Moro, which formed originally the palace gardens, but is now a wooded public park. Inside are superb views looking up towards the palace, and a modern museum containing a collection of old carriages, including a black seventeenth-century one which is known mysteriously as *Juana la Loca* and is possibly Europe's oldest surviving funeral carriage. Of similarly macabre interest is the processional carriage in which Alfonso XIII received in 1906 his explosive tribute from Mateo Morral.

You can climb back up towards the palace along the Cuesta de San Vicente, which skirts the northern side of the Campo del Moro, beginning its ascent alongside the Estacion del Norte, a railway station with a turn-of-the-century grandeur which belies the very modest nature of the railway traffic which passes through the place today. Near the top of the street, you will find steps to your right climbing up into attractive formal gardens that were laid out in the 1930s directly below the palace's northern façade. Due east of the gardens, on the other side of the Calle de Bailen which heads south towards the Plaza de Oriente, is the narrow Plaza de la Marina Española, dominated by a monument to Cánovas del Castillo, Spain's political leader after the restoration of the monarchy in 1874. This grand and exceptionally pompous work, featuring allegories of History and Fame, was perhaps a strange way of commemorating a man of unprepossessing appearance, with a squint and a nervous tic, and dressed so badly that one contemporary described him as a 'subaltern on half-pay'. Behind Cánovas stands the SENATE HOUSE, a neo-classical work created in 1820 out of a convent dated to 1581.

Still functioning as a convent, and indeed one of the finest in Madrid, is the CONVENTO DE LA ENCARNACIÓN, which lies on a quiet square just to the south of the Plaza de la Marina Española. Founded in 1611 by the wife of Philip IV, Doña Margarita, it was built by Juan Gómez de Mora, whose hand is evident above all in the austerely beautiful granite façade of the church. The supremely elegant church interior, with its delicate stucco-work and predominance of whites and pastel blues, was remodelled in the late eighteenth century by Ventura Rodríguez, but still retains its original organ, on which wonderful concerts are given every Sunday morning at 11.30. Guides from the Patrimonio Nacional will take you around the rest of the convent, where, among many lesser works of art, are a signed painting by José Ribera of John the Baptist (1635) and two sculptures by the seventeenth-century master of polychromed wood, Gregorio Fernández. Also here is a curious Flemish panel representing a marital swap between France and Spain, Louis XII of France receiving Ana of Austria, and the future Philip IV getting in exchange Isabel Bourbon, the whole ceremony taking place half-way across the estuary of Bidasoa, which lies in between the two countries. But all these works, however interesting, will fall to the back of your mind as soon as you enter the extraordinary Reliquary, which is the convent's greatest claim to fame. This comparatively small room is lined on every side with smart wooden cases as in an old library, but instead of books the cases display no less than four thousand relics, the whole collection bringing together every conceivable saint. A tiny vial contains the most sacred of these relics, a drop of blood from St Pantaleon, a fourth-century martyr and doctor whose blood was generously distributed among many reliquaries. However, this particular sample, little bigger than a pin-prick, has a special significance, for, every year, on the anniversary of the saint's martyrdom of 27 July, it liquifies, and only does so at other times of the year to warn of impending catastrophes, such as World War I, or the Spanish Civil War. Sceptics generally, and visitors from Protestant countries, in particular, tend to wince in such places, but most people will at least be able to appreciate the harmonious refinement of the setting, with its elegantly restrained reliquary cases, its altarpiece of *The Nativity* by Leonardo's follower Bernado Luini, and its superb coffered ceiling, which sparkles with classical grotesques painted by Vicente Carducho.

Heading north-east from the convent along the Calle de la Bola, you will pass to your left the short Calle de Guillermo Rolland, where, at number 7,

The terraced gardens below the northern side of the Palacio Real, with statuary intended originally for the palace's parapet.

Gómez de Mora's seventeenth-century convent of the Encarnación.

the great fantasist and lover of the absurd Ramón Gómez de la Serna was born in 1883. As you emerge eventually into the singularly ugly Plaza de Santo Domingo, the magical aura which hangs over the surroundings of the Palacio Real at last evaporates, and you return to a more mundane world, albeit only briefly. At the junction of the square and the unfortunately named Calle de Venereas, once stood the Café Varela, an establishment made famous by the poet and *costumbrista* Emilio Carrere. Madrid might lose the bodies of its famous poets, but it does not so easily forget their memories, for in the middle of the characterless Galician restaurant which has replaced the Café Varela can be found a memorial plaque touchingly inscribed with the words: 'This is where the great poet Emilio Carrere wrote his finest verses.'

4
The City of the Enlightenment

....

THE MUSEO DEL PRADO *to* THE GLORIETA DE ATOCHA

'The past is no better than the present, but it is lit by a suggestive, crepuscular twilight both poetic and distinct from the crude and sour reality of the present'. With these words, written at the outbreak of the Spanish Civil War, the elderly Pío Baroja embarked on a nostalgic evocation of the Buen Retiro, the park which forms the main setting of his romantic novel, *Nights of the Buen Retiro*. The world of aristocrats in their finery, parading carriages, and nocturnal brilliance that Baroja evoked may have gone forever, but a residue of aristocratic elegance, leisurely unconcern, and even poetry lingers on in the beautiful area of Madrid extending from the Retiro gardens down to the Paseo del Prado. This is the showcase heart of Madrid, exceptionally rich in monuments and museums, graced by the smartest of turn-of-the-century apartment blocks (including one in which Baroja himself lived), and featuring what is still one of the most enchanting of Europe's city parks. The initial development of the area is due to the presence here of the fifteenth-century monastery of San Jerónimo, from which was to evolve the Palacio del Buen Retiro of Olivares fame. However, this is essentially the Madrid of Charles III, whose memory will constantly be invoked in the course of the following itinerary, which begins outside the outstanding museum which he founded, the Prado, and ends at what is now the remarkable cultural centre named after Queen Sofia, an institution situated in one of the most ambitious buildings undertaken during Charles's enlightened reign.

The impact of Charles III on the appearance of Madrid is felt above all in the broad and shaded thoroughfare of the Paseo del Prado, which runs from the Calle de Alcalá down to the railway station at Atocha. Long before Charles III's time there had been grown up here the so-called '*prado*' or meadow of San Jerónimo, a large poplar-lined walk which had already emerged by the mid sixteenth century as a major recreational district, famed

OPPOSITE *A remote corner of the Parque del Retiro.*

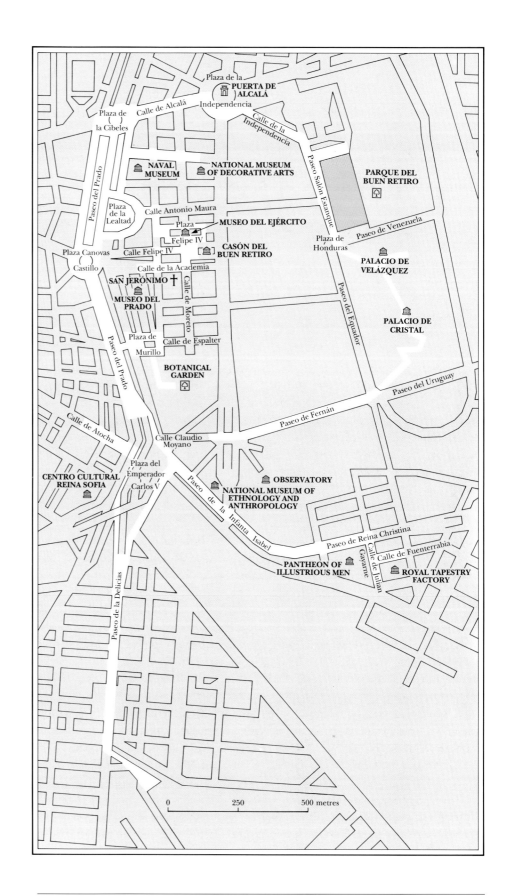

THE CITY OF
ENLIGHTENMENT

for its winter sun and summer coolness. Pedro de Medina, in a book of 1560 on the glories of Spain, wrote of this walk that

> It is fascinating and most entertaining to observe the crowds who go there, comprising some of the most splendid women, exquisitely attired gentlemen, and all sorts of lords and ladies in coaches and carriages. Here you can savour to the full the freshness of the wind on summer nights and evenings, and hear much good music, without any risk of being attacked, robbed or suffering any other harm, thanks to the good care and attention of the court mayors.

Medina's account of the original *paseo* was an idealized and rather optimistic one, for other authors of this period mentioned the fights that often broke out here and the sordid sexual encounters that relied on the density of the surrounding foliage and the various hollows and other natural deformities that pock-marked the terrain. What is more the beautiful embellishments referred to by both Medina and others amounted to little more than two insignificant fountains fed by a long and stagnant ditch which ran the whole length of the walk.

Reform of the Prado de San Jerónimo and of the adjoining prados of Atocha and Recoletos had clearly become a pressing necessity by the late eighteenth century, and in 1775, after seven years of planning, work on a new line of *paseos* was finally begun under the direction of the engineer José de Hermosilla. The ground was levelled, the ditch filled, new rows of trees planted, and a series of splendid fountains created, the latter designed by the great Ventura Rodríguez. The most elegant and popular part of this new avenue was the stretch in between the Calle de Alcalá and the Carrera de San Jerónimo, a stretch which begins at the north with the famous fountain showing Cybele seated imperiously in her chariot, and ends with the fountain of the trident-bearing Neptune pulled along by his horses. Known as the 'Salón del Prado', this was where most of Madrid would at times be seen to gather, and certainly all the fashionable young. Mesonero Romanos described it in 1830 as a place 'where amorous intrigues rule the day, where the confusion, the constant social intercourse, the ceaseless civilities, the variety of clothes and faces, the noise of the coaches and horses, the dust, the boys selling water and cinnamon, and, in short, the bustling life which is not to be found in any other of the city's *paseos*, all combine at first to irritate foreigners, who, however, end up by loving it all'. Even Théophile Gautier, whose snobbish French prejudices prevented him from being able to appreciate the elegance of the Salón del Prado, had none the less to admit that

> It was one of the most animated sights that can be seen, and it is one of the most beautiful promenades in the world, not because of the site, which is most ordinary (in spite of all the efforts of Charles III to correct its defects) but because of the astonishing assembly which gathers there every evening, from 7.30 until 10.00.

The Salón del Prado today, though still keeping its trees, fountains, and general air of sophistication, is a very different place to what it was in Gautier's day. By the turn of the century it had lost most of the old palaces that once flanked it, and had acquired its present stone benches and landscaped central reservation. But the most significant of the changes is that it is no longer the animated rendez-vous of Madrid, the noise and confusion of the place today being not the result of loitering crowds but of the constant flow of car traffic. Only in the Paseo de Recoletos, to the north of the Fuente de Cibeles, can you experience something of the social vitality of the Salón in its former days, but only if you go there during the summer months, when its pavements are lined with open-air bars that remain packed until the early hours of the morning.

The crowds that assemble in the southern half of today's Paseo de Prado are of a rather different kind to the summer ones on Recoletos, for they have come here not to drink or socialize, but to visit one of the world's most popular museums. This area immediately to the south of the Neptune Fountain was designated by Charles III less for pleasure than for instruction, specifically scientific instruction. The MUSEO DEL PRADO was conceived initially as a museum of natural sciences, and as a complement to the adjoining botanical garden, which was laid out in 1774 by the up-and-coming young architect Juan de Villanueva. The JARDÍN BOTÁNICO, which was greatly enriched in its early years by seeds collected in the course of numerous scientific expeditions to Latin America and the Philippines, was badly neglected in the nineteenth century, so much so that Richard Ford reported that it came to be inhabited by a brood of escaped boa-constrictors that bolted any unfortunate dog or cat that strayed in to study botany. Recently restored to its original state, the garden deserves a visit, not only for its botanical specimens, but also for its elegant terraced layout, and the sophisticated simplicity of Villanueva's architectural structures, which comprise Palladian-inspired entrance gates and a superlative pavilion and greenhouse.

Villanueva, having consolidated with the Jardín Botánico his growing reputation, was entrusted in 1775 with the design of the Museo del Prado itself. So as to make the museum a natural extension to the promenade alongside it, he created a structure which is enormously long in relation to its height, and indeed he had even toyed at first with the idea of building in front of it a long covered portico where strollers could take refuge in times of rain. The great scale on which he worked, and his use of granite and the Doric Order, could have led, in less capable hands, to a cold and monotonous structure. However, the building is instead a most lively composition, incorporating elements of a palace, a rotunda and a temple, and with a rich interplay of arcades, niches and colonnades. The end result, although described somewhat dismissively by Ernest Hemingway as being 'as unpicturesque as an American High School building', is one of the supreme achievements of European neo-classicism, and a structure which is far too

OPPOSITE *Ventura Rodríguez's Fountain of Neptune: one of the artistic highpoints of the Paseo del Prado.*

The main façade of the Museo del Prado with a nineteenth-century statue of Velázquez in the foreground.

little appreciated by those whose first reaction is to ignore the building and rush straight inside to see the paintings.

Charles III did not live to see his cherished museum completed, and the place never housed the intended natural science collections. Work on the building began only in 1785 and continued until 1808, but no sooner had it been finished than the museum was ruthlessly pillaged by the French, who even stripped it of the lead on its roof. Left to decay, the building was almost on the point of collapse when Ferdinand VII decided to have it adapted to house the royal collection of paintings, an idea which had already been suggested by his father, Charles IV. The new museum was inaugurated in November 1819 and made open to the public 'except on rainy days and when there is mud around'. Around the revolution of 1868 the museum was appropriated by the state, and its holdings greatly increased by the incorporation that year of the Museo Nacional de la Trinidad, which was made up of works of art confiscated from dissolved monasteries and convents.

This collection of religious works, combined with the fabulous treasures amassed by the royal family themselves, continue to form the basis of the museum today, despite numerous later donations.

Leon Trotsky, coming to Spain in 1916 after having been expelled from wartime France, paid a salutary visit to the Prado and was reminded again of the 'eternal' element in Art. Reactions to the museum have generally been as gushing as Trotsky's, and, from the time of Richard Ford onwards, a tour of the place has frequently constituted the high point of a stay in Madrid. It is unfortunate, however, that Madrid's tourism is concentrated to such a great extent on this one place that if you come here during the summer months the unbearable overcrowding caused by the invasion of huge tour groups is likely to make you reflect less on the 'eternal' element of Art than on the very mortal failings of the human body. The congestion is not helped by the very special nature of the museum's collections, which do not add up to a balanced survey of western art, but are focused instead on groups of outstanding paintings by a relatively select number of artists, several of whom – such as Bosch, Velázquez and Goya – are represented by most of their best-known works.

The unbalanced quality of the Prado collections is to a large extent a reflection of the idiosyncratic and at times obsessive tastes of the Spanish royal family. Isabel la Católica was passionate above all about Flemish art, which is why the museum has such a remarkable collection of early Flemish works, in particular by Roger Van der Weyden, whose sense of pathos and drama was especially close to Spanish sensibilities. Charles V had a great affection for Titian, admiring him for the emotional directness of his paintings, as is seen, for instance, in the Prado's magnificent equestrian portrait of the emperor. The Prado's holdings of Titian were further enhanced by Philip II, whose interest in the artist was rather different to his father's, being concentrated on Titian's mythological paintings featuring female nudes. Most of Titian's later mythologies were commissioned by Philip II, who referred to them as *poesie*, which was probably his euphemism for erotica. Despite, or perhaps because of, his bigotry and religious mania, Philip II seems to have had an obsession with the erotic, and on one occasion even requested Titian to send from Italy a female nude seen from the back to balance another work in his collection in which the nude was seen from the front. What is undeniable is Philip II's love for the bizarre, a love which expressed itself most blatantly in the avid way in which he collected the works of Hieronymus Bosch. He is known to have spent hours locked away in his bedroom at the Escorial contemplating such paintings as *The Garden of Earthly Delights*, undoubtedly revelling in its unrivalled wealth of sexual and macabre details. In contrast, an orthodox and distinctly wholesome attitude towards art was shown by his son Philip III, whose greatest contribution to the royal collections lay in his patronage of Rubens, another artist who is exceptionally well represented in the Prado. Philip IV inherited his father's interest in Rubens, but as a patron he is remembered principally for his extraordinary association with Velázquez, an association betwen a monarch and a painter which is virtually unique in the history of art. Every day the king would visit the artist in his studio, and as an outcome of this friendship, Velázquez felt emboldened to place himself on the same level as the royal family in *Las Meninas*, the work which attracts the Prado's greatest crowds.

For all the public exposure which they have received, the paintings of Velázquez continue to have a vividness which early writers on the artist have attributed to the miraculous. The uniform brilliance of these works certainly highlights the limitations of the museum's holdings of other Spanish artists, which are surprisingly patchy. The collection of Spanish medieval art, although making for a pleasantly quiet part of the museum, has not nearly the range or excitement of that to be seen in Barcelona's Museo de Arte de Catalonia. As for the paintings here by El Greco – which were mainly acquired at a comparatively late date – these will have less of an impact on anyone who has spent any time in Toledo. Trotsky, mysteriously, singled out the Riberas for special praise, but, with the major exception of a monument-ally powerful *Martyrdom of St Bartholomew*, you can see better examples of this artist's work elsewhere in Europe, as is also sadly true of the work of Velázquez's other great contemporaries such as Zurburán and Murillo. The relative paucity of the seventeenth-century holdings is a sorry indication of the way in which English and French travellers mercilessly plundered Spain's heritage in the wake of the Peninsular War, when Spanish art reached the height of its popularity.

It is with its vast collection of paintings by Goya that the Prado comes back into its own again, reviving wilting spirits, and ensuring that a visit to this building ends on a note of climax. The numerous loud-mouthed tour-guides also seem to perk up at this point, for Goya's works, in particular the Black Paintings, give an opportunity to voice the romantic and very clichéd view of the artist as a tormented soul. Personally I prefer to emphasize instead Goya's love of pigeon-shooting and the way he rarely failed to materialize at his shareholders' meetings. I have little sympathy too for the idea of Goya as a radically political artist, for although he depicted the horrors of Spain's War of Independence, he appears to have been quite happy to have worked for anyone who paid him, and indeed was under the pay of the French one moment, and of the tyrannical Ferdinand VII the next. Perhaps the least attractive aspect of the Goya legend, and one peculiar to the Spanish vision of him, is the way in which he has come to symbolize Spanish machismo. As you stand in front of the *Maja Desnuda*, you are almost certain to overhear someone talking gleefully about the affair which Goya is supposed to have had with the Duchess of Alba, who, even less plausibly, is said to have posed for the picture. In fact the only documentation to have come down to us about Goya's intimate life takes the form of a recent and scarcely publicized discovery of a collection of love letters written by Goya to a man. None of this information has of course any relevance to an enjoyment of the paintings, but

Described by Ortega y Gasset as a picture of 'a portraitist portraying the art of portraiture', Las Meninas now dominates the larger of the Prado's rooms devoted to Velázquez.

temples of art such as the Prado tend to enshrine mythologies about artists, and these mythologies need occasionally to be questioned.

Leaving the Prado by its northern door, you will find yourself confronted by a very pictorial monument to Goya by the turn-of-the-century sculptor Mariano Benlliure, the stone base of which is ridiculously carved with a group of demons hovering over a blissfully oblivious *Maja Desnuda*. At the top of the neighbouring flight of steps is the Calle de la Academia, which gently climbs east towards what was once the royal palace of the Buen Retiro. The first building which you come to on the right is the former monastery church of SAN JERÓNIMO, which stands on a terrace above the Prado, its gothic spires and pinnacles forming an unusual element in the skyline of a city otherwise little affected by this style. The monastery was founded by Ferdinand and Isabel in 1505, and in 1528 became established as the place where the nobility and Cortes of Castile swore allegiance to the crown princes of Spain. The basis of the future royal palace of the Buen Retiro was laid in the early 1560s when

The much-altered façade of the sixteenth-century church of San Jerónimo. The ruined arches of the monastery formerly attached to it can be seen on the right.

Philip II ordered the building here of a royal apartment, intended to provide lodgings for the king when he retreated to San Jerónimo for Easter services, or when he took part in the various state ceremonies that were organized here, such as solemn entries into the city. Badly damaged by the French in the early nineteenth century, the monastery was dissolved in 1835, and was used subsequently as a barracks and military hospital. The church and the adjoining ruins of a sixteenth-century cloister are all that is left today of the original complex, which was demolished after 1868, together with most of the royal palaces. Saved and thoroughly restored and remodelled during the reign of Isabel II, the present church has a strong nineteenth-century character, but none the less retains much of its original appearance, in particular its porticoed west portal, which is in the elaborate late gothic style known as the Isabelline plateresque. The building has continued to be used this century for important royal functions, such as the marriage in 1906 of Alfonso XIII to Victoria Eugenia von Battenberg, and, following the death of Franco, the religious ceremony inaugurating the reign of Juan Carlos I.

The parallel street to the north of the Calle de la Academia is the broad Calle de Felipe IV, which is blocked off at its upper end by the sturdy mass of the Casón del Buen Retiro, an annexe to the Museo del Prado. This and the nearby Museo del Ejército are the main and much altered architectural fragments of the Retiro palace, the grand and fantastical complex which had been dreamed up by Count Duke Olivares as a way of consolidating his hold over Philip IV. When work began on the building in 1630, the intention had been simply to enlarge Philip II's royal apartment in preparation for the ceremony in 1632 of swearing allegiance to Prince Baltasar Carlos. However, almost immediately, Olivares began imagining a vast centre of the arts and recreation, complete with a beautiful series of gardens where plays and pageants would be put on in the summer months. The palace, which was put up at great speed under the principal supervision of Juan Gómez de Mora and Giovanni Battista Crescenzi, inspired both extravagant eulogies and the most virulent criticism, the latter being voiced mainly by Olivares's growing number of enemies, who referred to the place contemptuously as the 'chicken-coop' after an aviary in its gardens. Olivares's eventual fall from favour led to the palace being neglected, but in the eighteenth century it acted as the permanent residence of the Bourbon kings during the period when the *alcázar* was being rebuilt. Left to ruin during the French invasion of Spain, it was largely pulled down after the collapse of the Spanish monarchy in 1868.

The CASÓN DEL BUEN RETIRO, built by Alonso de Carbonell in 1637 as the ballroom of the palace, was almost entirely remodelled in the late nineteenth century and given a neo-classical casing. The insipid back façade, which dates back to 1877, overlooks the Retiro park, and faces the park's one remaining seventeenth-century gate. Far more imposing is the main façade, which rises above a monument by Benlliure to Isabel II's mother María Cristina, and

The late nineteenth-century back façade shielding the former ball-room of the seventeenth-century Buen Retiro.

was built in 1891 by Ricardo Velázquez Bosco, whose splendid Palacio de Cristal and Ministry of Agriculture will be admired later in this itinerary. Much of the building is now given over to the nineteenth-century holdings of the Prado, which range from grand historical works of the Romantic period such as Carlos Luis de Ribera's *Daughters of El Cid* to delicate turn-of-the-century landscapes by artists such as Santiago Rusiñol. This part of the building is undeservedly little-visited, for those who come to the Casón today are primarily interested in the wholly separate section devoted to Picasso's famous canvas, *Guernica*. The story of this large canvas goes back to a commission which Picasso had received during the Civil War to decorate the Spanish Pavilion at the Paris World Exhibition of 1937. Undecided for several months as to what he was going to paint, Picasso was presented with the ideal subject-matter when, in April of that year, German planes of the Condor Division destroyed the Basque town of Guernica, a bombing which was purely vindicative and had no military significance. Picasso, sharing the general sense of outrage provoked by this attack, set about working on the canvas with his characteristic speed and passion, completing the work by late June. After the Civil War the painting was deposited by Picasso in the Museum of Modern Art in New York, and was only brought to Spain in 1981. When it was eventually hung in the Casón del Buen Retiro, members of the Guardia Civil carrying machine-guns had the task, ironically, of guarding the work from right-wing extremists, and even today there are formidable security arrangements in operation here, including the screening of visitors and the placing in front of the painting of a large and ungainly bullet-proof shield. As you contemplate this stark, monochrome testimony to the continuing emotive power of art, you might pause for a moment to reflect that you are standing in the very room where balls were held in Habsburg times. Indeed if you look up at the ceiling, which is usually ignored by visitors, you will find a colourful, triumphant fresco executed in 1694 by an artist as renowned as Picasso for the speed at which he painted, Luca Giordano, who was sometimes known as '*Fa Presto*'.

Whereas Picasso's *Guernica* chronicles the tragedy of war, the glories of war are celebrated in the absurdly anachronistic MUSEO DEL EJÉRCITO, which is situated just to the north of the Casón del Buen Retiro. The building which houses it is the main surviving section of the Buen Retiro palace, and has miraculously retained one of the grandest of the palace's original rooms, the ceremonial hall known as the Salón de los Reinos. For this room Zurburán painted a series of ten canvases of the Labours of Hercules, and Velázquez executed five of his equestrian portraits of the royal family, as well as his celebrated *Surrender of Breda*, which formed part of a series of twelve large battle scenes representing the victories of Philip IV. The paintings by Zurburán and Velázquez are now in the Prado, and the room's oriental carpets, silver lions, and other lavish furnishings have all disappeared. However, some of the pictures by Velázquez's followers are still in place, and,

The main surviving section of the palace of the Buen Retiro, the Salon de los Reinos preserves its original stuccoed grotesques on the ceiling. The room itself now forms part of the Museo del Ejército.

more importantly, the room has kept its magnificent gilded ceiling decoration, comprising the escutcheons of the 24 kingdoms of the Spanish monarchy, and elaborate classical grotesques.

The Salón de los Reinos in itself is sufficient reason for visiting this museum and should be an essential sight for anyone who wishes to understand the context for which some of Velázquez's greatest paintings were intended. Sadly, however, the notion of a military museum in a country which has only recently emerged from a military dictatorship seems to have put off all but school children and die-hard Francoists from coming here. The more sensitive and politically aware tourist might indeed find this an inappropriate place to visit immediately after seeing Picasso's *Guernica*, for, in its present layout, it is essentially a monument to Francoism, and has numerous busts and portraits of Franco and his generals, and even a reproduction of General Moscardó's horrendous study in Toledo's *alcázar*. Yet to anyone with a sense of humour and a taste for the ludicrous, this has to be one of Madrid's most entertaining museums. Confronted, in the empty, gloomily lit halls, with a compressed, symmetrical display of thousands of rifles, medals, swords, and tattered old flags and banners, you have the impression of having inadvertently opened a vast packing-case which has been left undisturbed for years. The necessary note of bathos is provided by the sense of chaos underlying all the would-be military precision, the models of soldiers who appear to be dressed for amateur theatricals, and the piped military music, which accompanies you throughout the museum, eventually depositing you in the cavernous basement, where you reel from the sight of a veritable ocean of cannons. You will be glad to know that the contribution made by women to all this glorious military history has not been forgotten, and there is a tiny vestibule grandly entitled 'Sala de las Heroinas', featuring a portrait of María Pita, who outwitted '*el pirata Drake*'.

From the Museo del Ejército you should head back west towards the Paseo del Prado, crossing the Calle de Ruiz de Alarcón, where at number 12 is the elegant residential block where the writer Pío Baroja lived. Despite the grandeur of his home surroundings, Baroja was often to be seen in the company of vagrants, and, during his Madrid years, was described by César González Ruano as 'resembling a beggar dressed in a suit snatched from a corpse'. Almost round the corner from Baroja's house, overlooking the Plaza de la Lealtad, is the palatial HOTEL RITZ, gleaming in its coat of icing-sugar plaster. Built in 1908 by the French architect of the London Ritz, Charles Mewes, it replaced the Hotel Paris as Madrid's most luxurious hotel, and also served as a model to the many other French-style buildings put up in Madrid over the following two decades. Mewes, taking into account the proximity of the neo-classical Museo del Prado, was unusually restrained in his design of the building's exterior, reserving his neo-baroque decorative exuberance for the reception hall and adjoining spaces. If you are smartly dressed you will be allowed to wander into the fabulously appointed main bar, where you might even be tempted to slouch into one of the armchairs and order a coffee, an experience which acts as a decompression chamber after the noise of the traffic outside, but which is likely to be less relaxing the moment you receive the bill. The young Salvador Dalí, short on funds but with his life-long fascination with the world of the very rich, ordered a cocktail here in 1926, made an impression by telling the barman to keep the very considerable change, and then, having cut his finger on the glass, created a special cocktail of his own featuring his blood and the cotton cherry from the hat of an elegant and bewildered blonde next to him. Afterwards he rushed out into the street, feeling, as he was later to relate in his autobiography *My Secret Life*, 'as greatly moved as Jesus must have felt when he invented Holy Communion ... The sky over Madrid was a shattering blue and the brick houses were pale rose, like a sigh filled with glorious promises. I was phenomenal. I was phenomenal.' He began to run, jumping with exaggerated leaps into the air, and shouting at the top of his voice, 'Blood is sweeter than honey'. In this state he stumbled across one of his fellow students, who told everyone the next day that 'Dalí is crazy as a goat'.

Making a less dramatic exit from the Ritz, you should walk over to the small shaded garden in the middle of the Plaza de la Lealtad to see the large obelisk designed by Isidro González Velázquez to commemorate the victims of 2 May. The idea for such a monument was proposed by the Spanish Parliament in 1814, but it was not until 1840 that the present one was finally completed. Covered all over with such stirring words as '¡*Honor eterno al patriotismo!*', it even incorporates at its base an urn containing the ashes of those killed by the French. The gilded silver keys to this urn are kept for some reason in Madrid's municipal archive. From here you should walk north along the Paseo del Prado, noting, on the other side of this avenue, the early nineteenth-century PALACIO DE VILLAHERMOSA, which is at pesent being adapted to house the remarkable art treasures of baron Thyssen-Bornemisza, which range from Carpaccio to Edward Hopper. Further north, at the half-way point between the Neptune and Cybele fountains, is another of the fountains designed by Ventura Rodríguez, this one featuring Apollo standing on a plinth surrounded by representations of the Four Seasons. Adjacent to this, at the junction of the Paseo del Prado and the Calle de Montalbán, is the MINISTERIO DE MARINA, the modern extension to which houses a MUSEO NAVAL featuring a chaotically arranged collection of model ships. The better organized but less entertaining MUSEO NACIONAL DE LAS ARTES DECORATIVAS stands further east along the Calle de Montalbán, occupying a late nineteenth-century residence at number 12. Excessive good taste, and an atmosphere of cold sophistication dull somewhat the impact of this museum's wonderful and wide-ranging collection, one of the high points of which is a colourful eighteenth-century Valencian kitchen entirely decorated with illusionistic ceramic scenes featuring servants, kitchen vessels, food, and such delightful details as a cat tugging at a large fish.

The Plaza de la Cibeles, presided over by its famous fountain of the charioted goddess, marks the busy intersection of the paseos del Prado and Recoletos with the equally broad Calle de Alcalá. This is the nerve-centre of modern Madrid, and it is here, at its south-eastern corner, that you will find one of the city's most spectacular and eccentric buildings. Gómez de la Serna speculated that one day this building might enjoy a more dignified function than its present one, and perhaps even be taken over as the headquarters of the Ministry of the Interior, as the prominence both of its architecture and situation surely deserved. For the moment, however, it remains what it has always been, namely the city's central POST OFFICE. Designed in 1904 by Antonio Palacios, and completed in 1919, its construction signified for Gómez de la Serna the 'official arrival in Madrid of unprecedented structures, built neither for God nor for the pure aristocracy of old'. It was, as he also noted, a curious mixture of the 'hybrid and the rational', a work which was daringly modern for the time, while at the same time outlandishly drawing on Spanish architecture of the past. Conceived as a colossal temple to Progress, its exterior of castellated towers thrown up to a great height earned the building the nickname of 'Our Lady of Communications'. As for the lavish decorative coating of the building, this can be described as 'neo-Churrigueresque', and is complemented by a wonderful row of large gilded bronze letter-boxes, evocatively inscribed with the main destinations in Spain.

Heading east from the post-office building towards the main entrance of the Retiro park, you briefly join the Calle de Alcalá, which was formerly the main road leading east of Madrid. On the other side of the street, at number 57, is the Café Lion, one of the last of the many famous cafés that once lined the street all the way west to the Puerta del Sol. Founded in 1929 as a replacement to the Café Lion d'Or, it attracted the two opposite extremes of the Spanish political world of this period, both of which were drawn to the café's basement section known as 'the Happy Whale'. One of its regulars was the founder of the Falange, José Antonio Primo de Rivera, who was constantly to be seen here with an admiring crowd almost until he was arrested and shot by the Republicans in November 1936. Another habitué was García Lorca, who, with the Chilean Communist poet Pablo Neruda, and members of the travelling theatre company called 'La Barraca', would come both here and to the neighbouring and still surviving Cervezería Correos. Higher up the street you will emerge into the circular Plaza de la Independencia, part of the perimeter of which is taken up by the gates to the Retiro park, and the rest by a harmonious group of residential blocks dating back to the 1870s. In the middle of all the traffic stands one of the most beautiful of Charles III's legacies to Madrid, the three-arched city gate, the PUERTA DE ALCALÁ, through which – in the words of Gómez de la Serna – 'the dawn threads each morning its golden point'. This was the most important of Madrid's gates, not only on account of its position alongside the royal palace of the Buen Retiro, but also because of its being the entrance to the city for those travelling here from Barcelona and France. Accordingly, Charles III took particular care in the choice of its design, rejecting no less than five projects by Ventura Rodríguez in favour of the present structure by Sabatini, a perfectly proportioned work of uncluttered simplicity, the sculptural decoration of which is set apart from the rest of the granite monument by being executed in white Colmenar stone.

If you were to continue heading east along the Calle de Alcalá you would skirt the northern side of the Retiro park, coming eventually to the large

The grand days of Madrid's postal service: one of the gilded bronze letter boxes from Antonio Palacios's 'Nuestra Señora de las Communicaciones'.

equestrian monument to the hero of the first Carlist War, General Baldomero Espartero, whose well-endowed horse has given rise to the popular Madrid saying, 'to have more balls than the horse of Espartero'. Entering instead the Retiro, you will find in front of the main entrance an alley of trees leading up to the large rectangular pond, or *Estanque*, which forms the main survival of the original royal PARQUE DEL BUEN RETIRO. The park was inaugurated in the autumn of 1632 with a mythological spectacular recreating the loves of Orpheus and Eurydice, the *Estanque* being filled with boats carrying members of the court, as well as musicians playing the music of Monteverdi. After 1767, the park was opened conditionally to the public, but it was not handed over to the municipality of Madrid until the reign of Isabel II, by which time it had been thoroughly restored following the devastation caused by the French . In its first 50 years as the city park of Madrid it acquired its present-day layout, as well as a superb series of architectural and sculptural embellishments, including what may be described as Madrid's answer to Rome's monument to Vittorio Emanuele II. This monument to Alfonso XII comprises a vast oval formed on one side by steps leading down to the *Estanque*, and on the other by two arms of a colonnade flanking the enormously tall plinth which supports the equestrian bronze of the monarch by Benlliure.

Pío Baroja may have looked back nostalgically to the Buen Retiro park of his youth, but the place today has changed remarkably little over the years, the greatest difference being that today few people other than vagrants would think of coming here at night. But from the late afternoon right up to dusk, a large cross-section of Madrid society swarms around the bosky shores of the *Estanque*, under the watchful eye of Alfonso XII. Open-air cafés, rowing-boats for hire, the ubiquitous street performers, pavement artists, portrait painters, fortune-tellers, flamenco-strumming gypsies, even an elderly man with a typewriter calling himself a poet, form part of the endlessly absorbing human zoo of the Retiro. Until comparatively recently there was also a real zoo, a legacy of the park's royal menagerie, and a place where miserable polar bears prowled in endless circles trying to avoid a decorative trickle of water and the taunts of a public who ignored the notices not 'to spit or throw sunflower seeds at the animals'. 'It is an indisputable fact', wrote Nina Epton in 1964, 'that all these cramped animals look contented and the bears are actually frolicsome'. Today the grounds of the former zoo are taken over every May and June by the hundreds of open-air stalls constituting Madrid's Book Fair, a genuinely frolicsome event marking the arrival of summer, and attracting almost the whole of Madrid, not for the books, but for the crowds of parading people.

The Retiro is fortunately sufficiently large and varied to accommodate all tastes. Lovers of peace, or indeed lovers, can escape the worst of the crowds by slipping off into the woods immediately to the south of the *Estanque*. Here you will also find two architectural marvels by Ricardo Velázquez Bosco, the first of these – the PALACIO DE VELÁZQUEZ – being a large pavilion in glass, brick and iron erected in 1882 for the last of a number of exhibitions that were once

Detail of Daniel Zuloaga's ceramics on the Palacio de Velázquez in the Retiro gardens.

held in the park on the lines of that of London's Crystal Palace. Profusely decorated with ceramics by Daniel Zuloaga, this pavilion is now used for temporary art exhibitions, as is the nearby PALACIO DE CRISTAL, the most endearing of Velázquez's works. One of the most stunning examples in Spain of a glass and ironwork structure, with two long sides inspired by a cathedral apse, this gains an added beauty from its position above a small and picturesquely planned lake, where gliding swans and a great central jet of water further enhance the cool and relaxing atmosphere. Less in harmony with the surroundings is the sculpture by the contemporary Basque artist Chillida on the lake's southern shores, a work which seems at first sight like the emptied contents of a lorry carrying building materials. Numerous other sculptures of a more traditional kind are scattered throughout the park, including, at the end of the main avenue running south from the *Estanque*, a monument by one Ricardo Bellver entitled *The Fallen Angel*. Although the style of this work is traditional, the subject-matter certainly is not, and it is claimed to be the only one in the world dedicated to Lucifer.

The Palacio de Cristal in the Retiro gardens, now used for art exhibitions.

Lucifer has been condemned to the bleaker, southern half of the Retiro, and from here you would be best advised to head to the park's south-western

exit, noting as you do so Juan de Villanueva's OBSERVATORY, a necessary corrective to Satanism which rises on the hill to your left. Commissioned in 1785 by Charles III, it is a temple to the spirit of the Enlightenment, its central telescope contained within a classical rotonda which sits proudly above a colonnaded portico. Leaving the park, and crossing over the Calle de Alfonso XII, you reach the sloping Cuesta de Claudio Moyano, the railings of which mark the southern edge of the Jardín Botánico. In front of these is a long row of recently restored turn-of-the-century book-stalls, where you can buy both new and second-hand books and experience daily something of the animated atmosphere of the annual Retiro book fair.

At the bottom of the hill the noise increases as you reach the southern end of the Paseo del Prado, where a whole series of radiating thoroughfares disgorge their traffic into a sprawling and untidy square dignified both by the name of Glorieta del Emperador Carlos V and by the grandeur of the surrounding buildings. In the case of the Ministry of Agriculture, immediately to your left on entering the square, rarely can a building of such majestic and glorious character serve such an earthbound function. Built in 1893 by Velázquez Bosco, it features much ceramic decoration by Daniel Zuloaga on its vast exterior, and a monumentally-sized porticoed frontispiece which seems almost to be borne on wings thanks to its crowning allegorical figure of Glory flanked by winged horses.

The history of Madrid itself soars off into flights of fantasy as you approach, on the south-eastern side of the Ministry of Agriculture, the neo-classical building housing the MUSEO ETNOLÓGICO Y ANTROPOLÓGICO. There is nothing remarkable about the actual building – a coldly academic structure – nor about its clearly if unimaginatively displayed collections of anthropological, ethnographical and prehistoric items. However, the building takes on an eerie fascination with a knowledge of the strange story of its founder, Doctor González Velasco, one of the most famously eccentric of Madrid's personalities. A distinguished scientist and master surgeon, Dr Velasco assembled in his house a cabinet of curiosities, and this was later to form the basis of the present museum, which was built next to his house and inaugurated in 1875, the year of his death. Until the outbreak of the Civil War, when it mysteriously disappeared, one of the objects displayed in the museum's hall was a skeleton belonging to a giant whom the doctor had encountered on a trip to Asturias and had promised free board and lodging in his Madrid home on condition that he could keep his body after his death. The doctor had various other human skeletons in his museum, including those of a 28-year-old mass murderer called Juan Tomás Blanco and of a consumptive young woman. It was the presence of the latter corpse in the doctor's collection which was to provide material for the best known story associated with him, a story where fact and fiction are difficult to separate, and which has been celebrated in a novella by Ramón Sender entitled, *The Daughter of Dr Velasco*. The daughter in question was a blonde called Gertrude who died young from tuberculosis, inspiring her stricken father to try and preserve her memory by embalming her corpse. There were even reports that the doctor had been seen taking this corpse with him on his carriage rides up the Paseo del Prado, a promenade which he had regularly undertaken with his daughter in happier days. Nothing remains to testify to the doctor's reputed skills as an embalmer, and the best which can be offered to the macabre-minded visitor to the museum today is a battered old camel with its stuffing falling out.

Those in search of memories of the dead will find only a short detour to the east of Dr Velasco's museum the Pantheon of Illustrious Men, which was planned in the 1890s in conjunction with the proposed reconstruction of the ruined sixteenth-century basilica and monastery of Atocha, famous for being the burial place of the missionary and champion of the Indians, Fray Bartolomé de las Casas. This pantheon, inspired by Pisa's Campo Santo, features a large cloister surrounded by cypresses, and a tall bell-tower built of bands of different coloured stone. It is interesting as the sole important example in Madrid of the influence of Italian medieval architecture, and as a repository of some fine monuments by Benlliure and other fashionable turn-of-the-century sculptors. As a place for honouring Spain's dead, however, it was almost as much of a fiasco as San Francisco el Grande had been, most of its corpses being later removed, leaving only among the ranks of the famous dead a group of political figures which includes the Andalusian lawyer and civilian Unionist Ríos Rosa, and the three assassinated statesmen, Práxedes Sagasta, Eduardo Dato, and Cánovas del Castillo. Funds ran out before the monastery and basilica could be rebuilt, and the present buildings, dating from after the Civil War, are depressing pastiches of the Herreran style. Perhaps the best reason for making a detour to this part of town is to visit the ROYAL TAPESTRY FACTORY, which is situated further to the east, at the junction of the calles de Fuenterrabía and Julián Gayarre. The original factory, for which Goya executed the numerous tapestry cartoons that are now in the Prado, had been founded by Philip V at the beginning of the eighteenth century, but the present building dates only from the 1880s. It still functions as a tapestry factory, and the fascinating guided tour through its small, decaying rooms – where working conditions seem to have changed little since Goya's times – will give you much insight into the patient process of weaving tapestries, and also make you sad at the realization of the amount of work which has gone into the generally hideous products of recent years.

The elderly Mesonero Romanos, in one of his characteristic outbursts of nostalgia, concluded a description of the Paseo del Prado by reflecting that the sonorous pealing of the bells of Atocha, San Jerónimo and Recoletos had given way to the whistle of locomotives and to great hisses of steam. He was referring to the recently completed railway station of Atocha, which had been built according to a plan which he himself had proposed on the southern side of the Glorieta del Emperador Carlos V. The original structure, inaugurated with the completion in 1851 of the railway line between Madrid and

Aranjuez (the second oldest in Spain), was succeeded in the 1890s by a splendidly elaborate ironwork structure. The latter, full of evocative memories for those who have set off from here down to the south of Spain, is now being restored, and a new station is going up behind it. Rafael Moneo, who achieved an international reputation in the early 1980s with his creation of the Museo Arqueológico at Mérida, is in charge of the new structure, which has as yet a singularly bleak look. Enthusiasts of the old days of railway travel will have today to satisfy their enthusiasm with a visit to the nearby Estación de Delicias, which can be reached by heading south from Atocha down the Paseo de Delicias. This fine ironwork structure of the 1880s was a shunting station which came popularly to be known as the Flea Station, a more appropriate name than its official one of Station of Delights. In keeping with the present universal trend of preserving the past by turning it into a museum or heritage centre, the station is now a railway museum, its tracks lined with old engines and carriages, including an old dining car where you can sit down for a drink in a setting of neo-baroque splendour.

A more imaginative transformation of an old building is to be seen at the CENTRO CULTURAL REINA SOFIA, which stands directly in front of the old Atocha railway station. This was originally the Hospital General de San Carlos, which was founded by Philip II and later rebuilt during the reign of Charles III, who entrusted the work to his favourite architect, Francesco Sabatini. Sabatini envisaged a building with seven courtyards, which would have made it even larger in size than the Palacio Real. Only one of these courtyards was completed, but this alone is of echoing proportions, as are the marbled rooms and corridors within the former hospital. Converted by Antonio Fernández Alba in the 1980s into the present cultural centre, the building manages to house the city's museum of modern art and still have room to put on some of the most ambitious and spaciously laid out art exhibitions in Europe today. I remember in particular an exhibition of Alberto Giacometti in which one of this sculptor's tiny striding figures had been the sole work placed in a hall over 50 metres long.

In the tradition of Herrera's Escorial, Sabatini's hospital was a building combining monumental proportions with a considerable austerity. However, those who financed the reconstruction of the building in the 1980s were anxious to create a lively structure which would express the optimism of the city as it approached the end of the milennium. Not content with the way Fernández Alba had respected the severe character of the building's original exterior, they turned to other architects to try to lighten the façades. The solution eventually adopted was the application to the front and back façades of glass lift shafts which shine with dazzling modernity against Sabatini's great expanses of brick. Visitors ascending in these lifts have the sensation of rising in the air above an ever expanding panorama of Madrid, a sensation also of being effortlessly projected from the world of Charles III into that of the present day.

The bold lift-shafts recently added to the eighteenth-century block which now forms the Centro Cultural Reina Sofia.

5
Parks and Gardens

....

THE PLAZA DE ESPANA *to* EL PARDO

The story of Madrid as it expands at alarming speed from the 1860s onwards is best told as you move into the northern half of the city, progressing through the changing city evoked by Pérez Galdós into a landscape of skyscrapers suggestive of America. A foretaste of Madrid's development since the 1930s will be had in the course of this chapter, which, covering an area extending north-west of the Palacio Real passes two of the earliest of the city's skyscrapers, and later heads off through the modern university. Yet the principal theme of the itinerary is not the city's modern aspects, but its green spaces, which in turn bring back memories of the seventeenth and eighteenth centuries. Goya too makes a prominent appearance in these pages, some of his greatest works being found in the former isolated hermitage in between the Parque del Oeste and the vast green expanses of the Casa de Campo. The reader will finally be left in the forested grounds of the Pardo, an appropriate conclusion to a chapter intended largely as a rural interlude before the urban onslaught to come. This is the Madrid which Ramón Villaamil, the tragic protagonist of Galdós's novel, *Miau*, comes to appreciate only in the sad, closing stages of his life. On the premature summer's day which he chooses for his suicide, he goes to what is now the Plaza de España and stares north towards the distant Sierra de Guadarrama, relishing the green and wooded landscape which lies in between. The horse-chestnuts, the plane trees, and the black poplars are on the point of sprouting, the privet hedges are already showing their new leaves, and small pink flowers dot the Judas trees. '"How lovely that is!" he said to himself, loosening the neck of his cloak, which was making him very hot, "It's as if I were seeing it for the first time in my life, or as if the sierra and those trees and this sky have only just been created."'

Villaamil lived – as shall be seen in the following chapter – off the Plaza de la Comendadoras, and on his way to the Plaza de España would have passed

OPPOSITE *The bronze figures of Don Quixote and Sancho Panza provide the foreground to the monument to Cervantes in the Plaza de España.*

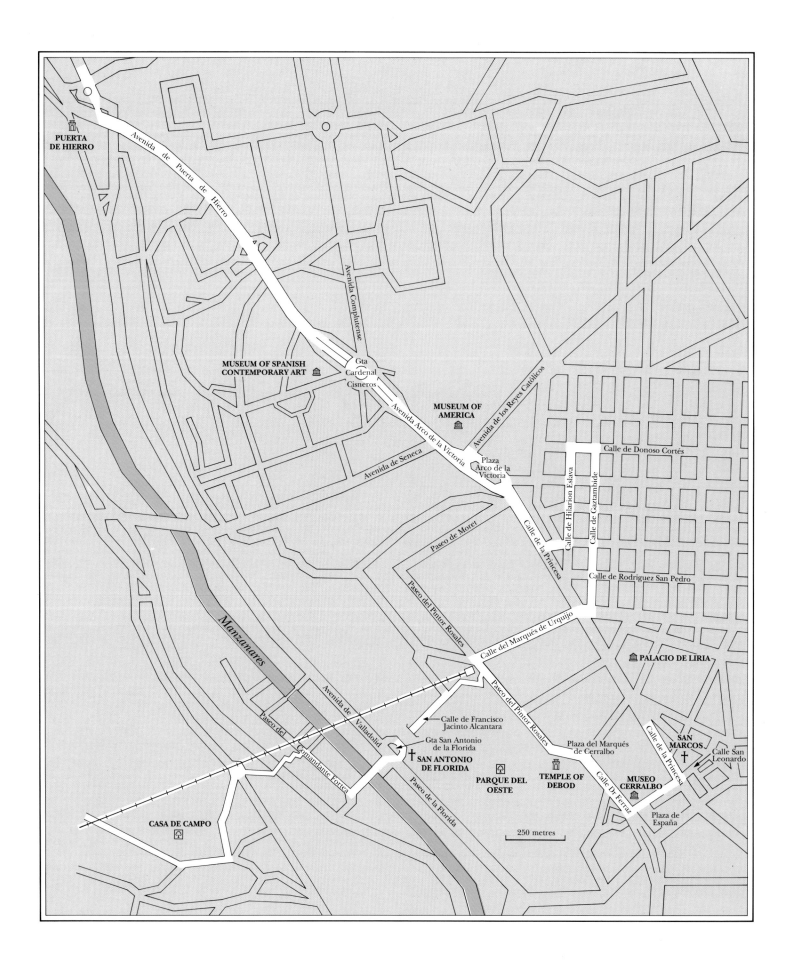

PUERTA
DE HIERRO

Avenida de Puerta de Hierro

Avenida Complutense

MUSEUM OF SPANISH
CONTEMPORARY ART

Gta
Cardenal
Cisneros

MUSEUM OF
AMERICA

Avenida Arco de la Victoria

Avenida de los Reyes Católicos

Avenida de Seneca

Plaza
Arco de la
Victoria

Calle de Donoso Cortés

Calle de Hilarion Eslava

Calle de Gaztambide

Paseo de Moret

Calle de la Princesa

Calle de Rodriguez San Pedro

Manzanares

Paseo del Pintor Rosales

Calle del Marqués de Urquijo

PALACIO DE LIRIA

Avenida de Valladolid

Paseo del

Paseo del Pintor Rosales

Calle de Francisco
Jacinto Alcantara

Comandante Fortea

Gta San Antonio
de la Florida

Plaza del Marqués
de Cerralbo

Calle de la Princesa

SAN
MARCOS

Calle San
Leonardo

† SAN ANTONIO
DE FLORIDA

Paseo de la Florida

PARQUE DEL
OESTE

TEMPLE OF
DEBOD

Calle Dr Ferraz

MUSEO
CERRALBO

CASA DE CAMPO

250 metres

Plaza de
España

near the PALACIO DE LIRIA, which I have chosen as the starting point of this itinerary. Standing in a large garden off the long and busy modern Calle de la Princesa, this palace is an enclave of the eighteenth century containing perhaps the richest of the city's private art collections. The building, which recalls in its elevation both the Palacio Real in Madrid and the Bourbon palace of La Granja, was commissioned in 1762 by James Stuart Fitz-James, 3rd Duke of Berwick and Liria, and someone who was later to marry into the house of Alba, one of Spain's most important aristocratic families. The original architect was the Frenchman A. Guilbert, but he was replaced in the 1770s by Ventura Rodríguez and Francesco Sabatini. The English architect Edwin Lutyens carried out reforms within the house around 1900, and the place was extensively reconstructed following severe damage in the course of the Civil War. Lutyens is sometimes thought to have been responsible as well for the staff quarters adjacent to the main entrance gates, outside which gather, every Friday morning, the small groups of people who have made appointments to visit the palace.

These Friday morning tours seem to attract principally those with a hankering for the world of privilege, and clear signs of delight are shown as an elderly liveried retainer takes you across the beautiful lawn and into the marbled vestibule, from where a grand staircase by Lutyens leads up to the lavish suite of first-floor rooms. Amidst all the porcelains, tapestries and gilded furniture is displayed a collection of paintings of uniformly high standard, including a panel of the Virgin by Fra Angelico, one of the relatively rare oil landscapes by Rembrandt, a superb self-portrait by Mengs, and works by Fra Bartolommeo, Titian, Palma Vecchio, Andrea del Sarto, Francesco Guardi and Rubens. Most of Spain's leading sixteenth- and seventeenth-century painters are represented, and there is an exceptionally rich group of family portraits, ranging from Titian's portrait of the 3rd Duke of Alba up to portraits of members of the Stuart family by Reynolds, Gainsborough and Raeburn. One room is dedicated to Goya, and features a celebrated full-length portrait of the 13th Duchess of Alba, one of the hands of her puppet-like body pointing to an inscription in the ground bearing the enigmatic words, 'Only Goya'. Among the portraits of more recent members of the family are works by Federico de Madrazo, Winterhalter and Augustus John, and a horrendous Velázquez pastiche by Zuloaga showing the present Duchess as a child, seated on horseback, behind a large Mickey Mouse.

The figure of Mickey Mouse prepares you for the shock of returning to the twentieth century the moment you leave the house and make your way south down the noisy Calle de la Princesa towards the nearby Plaza de España. Immediately before entering the square you could make a short detour back into the eighteenth century by turning left on to the Calle de San Leonardo to visit the church of SAN MARCOS, which sits incongruously alongside ugly apartment blocks of the 1950s. Founded in commemoration of the Battle of Almansa – in which the 1st Duke of Berwick had taken part – this church is

OPPOSITE
PARKS AND GARDENS

one of the finest ecclesiastical works by Ventura Rodríguez, and a real masterpiece of the Madrilenian late Baroque. The curved arms of its severe façade pull you in to a gilded polychromed interior conceived as a succession of five unevenly sized ellipses, the largest of which has a dome covered in frescoes featuring a scene of the Duke of Berwick mounted on a white steed.

The Plaza de España, marking the site of yet another convent pulled down by Joseph Bonaparte, once formed part of a piece of land belonging to the dukes of Alba, who sold it to the municipality of Madrid on condition that a children's garden was built in the middle of it. The long square, sloping down towards the viewpoint admired by Villaamil, is taken up today by a large terraced garden although, instead of any attractions for children, there is in its centre a huge monument to Cervantes. With pretensions as soaring as its size, this multi-figured work of the 1920s rises up above a large pool, the centrally-seated figure of Cervantes surrounded by a nightmarish melée of his creations, as well as by allegorical figures symbolizing his essential 'Spanishness'. The upper half of this memorably vulgar square is redolent of the 1950s, and is given a strong South American look by its two skyscrapers, at one time the largest in Europe. The earlier and architecturally more interesting of the two is the EDIFICIO ESPAÑA, which was designed in 1947 and occupies the whole of the square's eastern side. A typically megalomaniac product of the early Franco years, it has a grandiose tiered elevation comparable to that of Moscow's University Building, but is unmistakeably Spanish on account of the elaborate neo-baroque ornamentation applied above its entrance portal. The adjacent TORRE DE MADRID, at the north-eastern corner of the square, dates from the mid 1950s, and, with its 32 floors, is slightly higher than its neighbour. This was the first of Madrid's truly tall buildings to abandon all neo-baroque trappings, but the end result today is a structure of remarkable tackiness, its futuristic pretensions gone grey and mouldy. The interior, the first in Spain to have air conditioning throughout, is worth visiting solely to take the lift up to its top-floor bar, from where an incomparably extensive view of Madrid can be enjoyed.

At the south-western corner of the Plaza de España is the former building of the Asturian Mining Company, a fine turn-of-the-century structure which has recently been boldly converted inside to create one of the city's many exciting new venues for art exhibitions. The ironwork structure of the original hall, incorporating rows of spindly Corinthian columns, is strikingly contrasted with white tubing for air conditioning, curved walls of coloured steel, and gang-walks in light wood. For an unchanged interior of the last years of the nineteenth century you have to head due north-west of the square along the Calle de Ferraz, and take the first turning to the right. Behind the eclectic red-brick exterior at number 17 Calle Ventura Rodríguez, lies the Aladdin's treasure-trove constituting the MUSEO CERRALBO. This was the palace of the 17th Marquis of Cerralbo, a politician, collector, and pioneering student of archaeology who died heirless in 1922, leaving the house and its contents to

Palatial architecture of the early twentieth century in a luxurious residential district north of the Plaza de España.

the state. The house, virtually untouched since the Marquis's day, was built in the 1880s and decorated and furnished in a style which can only be described as neo-baroque. This is not a place which will appeal to genteel English tastes, though it is difficult to imagine how anyone could be unmoved by its atmospherically lit rooms, where the sun peers through the gaps between great swathes of heavy drapery, illuminating a gilded profusion of paintings, columns, swollen mirrors, dusty family mementoes, marble-topped tables and the restless arabesques of silk and velvet-lined furniture. The *horror vacui*, or fear of empty spaces, which characterizes the decoration of this palace is balanced by its near-sepulchral silence. This is one of the least-publicized of Madrid's great museums, and the little that is written on the museum in the existing guide books gives greater emphasis to its art treasures than to its setting, which is by far its greatest attraction. Few of the works by the many famous artists supposedly represented here are of more than minor interest, and the sole paintings that stand out afterwards in the memory are the wall and ceiling decorations by the eccentric and virtually unknown Máximo Juderías Caballero.

Juderías Caballero, a native of Zaragoza, attracted the attention of the marquis at an early age, and was a guest in the palace for seven years while engaged in its decoration. He was later offered commissions from other aristocrats, but became disillusioned with Madrid after the elderly Duchess of Castro Enríquez asked him to cover up the nudes on some decorations that he had planned for her house on the Calle del Arenal. Settling subsequently in Paris, he returned to Spain only at the end of his long life, dying eventually in a remote Aragonese village in 1951, by which time he had long been forgotten by the Spanish art establishment. An academic artist who showed no originality either in his style or subject-matter, Juderías was none the less a painter of stunning technical virtuosity, and, as you enter one of the rooms that he decorated in the Palacio Cerralbo you suddenly emerge from the all-pervading baroque gloom into the brilliant sunlight of an illusionistic decoration portraying peasants at work in the fields. He reserved his greatest technical feats for the palace's extraordinary ballroom, where, competing with a gilded, mirrored and marbled setting of overwhelming lushness, he produced a Tiepolo-inspired ceiling in which historical and mythological figures co-exist effortlessly with people in everyday dress, such as a group of realistically observed musicians placed directly above the musicians' gallery.

Returning to the Calle de Ferraz and continuing to head north-west, you will skirt to your left the long and very beautiful gardens of the PARQUE DEL OESTE, which were laid out at the beginning of this century and have wonderful views towards the Sierra de Guadarrama. Your mind still dazzled by the Museo Cerralbo you might well feel that you are suffering from an illusion the moment you see, at the southern end of the park, what looks unmistakably like an Egyptian temple. This is not an illusion but the Temple of Debod, a structure of the fourth century BC presented to the Spanish government in 1968 as a gesture of thanks for the efforts of Spanish archaeologists in preserving monuments threatened by the lake created by the Aswan High Dam. This venerable survival from ancient Egypt stands at the heart of what is now, during the summer months, the most fashionable night-time district of Madrid, for the parkside promenade which passes directly in front of it – the Paseo del Pintor Rosales – is lined from June to September with open-air bars or *terrazas* that are thronged until the early hours of the morning with the young and elegantly dressed. The Paseo del Pintor Rosales is the northern continuation of the Calle de Ferraz, and if you

An avenue in the modern Parque del Oeste bordering on the fashionable terrazas of Las Rosas

keep walking north along it, you will come, near the junction of the Calle Marqués de Urquijo, to the Estación Teleférico, from where you can descend by cable-car to the distant Casa de Campo. However, if you want to see Goya's frescoes in the hermitage of San Antonio de Florida, you should descend instead by foot down the Calle de Francisco y Jacinto Alcántara. This will take you through the wooded centre of the Parque del Oeste, and past the Ceramics School where the Zuloaga family once had a studio. Next to this shaded and quietly situated building is a gate through which you can see a short alley of cypresses leading to a distant column. The column marks the site of the common grave where 43 of the Spaniards executed by the French on 3 May 1808, lie buried. The day after the execution, members of the lay confraternity of San Antonio de Florida applied for permission to recover the bodies from the pit in which the French had left them, and bury them in sacred ground near their church. On the wall beside the grave is a ceramic reproduction of V. Palmaroli's dramatic painting of female mourners now in Madrid's Town Hall, while Goya's more famous version of the execution is reproduced at the entrance to this intimate and quietly affecting cemetery.

The railway tracks leading to the Estación del Norte now separate the cemetery from the former hermitage of SAN ANTONIO DE LA FLORIDA, which stands at the bottom of the hill, within sight of the Manzanares. Since 1927 the original church of the hermitage has not been used for services, which are held instead in the twin building adjoining it. The church, which was commissioned by Charles IV in 1792 in response to the growing cult of St Anthony, is a neo-classical jewel by the little known architect Francisco Fontana. The fame of this tiny church, however, is due entirely to its frescoes by Goya, who received the commission from Charles IV in 1798, the year of the building's consecration. Goya took 120 days to complete these frescoes, painting vividly lit angels and ecclesiastical symbols on the spandrels, and covering the whole of the dome with a scene of St Anthony raising a murdered man to life to exonerate the saint's father by identifying the true murderer. This uninspiring-sounding scene was set by Goya behind a fictive balcony, around which he portrayed a crowded cross-section of contemporary Madrid society. The general animation and glistening areas of white reveal the influence of Giovanni Battista Tiepolo, but the darkly satirical and boldly expressive quality of some of the figures look ahead to the Romantic era. It is also a remarkably secular depiction of a religious scene, with no heavenly onlookers to balance the realistic world below. The only god who is to be found in this hermitage today is Goya himself, whose corpse was brought here in 1919 from Bordeaux, and who lies where one would normally expect in a church to find the high altar.

The shaded banks of the Manzanares, where crowds of washerwomen used to gather, were deprived early this century of all remaining elements of the picturesque by being contained by large walls of stone and lined on both sides by characterless buildings. None the less, with the disappearance of the washerwomen, this area emerged as a popular place to spend a leisurely summer's afternoon, and a number of cheap and modest eating establishments grew up along the river's banks. Near the hermitage is the only one of these establishments to survive, Casa Mingo, where many Madrilenians come during the summer months to eat roast chicken and the delicious Asturian cheese called *Cabrales*, accompanying all this with a bottle or two of Asturian cider, which is traditionally poured out into the glasses from a great height. Another attraction, now gone, was the nearby swimming-pool of El Lago, a quiet and luxuriant pool much frequented by transvestite prostitutes during their work breaks. By crossing the bridge directly in front of the hermitage and then negotiating the rather more ominous-looking dual carriageway of the M-30, you will reach Madrid's largest recreational area, the CASA DE CAMPO. Originating in a hunting ground acquired by Philip II, this is a vast undulating park, rather frayed at the edges, and containing such attractions as tennis-courts, a fairground, woods, and a large lake for swimming and boating. From the top of one of its mounds you are offered one of the finest views of the Madrid skyline, the cliff-top bulk of the Palacio Real framed on one side by the skyscrapers of the Plaza de España, and on the other by the huge dome of San Francisco el Grande. Near the highest part of the park you will find the terminal of the cable-car which will take you back up to the Paseo del Pintor Rosales, affording vertiginous views to the Manzanares.

Between the Paseo del Pintor Rosales and the parallel Calle de la Princesa extends an oblong grid of streets laid out in the late nineteenth century but lined today mainly with elegant residential and office blocks dating from the 1920s onwards. Heading east of the paseo along the broad Calle Marqués de Urquijo you will pass at number 47 a block marked by a recent plaque to the leading member of the Generation of 27, Rafael Alberti, who lived here between 1931 and 1936, during the years in which his acivities as a poet came to be subservient to his involvement in Marxist politics. You eventually come out at the main commercial stretch of the Calle de la Princesa, where you should turn left. One of the long parallel streets running north of here is the Calle de Gaztambide, where at number 65 is a grey and grimy modern college and residence belonging to the Escolapian Fathers, a teaching order founded in the seventeenth century by St Joseph of Calasanz. This unpromising building will feature in the itinerary of anyone seriously interested in Goya's works, for, since 1990, its chapel has housed one of this artist's most powerful religious works. Commissioned from him in 1819, it represents *The Last Communion of St Joseph of Calasanz*, a subject of particular significance to him, and not only because he had been born, like the saint, in Aragón and had been educated at an Escolapian School. In 1819 Goya was struck down by a serious illness, and thoughts of his own last communion must certainly have entered his head. The kneeling saint, illuminated by a solitary beam of light, and with his eyes closed as his lips touch the holy wafer, is a literal and especially moving portrayal of blind faith, frightening in its fanatical intensity and yet

OPPOSITE *View from the cable-car over the much-maligned river Manzanares, with the Palacio Real and the as yet incomplete Almundena cathedral in the background.*

also offering a glimpse of hope in the darkness. The following year Goya's mood was to take a more pessimistic turn, the lingering effects of his illness triggering off the first of his 'Black Paintings'.

The last years of Pérez Galdós's life were spent at a red-brick residence which once stood at number 7 on the Calle de Hilarión Eslava, the parallel street to the west of the Calle Gaztambide. Blind, embittered, and virtually insolvent, he died here on 5 January 1920, out of favour with both the political and literary establishments, but still commanding an enormous respect among the people of Madrid. The house, which had been built in 1910 for one of his cousins, was pulled down as late as 1976, the efforts to save it as a museum to the writer having resulted only in the keeping of its plaque, which now adorns a modern apartment block. The area of Madrid most marked by Francoist architectural ideals is reached as you continue walking north along the Calle de la Princesa and come out into the Plaza de la Moncloa. To your

The Air Ministry – a famous example of the way in which fascist architects adopted the spirit and form of Juan de Herrera's Escorial.

left, rising like a monster above the northern end of the Parque del Oeste, is the MINISTERIO DEL AIRE, a triumphantly sized monument of which Hitler would have been proud. Its architect, Luis Gutiérrez Soto, established his reputation in the 1920s as a pioneering representative of functionalism, but later came under the influence of the primitive neo-classicism purveyed by Hitler's architects P. L. Troost and Albert Speer. The architecture of the Nazis was greatly admired by the Falange, and elements from such buildings as Troost's Haus der Kunst in Munich and Albert Speer's Zeppelinfeld in Nuremberg were imitated in the initial design of the Air Ministry, work on which was begun in 1942. The collapse of Nazi Germany, however, led to a major change of plan, and the building ended up in 1951 as such a pastiche of the Escorial that it came popularly to be known as the 'Monasterio del Aire'.

On the opposite side of the Plaza de la Moncloa is a tall rounded temple to Franco's war dead, while the square culminates at its northern end in a fascist-style triumphal arch bearing a Latin inscription recording Franco's military victory. The arch has at least some practical value, for inside is kept the archive of Madrid's University, the enormous campus of which begins immediately below the monument, extending far into the northern horizon. The University City, which is spaciously laid out in pleasant verdant surroundings, was founded by Alfonso XIII in 1927, but was severely damaged during the Civil War, and replanned in the 1940s as yet another monument to the greater glory of Franco. The main attraction for tourists is the MUSEO DE AMÉRICA, which is the first large building which you come to as you descend from the arch down the broad and busy Avenida Arco de la Victoria. Housed in a neo-Herreran complex which incorporates also a library and church, this museum features a celebrated collection of ancient finds from Latin America, many of which were amassed in the course of the scientific expeditions launched during the reign of Charles III. Further down, just to the west of the intersection which joins the Avenida Arco de Victoria with the Avenida de Puerta da Hierro, is the tall block which was built in 1969 to house the MUSEO ESPAÑOL DE ARTE CONTEMPORÁNEO. One of the major and bolder commissions of the last years of the Franco regime, this structure was much admired in its time, although it is generally considered today as being more suited for use as a multi-storeyed car park than as an art gallery. A number of fine modern sculptures lie around its attractive gardens, but the bulk of the collections have now been moved to the Centro Cultural Reina Sofía. Unoccupied and of uncertain future, the building stands today as a monumental folly commemorating a bygone era in both politics and architectural taste.

Frequent buses starting from near the Plaza de la Moncloa ply down the Avenida Arco de la Victoria in the direction of El Pardo, a journey of some fifteen minutes. On the way you will pass near the residences of both the president and king of Spain, and will also skirt the exclusive residential district of Puerta de Hierro, which numbers among its many luxurious modern villas

François Carlier's eighteenth-century chapel attached to the extensively remodelled palace of El Pardo.

the colourful high-tech structure comprising the house–museum of the Moroccan-born millionaire Jacques Hachuel. The PUERTA DE HIERRO itself, sitting today in between the two lanes of the La Coruña motorway, is an elegant baroque gateway commissioned by Philip V to mark the entrance to the hunting grounds of EL PARDO. These grounds, which have been exploited by Spanish kings from at least the early fifteenth century onwards, are formed of gently undulating terrain covered with what is now a rather threadbare carpet of oaks and junipers, populated by a great variety of game. The nearest area of natural beauty within easy reach of Madrid, the place is very popular with daytrippers, who come here to take their siestas under the shade of trees, preferably after having had a filling lunch of game served in the many bars and restaurants of El Pardo village. The village, founded by Charles III, has a lively appeal at weekends, but would otherwise be unremarkable were it not for the large palace which dominates it, and the nearby summer pavilion of the Casita del Príncipe. The palace has its origins in a hunting lodge built by

Henry III of Castile and Léon in 1405, which was replaced in 1547 by a grander structure commissioned by Charles V, a great enthusiast of hunting. Rebuilt in the early seventeenth century by Francisco de Mora and Juan Gómez de Mora, it was remodelled and enlarged by Francesco Sabatini, during the reign of Charles III. Elements of the seventeenth-century structure, such as the high-pitched slate roofs and the corner towers, are clearly apparent as you stare at the main façade from across a vast forecourt, but the interior has a highly restored eighteenth-century character, as well as a number of nineteenth-century and later additions. Many of the royal family Titians were once kept in the palace – including the portrait of Charles V at the Battle of Mühlberg – and it was for here that Velázquez painted his famous hunting portraits that are also now in the Prado. Today the building contains numerous canvases by Luca Giordano, ceiling paintings by Goya's teacher Bayeu, and a beautiful folding screen by the most successful Catalan artist of this century, José María Sert. However, the interest of the palace is primarily historical, and, in the course of the guided tour around it, you will be shown the room where Alfonso XII died, and numerous mementoes of Franco, who took over the building as his main residence immediately after the Civil War, when it served as the headquarters of the International Brigade. Among the Franco mementoes are the heavy desk used by him for writing Christmas cards, the neo-gothic chapel where he prayed, and the eighteenth-century theatre which he transformed into a cinema, complete with air-conditioning hidden in a row of lions' heads around the cornice.

The CASITA DEL PRÍNCIPE lies a few minutes walk to the north of the palace, and is a tiny neo-classical masterpiece, commissioned from Juan de Villanueva in 1782 by the future Charles IV. The exterior is exceedingly simple, but the interior is of exquisite richness, with a central marbled hall and a suite of rooms on either side decorated by the likes of Bayeu and Maella, and with some outstanding portraits by Mengs. Another eighteenth-century building which can be visited in the grounds of El Pardo is LA QUINTA, but this is situated 3 kilometres south-east of the village, and is inaccessible by public transport. Used as an office by the present king, Juan Carlos, before he ascended to the throne, the building occupies a fine hill-top position and is covered throughout with a remarkable series of hand-painted mid nineteenth-century wallpapers. Those who have made the walk here from the village can pick up the Madrid bus by heading due west as far as the main road, a distance of just over two kilometres. The descent through the forest is pleasant enough, but to those who are already beginning to long again for the city, you will feel reassured as you suddenly catch sight once more of that by now familiar profile of Madrid looming enticingly above the Manzanares.

6
Churches and Tenements

....

THE GRAN VÍA *to* SAN PLÁCIDO

Back once again at the Puerta del Sol, you will find that there is still much to be seen at the very centre of Madrid, and that you have by no means exhausted even its seventeenth- and eighteenth-century monuments. You need only walk down the western end of the Calle de Alcalá to be confronted by a rapid succession of sights from the seventeenth century right up to the 1920s. However, what might be described as the heartland of this chapter lies just to the north of this street, in between the vulgar but splendid swathe of the Grand Vía, and the long line of French-style boulevards which extends west from the northern end of the Paseo de Recoletos. This area, relatively little visited by sight-seers, contains a remarkably wide range of monuments, but its appeal will be primarily to those who are interested in the Madrid known to Pérez Galdós, specifically in the world of artisans, shop-keepers and minor officials in which he felt most at home. The more elegant developments that took place in Madrid from the late nineteenth century onwards will be dealt with in the next and final chapter, but here I shall be looking at a part of the city characterized by considerable urban decay. The process of smartening up this area will doubtless soon begin in earnest, but until this happens, the visitor who comes here will have the uncanny sensation of walking into one of Galdós's novels, and being faced with the very scenes that he described with affectionate but unflattering realism.

The Calle de Alcalá, the longest of Madrid's streets, has it origins in an ancient drover's road along which shepherds from Extramadura led, until comparatively recent times, their transhumatory flocks towards northern Spain. Its subsequent development was closely similar to that of the nearby Carrera de San Jerónimo, convents and palaces being built along its western end in the course of the sixteenth century, followed by cafés in the nineteenth century, and, in more recent times, the headquarters of large banks. In contrast to the Carrera de San Jerónimo, however, this western end of the

OPPOSITE The granite façade of the late baroque convent church of Las Salesas, one of the most important commissions from the reign of Ferdinand VI.

BARRACKS
OF THE
CONDE
DUQUE

SANTA MARÍA LA REAL
DE MONTSERRAT

LAS
COMENDADORAS

Calle del Conde Duque

Plaza de las
Comendadoras

Calle de Quinones

Calle de San Bernardo

Plaza Dos
de Mayo

Calle de Sagasta

Plaza
Alonso
Martinez

Plaza Guardias
de Corps

Calle del
Cristo

Calle

Calle de Daoiz

Calle de San Andrés

Calle de Fuencarral

Plaza de
Santa Bárbara

Travesia del Conde Duque

Calle del
Universidad

Calle de San Vicente Ferra

MUSEO
MUNICIPAL

MUSEO
ROMÁNTICO

Calle de San Mateo

Calle Mejia Lequerica

Calle Fernando VI

CONVENTO
DE LAS SALESAS

Calle de Hortaleza

Plaza de la
Salesas

SAN ANTONIO

Calle Bárbara de
Braganza

Calle del Pez

SAN PLACIDO

SAN ANTONIO DE LOS
PORTUGUESES

Calle San
Tomé

Calle de Barquillo

Calle de la Puebla

MERCEDARIAN
CONVENT

Calle de
Libertad

Calle de
Augusto Figueroa

Calle de Prim

Calle de Valvere

Calle de
Barbieri

Calle de las Infantas

Calle de Gran Vía

SAN JOSÉ

Calle Montera

Calle Virgen de los Peligros

CONVENTO DE
LAS CALATRAVAS

REAL ACADEMIA DE
SAN FERNANDO

BELLAS ARTES

Calle de Alcalá

Puerta del Sol

Calle de Sevilla

Carrera de San Jerónimo

250 metres

street has kept many of its old buildings, beginning, at number 3, with the imposing former CUSTOM HOUSE commissioned in 1761 by Charles III. This Italianate structure, with its rusticated basement, was the first of the many works built in Madrid by Francesco Sabatini, and one with a design clearly derived from that of a Roman palace.

Further down the street, at number 13, is the seat of the REAL ACADEMIA DE SAN FERNANDO, an institution founded by Philip V in 1752 as Spain's first academy of the fine arts. The building which it occupies, originally the home of the banker Juan de Goyeneche, was built in the 1720s by the baroque architect José de Churriguera, but, following its acquisition by the Royal Academy in 1774, was stripped of its baroque embellishments so as to be given an appearance more in keeping with the academy's Enlightenment ideals. Entering through the severe neo-classical portal which replaced an exuberant baroque one by Churriguera you will come to a dark vestibule, from where a heavy flight of steps will lead you up to the museum housing the academy's extensive art collections.

The recently restored museum is arranged on two floors around a large stuccoed hall where the academy's official sessions are held, presided over by busts of Philip V and Charles III. The paintings are the museum's greatest treasures, but these are displayed in what becomes an increasingly unselective and chaotic way in rooms crowded with furniture and other objects. Perhaps the most impressive of the rooms is the first one, which is devoted to Goya, and contains thirteen of his paintings, including two small self-portraits from opposite ends of his career, and a strikingly eccentric portrait of Manuel de Godoy, who, although portrayed with all the usual official trappings, is shown slouching in an armchair. Goya's satirical vision of human folly and fanaticism is evident in a sinister depiction of the popular festival of the Burial of the Sardine, and in three late works representing the Inquisition, a madhouse, and a procession of flagellants. Beyond this room is a long gallery filled with Spanish seventeenth-century paintings, among which are an austerely powerful picture by Zurburán of the Blessed Alonso Rodríguez, and a fantastical *memento mori* by Antonio Pereda which might have influenced Goya's famous etching entitled *The Sleep of Reason Produces Monsters*. An extensive collection of fifteenth- to eighteenth-century foreign paintings comes next, mainly minor or school works but with a truly memorable full-length portrait by Mengs of the Marchioness of Llana dressed as a *maja*. With the placing of Arcimboldo's characteristically bizarre representation of *Spring* in room featuring Japanese *netsuke*, the layout of the museum begins its decline into chaos, while with the works of some of the more recent academicians, the artistic quality of the collections also starts to fall. All evidence of logic or discrimination has vanished completely by the time you reach the upper floor, where silverware, fans, Picasso prints, lace, academic pictures, and everything else which once lurked in the Academy's deeper recesses has been thrown together in a way best appreciated as one big joke.

OPPOSITE
CHURCHES AND
TENEMENTS

BELOW *Goya's* Burial of the Sardine *typifies the way the artist exposed the grotesque element in Spanish popular traditions. The painting later inspired a play by the leading dramatist of the absurd, Fernando Arrabal.*

The essential character of the Calle de Alcalá is due above all to its exuberantly grand buildings of the early years of this century, one of which is the CASINO DE MADRID, which stands next to the Real Academia, at number 15. A fashionable French architect called Tronchet won the competition to design this building, but Spaniards had protested about the way in which his design reinforced foreign stereotypes of their nation by including reliefs of castanets and guitars on the façade. In the end the commission went in 1903 to a Spaniard, who produced a very French design featuring an interior of Monte Carlo-like opulence, with a quite magnificent grand staircase which flows down into the hall as if it were a billowing drapery. It is typical of the many contrasts of this idiosyncratic street that only a few doors away from the casino you will come to the former convent church of LAS CALATRAVAS. Dating back to 1670, this was saved by the intercession of General Prim in 1870, after which its façade was remodelled in a terracotta-pink style imitative of the Lombard Renaissance. Of the original church, the finest survivals are the tall dome, and the elaborate altarpieces by José de Churriguera, which are just about visible in the exceptional gloom of the severely planned interior.

The other side of the street is dominated lower down by the soaring art deco pile of the BELLAS ARTES building, which was designed in 1919, and continues to function today as an arts club and cultural centre. It is another work by the extraordinary Antonio Palacios, who abandoned here both the hieratic symmetry and neo-baroque ornamentation of his post-office building in favour of more solid cube-like forms and a bizarrely asymmetrical composition which culminates in a tall tower intended as an urban light-house casting its beams throughout nocturnal Madrid. The interior, gleaming with dark marble and Tiffany glass, was conceived as a city within a city, and its many floors embrace a series of theatres, exhibition halls, cinemas, conference rooms, and a large and luxuriant bar lined with enormous canvases by Muñoz Degrain, an artist sometimes considered to be Picasso's first master. The main entrance to the building is on the short and quiet Calle de Marqués de Casa Riera, where you will also find the luxurious HOTEL SUECIA. Owing to the presence on its premises of the Swedish consulate, this Swedish-run hotel played an important role in the cultural life of Madrid during the Franco era, offering a sort of sanctuary to controversial writers and intellectuals. In its recently refurbished bar, where dissidents once gathered, can still be seen the occasional intellectual from that generation, taking refuge from the younger crowds who favour the bar at the Bellas Artes.

Directly across the Calle de Alcalá from the Bellas Artes is the opening of the Gran Vía, its slope lined with a further succession of overblown buildings, shielding in their case a number of luxury shops of old-fashioned appearance. The construction of the street in 1910, involving the pulling down of a large area of central Madrid, aroused considerable controversy, and sentimentalists such as Díaz-Cañabate felt that the character of the city had been irrevocably destroyed by this 'horrible series of buildings and traffic jams.'

OPPOSITE *An art deco commercial block contrasts with an isolated survival of one of the Calle de Alcalá's seventeenth-century churches, this one belonging to the convent of Las Calatravas.*

The bronze Winged Victory crowning the Metropolis building at the junction of the Gran Vía and the Calle de Alcalá.

However, long before the street had been built, the hearts of many other Madrilenians had been warmed to it by a comic and fantastical *zarzuela* entitled *La Gran Vía*. The tunes of this enormously popular work by Frederico Chueca, although dating back to 1886, are still hummed today by many elderly Madrilenians, and form the *leitmotif* of one of the stories within a story of Felipe Alfau's eccentric novel *Chromos* (1948), a vision of Spanish life through the eyes of Spaniards living in America. It was only a matter of time before the street came to be regarded as representing the quintessential charm of Madrid, one of its greatest enthusiasts being the writer Francisco Umbral, who was reminded by it of New York and Chicago, and would experience daily an enormous elation as he began slowly ascending its slope from the Calle de Alcalá, eyeing its cosmopolitan procession of shops and people as if it were a cinematic spectacle.

The Gran Vía undoubtedly presents its finest profile when seen from just below its fork-like intersection with the Calle de Alcalá, the point where the two great thoroughfares meet being marked by one of the most popular of Madrid's buildings, the very name of which is evocative of turn-of-the-century cosmopolitanism, the EDIFICIO METROPOLIS. Built in 1905 by the French architects Jules and Raymond Fevrier, it celebrates the joining of the two streets with a cylindrical frontage comprising a ring of paired giant columns, an attic level of richly carved statuary, and a tall crowning dome highlighted in gold and bearing a bronze representation of Winged Victory. Tucked away on the side overlooking the Gran Vía, is the entrance to the narrow street of the Caballero de Gracia, where, in the words of Alfau, 'a delicate romance still dwelt in wandering shadows . . .'. This street, which gave its name to one of the best known songs from Chueca's *La Gran Vía*, hides at its northern end an outstanding neo-classical oratory by Juan de Villanueva, the back of which, overlooking the Gran Vía, has been subject to a recent and drastic alteration. Adjoining the Edificio Metropolis, at number 1 Gran Vía, is a luxuriously appointed shop belonging to the jewellery firm of Grassy, who keep in the basement here a museum featuring a superb collection of art nouveau clocks.

One of the longest running and most endearing institutions on the Gran Vía is to be found on the northern side of the street, at number 12. Misleadingly called the Museo Chicote, this is in fact an elegant bar founded in 1931 by Perico Chicote, a well-known Madrid personality who came to be known as 'the king of the cocktails'. While working as barman at the Ritz, Chicote had been presented by the Brazilian embassy with a bottle of the Brazilian rum called Paraty, and this inspired him to form a collection of drinks from all over the world, which were displayed in the bar's cellar and gave the place its title of museum. This museum soon came to be known as the most popular in Madrid after the Prado, but, sadly, the collection has recently been sold, reputedly to the Walt Disney Company. Even without its 'museum', however, the bar is well worth visiting, both for its architecture and special atmosphere. In the middle of its simple art deco façade – designed, incidentally, by the Air Ministry architect, Luis Gutiérrez Soto – is a swing door leading to a perfectly preserved art deco interior, gleaming with chrome and mirrors, and with a row of semi-circular alcoves. The courteous elderly waiters seem in themselves to be survivors from the 1930s, and are matched by one of Madrid's few remaining bootblacks, a man who began his career 50 years ago on the pavement outside the Palace Hotel, and continues to wear the striped jacket once common to those in his profession. You might well wonder what type of person frequents a place such as this. The travel-writer

Archibald Lyall, describing the atmosphere of the bar in 1960, wrote that 'up to about eight in the evening it is a respectable bourgeois resort but then, by a sort of tacit and accepted convention, the ladies of good society clear out and the ladies of the town come in and take over'. A similar transformation occurs today, the place having a somewhat sedate and reactionary character by day, and a young and fashionable one by night. Hemingway, needless to say, often came here, and the bar still attracts numerous literary personalities.

The time has finally come to plunge into the warren of dark and decayed streets that extend to the north of the Gran Vía. To do so you should start back at the lower end of the street, turning left into the Calle de Marqués de Valdeiglesias. The latter street begins around the corner from the church of SAN JOSÉ, which has a façade by Pedro de Ribera and a dark interior featuring a plaque commemorating the marriage in May 1802 of Simon Bolívar. The short street emerges into the Calle de las Infantas, where, on turning right, you will see the CASA DE LAS SIETE CHIMENEAS. Although heavily restored and altered over the centuries, this palace is still recognizable as the late sixteenth-century structure built by the two architects of the Escorial, Juan Bautista de Toledo and Juan de Herrera. In the eighteenth century the building was inhabited by Charles III's notorious minister Squillace, but English visitors will prefer to remember this as the place where in 1623 the future Charles I of England stayed, together with the Duke of Buckingham, Sir Kenelm Digby, and Endymion Porter.

The area you are now in is filled with restaurants, and you will find at the western end of the Calle de las Infantas a tiny, crowded and once famously cheap Cuban establishment, Zara. This was founded by one of the many refugees fleeing from Fidel Castro in the early 1960s, a period when Cuban food began having a considerable influence on local cuisine. The dish of rice, fried banana and tomato sauce known as *Arroz a la Cubana* became one of the staple offerings in Madrid restaurants, and inspired Francisco Umbral to write a whole page describing how the Gran Vía came to smell of it. One restaurant where you will not be finding *Arroz a la Cubana* is the nearby Salvador, which is one of the most traditional of Madrid's restaurants, and a place where the menu has changed little since it was opened in 1941. Situated at number 13 Calle Barbieri, which runs north of the Calle de las Infantas, it has pleasant, intimate dining rooms covered all over with photographs of the many bullfighters and other celebrities who have eaten here, Hemingway, of course, among them. The founder, Salvador Blázquez, had numerous distinguished friends, and there is even a photograph showing him as a young man in the company of the aged and near-blind Pérez Galdós. The great speciality of the place is breaded hake or *merluza rebosada*, a dish of characteristically Madrilenian simplicity but one requiring a considerable skill to achieve the subtle, succulent results to be tasted here.

At the northern end of the Calle Barbieri you emerge into the Calle de Augusto Figueroa, almost directly in front of another famous eating establishment, although of a different kind to Salvador's. Its dirty peeling façade – at number 35 – simply bears the words '*Tienda de Vinos*' (wine store), but it is known by everyone as 'El Comunista', supposedly because every dish on offer carried the same cheap prices. The establishment, which has been in the same family for over 100 years, became a renowned literary and artistic meeting-place in the 1950s and 1960s under the ownership of Angel Miguel, who still runs the place today. Francisco Umbral remembered the restaurant as being 'a bit prison-like and a bit railway station-like' but redeemed by a 'naïve and almost anonymous' decoration and above all by the near continual presence of a charismatic and enigmatic woman called Sandra around whom there always gathered a crowd of 'poets, painters and homosexuals'. The look of the place is unchanged today, down to the grime on its high, yellowing walls, the wooden panelling below, the simple benches that serve as seats, the poorly washed glasses, and the odd print and amateurish painting with which someone began an attempt long ago to bring some colour to the otherwise bare surfaces. The service is brusque, and the prices remain ridiculously if not uniformally cheap.

The run-down district which you are now in, popularly known as Chueca, was formerly referred to as that of the '*chisperos*', which is both the word for 'blacksmiths' and the old Madrid slang for 'underworld characters'. Bronze and iron foundries could once be found here, but this traditionally poor area has also maintained over the years a lowlife character, and up to very recently was a favourite haunt of drug addicts and other marginal elements of Madrid society. At the eastern end of the Calle de Augusto Figueroa, however, you come out on to the long Calle de Barquillo, which though dark, dirty and narrow, is an animated thoroughfare with vestiges of grand residences, such as that at number 34, which was the birthplace in 1756 of Francisco Castaños, whose victory at the Battle of Bailén in 1808 was the first major setback in Napoleon's career. The street was also the route used by royalty on their way to the magnificent CONVENTO DE LAS SALESAS, which was founded in 1747 by Barbara of Braganza – the wife of Ferdinand VI – as a retreat for her widowhood. This forms the centrepiece of a smart residential district which you will reach as soon as you emerge from the northern end of the Calle de Barquillo. The church of the former convent, which was built between 1750 and 1758 to the designs of the French architect François Carlier, is one of the most sumptuous and harmonious in Madrid, combining French classicism with baroque pomp. Rising on steps above a large forecourt, its granite porticoed façade is articulated by a giant order of piers and enriched by statuary in marble and white Colmenar stone, including a central medallion containing a relief of the Visitation. The best time to come here is on a fine late afternoon, when the rays of the sun dramatically highlight the relief carvings on the façade, and give to the dignified interior a warm suffused glow in which the wealth of marbled furnishings acquire an added radiance. The decoration of the interior, which includes altarpieces by the Italian artists Cignaroli and

Giaquinto, has a carefully orchestrated unity culminating in a high altar resplendent in green serpentine marble. Later in the century Charles III commissioned Sabatini to design the tombs of Ferdinand VI and Barbara of Braganza, which stand respectively in the south transept and in a side chapel adjoining the presbytery. These flamboyant baroque works, with their richly carved statuary by Francisco Gutiérrez, contrast markedly with the neo-renaissance tomb of the nineteenth-century military hero, General O'Donnell, which is situated in the north transept. The convent itself, now adapted inside to house the city's Law Courts, was never used by Barbara of Braganza, who died before she could become a widow.

From here the Calle de Fernando VI ascends in a north-westerly direction towards the Calle de Hortaleza, passing a fish-shop with its abundant contents arranged like some Rubensian still-life, and an equally enticing fruit-shop, where tightly-packed, symmetrical displays of the product bask in multi-coloured glory under a large sign inscribed with the words 'Eat a lot of fruit'. As you near the top end of the street, however, your attention will be absorbed entirely by the inflated and fantastical organic forms that ooze down the walls of the remarkable building which appears to your left. With its predominance of undulating lines, and restless overall decoration which appears to have been moulded in putty, this building is one of the few genuine examples of art nouveau in Madrid, and by far the most distinguished. Though it is not by Gaudí, as is popularly thought, it is by another Catalan, Grases Riera, who built it in 1902 as both an office and residence for the banker Javier González Longoria. The exterior, with its surrounding art nouveau ironwork, has today a slightly disintegrated look, while the interior has been largely transformed for its present use as the headquarters of the SOCIETY OF AUTHORS. None the less, if you come here on a weekday morning, you should step inside to see the grand staircase, a painted ironwork structure which lies immediately beyond the main entrance, enhancing the building's overall sense of movement with serpentine forms that soar with spiralling elegance up to a stained-glass dome bursting with myriad colours.

At the end of the Calle de Fernando VI there opens up to your right the long Plaza de Santa Barbara which slopes gently up to the noisy line of boulevards to the north, its shaded central reservation being covered with café tables. To your left meanwhile begins the long Calle de Hortaleza, a dark, narrow and very noisy thoroughfare of little architectural distinction, but with several interesting old shops, and a number of fashionable discothèque bars that cater for the incessant nocturnal flow of people. At this northern entrance to the street is the most exclusive of these bars, Hanoi, where, if you manage to look sufficiently interesting to persuade your way past the doorman, you will find yourself in a post-modernist marble coffin of a room, where booming music, a row of video screens, and posing groups of design-conscious *yuppis* all compete for your attention. On the opposite side of the street, at number 104, is the building where Peréz Galdós, fed up with his

Detail of the art nouveau ironwork surrounding the Society of Authors building.

publishers, bravely decided in 1897 to set up a publishing and printing company dedicated solely to the bringing out of his own works, an ill-fated enterprise which lasted until 1905. Further down the street, at the junction with the Calle de Farmacía, are the late eighteenth-century college and church of SAN ANTONIO which formed the first institution established in Madrid by the Escolapian fathers. This is where Goya's *Last Communion of San José Calasanz* used to hang before being transferred to the Escalopian College on the Calle de Gaztambide (see p. 130). In the absence of this work, the only good reason for making a special journey to this singularly lugubrious building is to see the bizarre ceremony which takes place here every year on 17 January. On that day a long procession of mules, horses and other animals file past the church to be blessed by a monk, who doubly ensures that they leave in a state of holiness by selling 'holy straw' to the owners.

The northern continuation of the Calle de Fernando VI is the Calle de Majía Lequerica, where you will find, at the junction with the Calle de Hortaleza, a building of 1912 with an unusual and grotesque decorative feature in the form of a line of enormous lizards supporting the upper balcony. From here you should take the first turning to the left, leaving the bustle which surrounds the Plaza de Santa Barbara for the dark and quiet Calle de San Mateo. Half-way up this street, at number 13, you will come to an attractive palace in dark red brick, which was built for the Marquis of Matellana by Manuel Martín, a cousin of Ventura Rodríguez. In 1924 this building was transformed into the MUSEO ROMÁNTICO, the brainchild of the Marquis of Vega-Inclán, who left to it his own miscellaneous collections, which included minor canvases by Spanish seventeenth-century artists, paintings of his own after El Greco, and a reproduction of a Toledan interior of the sixteenth century. Vega-Inclán was a romantic in the popular sense of the word, and his nostalgic view of the past led him to establish as well the famous El Greco House in Toledo, and the equally bogus Cervantes House in Valladolid. The Museo Romántico is as much of a fake as these last two institutions, its principal intention being to recreate a typical Spanish house of the Romantic era. None the less it has considerable charm, and, as you walk along its creaking floorboards through a series of mellowed rooms, you might well feel that you have stumbled across an atmospheric survival of the last century. The artistic high point is a painting by Goya of *St Gregory*, which hangs in the chapel. But, amidst all the esoterica and heavy dark furniture which take up the rest of the rooms, you will see works by most of the leading Spanish artists of the early nineteenth century, from the society portraitist Federico de Madrazo to the Sevillian *costumbrista* Valeriano Bécquer. The most genuinely 'Romantic' painting is a small expressive canvas by Leonardo Alenza representing a wild-looking man on the point of plunging a dagger into himself while jumping off a cliff into a landscape featuring a man hanging from a tree. There is a certain element of bathos as you move from Alenza's witty satire of the Romantic fashion for suicide to the nearby room dedicated to the most famous of Spain's suicide victims, Mariano José de Larra. The ultimate object of pilgrimage on any Romantic tour of Madrid must surely be this room's display case containing, among other personal mementoes of Larra, the pair of duelling pistols used to shoot himself in 1837.

At the top of the Calle de San Mateo is the long Calle de Fuencarral, which grew up in the course of the seventeenth century as the city extended its boundaries north to what is now the Glorieta de Bilbao. The street, lined today mainly with buildings of the turn of the century, has kept an old-fashioned commercial character, with numerous small shops that have survived despite growing threats from the large department stores to the south. Its one outstanding monument – to be seen to your right as soon as you emerge from the Calle de San Mateo – is the former HOSPICIO DE SAN FERNANDO, a hospital for the poor begun in 1722 by Pedro de Ribera. Even for those who have just seen the fantastically decorated Society of Author's Building on the Calle de Fernando VI, the shock of being confronted by Ribera's frontispiece for this hospital is a considerable one. By far the most elaborate of Ribera's creations, this frontispiece displays a baroque exuberance which is not only very uncharacteristic of Madrid, but also worthy of comparison with the extreme examples of the baroque style to be seen in Galicia and Andalusia. A sculptural group of St Ferdinand receiving the keys of Seville acts as the pivot of a composition bursting with garlands, draperies, shields, urns and every other conceivable ornamental detail, the whole pushing up the entablature of the façade to create a broken pediment of Borrominesque derivation. A characteristic feature of Ribera's work, and

OPPOSITE *The frontispiece of the Hospicio de San Fernando, the ornamental climax to the work of Pedro de Ribera.*

indeed of Spanish architecture as a whole, is the placing of such an exceptionally elaborate work in the middle of an otherwise severe façade, built in this case of dark red bricks. The simplicity of this façade is matched also by the chapel to be seen inside, a typically Madrilenian single-aisled structure, with barrel-vaulting and shallow transepts.

From the late eighteenth century onwards the frontispiece of the hospicio was pilloried by critics, historians and architects, who held it up as the supreme example of bad taste, and would doubtless have loved to have seen it pulled down. An opportunity to do so presented itself early this century, when the building was in such a terrible condition that its remaining inmates had to be transferred elsewhere pending its demolition. Fortunately the Academy of Fine Arts interceded at this point, and the building was saved for use as a Madrid's MUSEO MUNICIPAL, the first director of which was the poet Manuel Machado, who is commemorated by a plaque near the entrance. The museum, which has recently been refurbished, has a chronologically displayed collection relating to the history of Madrid, and has exhibits ranging from models of the medieval city to a drawing of Pérez Galdós on his death-bed. Among its many works of art is an allegorical painting by Goya, featuring initially a portrait of a triumphant Napoleon, which was replaced at a later stage of the War of Independence with the words 'Dos de Mayo'. The most remarkable part of the museum is the room housing an enormous wooden model of Madrid, commissioned by Ferdinand VII in 1828. Madrid was very lucky in its early topographical representations, and in 1656 had been the subject of a detailed plan by Pedro de Texeira which is considered today to be one of the masterpieces of urban cartography. The wooden model, executed over a period of nearly two years by an army officer called Gil de Palacio, is one of the greatest examples of its kind, and enjoyed such a success at the time that the French ambassador in Madrid invited Palacio to do a similar model of Paris. Peering closely at it, you will be drawn back into the streets of early nineteenth-century Madrid, observing the city before its dramatic transformation after the second half of the century.

After leaving the museum, you should make your way to the back of the building, where you will find a quiet square named after Pedro de Ribera, in whose honour has been transferred here the only one of his Madrid fountains to have survived. Known as the Fuente de la Fama, it is a further reminder of this architect's ornamental genius, and has a lively design of dolphins and angels supporting the trumpeting figure of Fame. A short detour to the north of here will take you to the Glorieta de Bilbao, the site of the seventeenth-century Puerta de Fuencarral, and now a busy intersection. On its southern side is the cavernous Café Comercial, which became popular with journalists after the Civil War, and was later the scene of numerous literary and political *tertulias*. One of its habitués in the 1950s and 1960s was the writer and *costumbrista* César González Ruano, who used to arrive at 9.30 each morning, glance at the papers, and then set about writing at least two of his own articles, fuelling himself for the task with constant cigarettes and cups of coffee. Previously he had been a mainstay at the Café Gijón, but he gave up that place supposedly as a result of a quarrel with the owner and of being pestered there by so many people that he had been unable to do any writing. The Café Comercial, as well as being an important testimony to Madrid's cultural life during the Franco period, is one of the city's most popular meeting-places, particularly for visitors from other parts of Spain. An evening's rendez-vous with friends here is likely to end up in the bars of neighbouring Malasaña, a district which is also reached by heading due west of the Museo Municipal on the Calle de San Vicente Ferrer.

Popularly referred to today as Malasaña, this district was once known as the 'Barrio de Maravillas' ('The District of Marvels'), a poetic name which had a certain ironic resonance in view of the terrible poverty which the area has experienced. With its former population of *manolos*, this has traditionally been a working- and lower middle-class district, the life of which in the early years of this century was beautifully evoked by Rosa Chacel in her autobiographical novel, *Barrio de Maravillas*. After the Civil War, the district became increasingly run-down and impoverished, as many of its older members saw their children leaving it in favour of the huge residential blocks on the city's outskirts. Property speculators soon began threatening to demolish it altogether, although their plans were fortunately stopped as a result of intensive neighbourhood protests. These protests had also the effect of drawing this district to the attention of the city's young, who soon began occupying the many empty flats and garrets, delighted to find such cheap accommodation in a quiet central area which was only a few minutes' walk from the Gran Vía. From the early 1960s onwards Malasaña acquired an increasingly Bohemian and student character, and bars and discothèques began proliferating. Its overall seediness none the less remained, and by the mid 1980s the area was in danger of being taken over almost entirely by drug addicts. Attempts to tidy the place up have only been partially successful, and this is still a poor and decayed area, criss-crossed by dark and narrow streets crammed with nineteenth-century terraces uniformally streaked in grey. It is still one of the livelier nocturnal districts of Madrid, though the protagonists of this night-life are not so much the smart *yuppis* of other areas, but rather ageing hippies and Bohemians. The appearance of Malasaña, however, should not put you off from coming here, for this district is a wonderful survival of old Madrid, with a virtually unrivalled range of old shops and bars, and a neighbourly intimacy which is rapidly disappearing elewhere.

The Calle de San Vicente Ferrer, where Rosa Chacel spent her childhood, is by night one of the more animated of Malasaña's streets, with numerous night-spots such as Manuela, a well-known alternative bar which seems to have remained stuck in the 1960s. As with all this district, however, it is remarkably quiet by day, barely disturbed even by traffic. At number 28, on the corner with the Calle de San Andrés, you will come to the LABORATORIO

The Laboratorio Juanse with ceramics with advertisements aimed at smokers and those with poor dental hygiene.

DE ESPECIALIDADES JUANSE, a pharmacy covered on the outside with some of the most famous of Madrid's surviving ceramic decorations. Dating back to 1925, these highly entertaining and colourful works are all advertisements for the products once sold within, and comprise absurd scenes of people suffering from symptoms ranging from tooth-ache to rheumatism, and even diarrhoea. Next door, marking a shop which once specialized solely in eggs, are some equally spirited if rather more tasteful ceramics representing hens.

From here you should descend north down the Calle de San Andrés to the Plaza del Dos de Mayo, which is at the centre of Malasaña, and was also the site of the most important event in this district's history. The square was at one time occupied by the military barracks of Monteleón, and it was to here, on that fateful day of 2 May 1808, that the young artillery officer Pedro Velarde made his way immediately on hearing the shots fired by the French in their attempts to subdue the uprising centred on the Puerta del Sol. On the orders of the French military government the barracks were firmly closed, but Velarde was able to persuade his way in and convince its commander Captain Daoíz of the necessity of distributing arms to the crowd of compatriots outside. A violent skirmish then ensued as the Spaniards attacked the French garrison stationed here, launching themselves against the superior forces with a bravery verging on despair. The fighting, which lasted for several hours, ended with the taking of the barracks, by which time the losses on both sides had been considerable. Velarde was killed outright, and the wounded Daoíz was taken home, where he died a few hours later. The two heroes were buried in the nearby church of San Martín, but their remains were transferred soon afterwards to San Isidro and later to the sarcophagus which lies at the foot of the 2 May Monument in the Plaza de la Lealtad. Their memory was further commemorated by the revolutionary government of 1869, who decided in that year to erect a monument to them in the middle of the Plaza del Dos de Mayo. In this they are shown in classical guise, standing underneath the arch which once formed the entrance to the destroyed barracks.

The classical apparitions of Daoíz and Velarde haunt a square bordered by tall rows of greying nineteenth-century residences, the whole characterized by a seedy charm which can take on a more sinister aspect late at night, when it is frequented by a dark and dissolute-looking crowd spilling over from the surrounding bars. One of the older of these bars is the mirrored and intimate Dos De on the square's eastern side, where a strange and solitary Californian, El Pollo Colorado, is to be heard giving the most entertaining renditions of Flamenco that you are ever likely to hear. Brought up among the gypsies of Granada, he is now one of the personalities of Malasaña, living the life of a vagrant and singing Flamenco in a way which seems at first to be a parody but ends by deeply moving you. Few other *payos* or non-gypsies have captured so well the complex rhythms of Flamenco.

The western limits of Malasaña are marked by the wide and ugly Calle de San Bernardo, which is reached by walking due west of the Plaza del Dos de Mayo on the Calle de Daoíz. The buildings of this street's northern half are mainly modern, the principal exception being the monastery church of SANTA MARÍA LA REAL DE MONTSERRAT, which rises up directly in front of you, its exterior distinguished by the crowning bulbous forms of a splendidly elaborate tower, a baroque structure of the early eighteenth century generally attributed to Pedro de Ribera. Continuing west from here along the narrow Calle de Quiñones, you will enter a district with much of the grimy nineteenth-century look of Malasaña, and with much of the latter's fascination. The street which you are on skirts the southern façade of the Montserrat monastery, a building which in Galdós's day served as a women's prison. It was directly in front of this façade that Galdós situated the house of Don Ramón de Villaamil, the tragic protagonist of his novel *Miau*.

Written in 1888, immediately after *Fortunata and Jacinta*, this book is the story of an unremarkable civil servant who, only a few months before becoming entitled to a pension, loses his post as a result of one of the many falls of government which Spain experienced in the late nineteenth century. The '*Miau*' of the title, so evocative of the pathetic and ineffectual cries for help of its hero, is also a reference to the cat-like features of his wife, sister-in-law and daughter, with whom he is irrevocably saddled and yet who are too absorbed

The façade of the eighteenth-century monastery church of Santa María la Real de Montserrat, with an ornamental tower attributed to Pedro de Ribera.

in their own mediocre lives to show much of an interest or understanding of his. The one member of his family with whom he enjoys any closeness is his young and sickly grandson, Luisito, who suffers from blackouts during which he has conversations with God. Reflections on the cruelty of divine providence punctuate the narrative, which ends, as we have seen, with the deranged Villaamil shooting himself near the present Plaza de España, saying to himself beforehand that the gun would not go off:

> The shot echoed in the solitude of that dark and deserted place. Villaamil gave a terrible leap, his head plunged into the shifting earth, and he rolled straight down into the gulf. He retained consciousness only for enough time to say: 'Well . . . it did . . .'

Miau lacks the panoramic vision of Madrid shown in *Fortunata and Jacinta*, but as a telescopic view of a particular area of the city it is perhaps without equal in Galdós's work. Almost every street and monument in that evocative district which extends to the west of the Calle de San Bernardo features in the novel, an especially important role being played by the churches of Montserrat and las Comendadoras, the latter bing situated at the opposite end of the Calle de Quiñones, overlooking the square named after it. These are the places where the pious womenfolk of Villaamil's family regularly attend mass, where Luisito has his visions, and where Villaamil vainly attempts to find some consolation for his plight. Whereas the Montserrat church is described as having a 'cold and bare' interior, that of LAS COMENDADORAS is referred to as 'one of the most beautiful and serene in Madrid'. This latter building, dating back to the 1660s, has retained its original appearance, even though the convent to which it is attached was remodelled by Sabatini in the middle of the eighteenth century. Its brick porticoed façade is flanked by two Herrera-style towers, behind which rises a large and elegantly simple dome. Once inside you will find yourself in the south transept of a building shaped like a Greek cross and covered all over in grey and white stucco. The harmonious interior – the ornamentation of which is largely concentrated on the consoles supporting the elaborate entablature – has a fine high altar by the ubiquitous Luca Giordano, of St James the Moor-Slayer. Meetings of the Knights of Santiago are still held in the church, and the numerous banners of this order that are hung inside not only give this place an added solemnity, but also provided on one occasion a distraction for the restless Luisito.

Playing children and elderly people seated on benches are the main signs of life on the homely if slightly faded Plaza de las Comendadoras, from where you should head west on the short Calle del Cristo, setting off in the same direction in which the by now confused and paranoid Villaamil embarked on the last journey of his life. The small Plaza de Guardias de Corps, known in Galdós's time as the Plazuela del Limón, is where *Miau* begins, with a devilish rush of school-children out of which emerges the shy and unfortunate Luisito. The square reappears again in the closing pages of the book, as Villaamil resolutely approaches it with a mounting hatred for his family bordering on frenzy. He would certainly have been in no mood to appreciate the magnificent and profusely ornamented main portal of the BARRACKS OF THE CONDE DUQUE. Commissioned from Pedro de Ribera in 1720 as a barracks to house the newly formed bodyguard of Philip V (a regiment to which Manuel de Godoy later belonged), the Conde Duque is one of the largest of all Madrid's buildings and comprises three enormous courtyards of an essentially austere character. Destroyed partially by fire in 1869, the building was left to ruin, but has recently been restored by the municipality of Madrid to serve as a library, archive and cultural centre. The work of transformation was entrusted to Julio Cano Lasso, who came up with an eccentric, post-

Roofscape of old Madrid

The barracks of the Conde Duque seen from the Torre de España with the Sierra de Guadarrama in the background.

modernist solution for the half-destroyed frontispiece seen inside the main courtyard. Instead of restoring it to its original condition, he strengthened its appearance as a ruin by applying brash modern elements such as large cubes of glass to a structure which has been left with cracks, exposed sections of masonry, and even a half-broken urn from which weeds grow.

Descending to the southern corner of the former barracks, and turning left on to the Travesía Conde Duque, you will come out again on to the Calle de San Bernardo, next to an austere classical building marking the site of a Jesuit college. With the decision made in 1842 to transfer the Complutense University from the nearby town of Alcalá de Henares to the centre of Madrid, this former Jesuit college was rebuilt as the main university building, which it remained until the creation of the Ciudad Universitaria from 1927 onwards. Across the street from it, at number 44, and immediately below at number 45, are the two remaining palaces of a street once lined with aristocratic seventeenth- and eighteenth-centuries residences. A similar decline in fortunes characterizes the Calle de la Pez, which runs east of the Calle de San Bernardo from a point immediately below the palace at number 44. This was until the 1930s one of the liveliest and smartest streets in central Madrid, inhabited by a remarkable cross-section of the city's society, from the aristocracy down to the lower middle classes. Its animation stemmed both from the nearby presence of the university and from its numerous shops, which made it a popular place for strolling, as Galdós sugested in *Miau* when he described how Luisito came here one day to browse in its tantalizing shop-windows. The departure of the university in 1927 initiated the decline, and it later became absorbed into that area of urban decay centred upon Malasaña. Near its eastern end it crosses a narrow and attractive sloping square, overlooked by one of the more interesting and least visited convents in the centre of the city.

The Benedictine convent of SAN PLÁCIDO was founded in 1623 by Doña Teresa Valle de la Cerda under the patronage of Philip IV's secretary of state, Jerónimo de Villanueva. Almost immediately the place came to acquire a scandalous reputation, due initially to rumours that numerous nuns, including Doña Teresa herself, had come to be possessed by the devil and had had to be exorcized by their confessor, Juan Francisco García Calderón. Under torture Calderón confessed to having indulged in sexual practices with his spiritual daughters, and was subsequently condemned by the Inquisition to life imprisonment. Doña Teresa was released without punishment, thanks doubtlessly to her friends in high places. The story of the convent's corruption does not end there, however, for shortly afterwards Philip IV fell in love with one of the nuns, and connived to see her with the help of Villanueva, who lived in an adjoining house. Thanks to a secret tunnel built expressly for the purpose, the king managed to gain entry into the convent, but his plans to seduce the nun were thwarted by Doña Teresa, who having had previous warning of the nocturnal visit, had persuaded the nun to lie on a funeral bier and pretend to be dead. News of all these doings came none the less to the attention of Inquisition, and eventually to the Pope, who demanded to see the documents relating to the case. This time the Count Duke Olivares came to the rescue, and arranged for henchmen to arrest and throw into prison the messenger whom the Inquisition had sent to Rome. Philip IV meanwhile, repenting of his misdemeanours, commissioned Velázquez to paint for the convent church the beautiful *Christ on the Cross* which is now in the Prado.

Although it no longer possesses this painting by Velázquez, the convent church has several other impressive works of art, including a superb high altar of the *Annunciation* by Claudio Coello, a dome painted by Francesco Rizi, and a polychromed statue of the dead Christ by Gregorio Fernández. These works gain greatly from their harmonious setting, which has been barely disturbed since the early seventeenth century. An almost undecorated brick wall characterizes the entrance façade on the Calle de San Roque, and a similar

Detail of Luca Giordano's frescoes in the church of San Antonio de los Portugueses.

sobriety and simplicity are to be found inside, where you are guided around by nuns of an apparently more respectable kind than those of Doña Teresa's time. The restraint of the interior contrasts markedly with the decorative brilliance of that of another nearby seventeenth-century monument, which you will reach by walking to the very end of the Calle de la Pez and joining the narrow and descending Corredera Bajo de San Pablo. A large group of dishevelled people, very much in keeping with the character of this street, is to be seen daily outside the building at number 16, which has been, since the eighteenth century, a charitable institution devoted to the feeding of the poor.

Originally this was a Portuguese hospital founded by Philip III in 1603, but of this institution there survives only the church of SAN ANTONIO DE LOS PORTUGUESES, which is situated at the corner of this street and the Calle de la Puebla. This centrally planned structure, designed by Juan Gómez de Mora in the 1620s but remodelled in the late nineteenth century, seems from the outside like an elegant gasometer, but the recently cleaned interior is covered with some of the most extensive fresco decorations in Madrid. The walls, painted at the end of the seventeenth century by Luca Giordano, feature scenes from the life of St Anthony, whose apotheosis is represented on the dome in an elaborate Bolognese-inspired illusionistic decoration executed in the 1660s by Francisco Rizi and Juan Carreño de Miranda.

The Calle de la Puebla, another important street of Habsburg origin which has recently fallen into decay, heads east towards an austere Mercedarian convent of the early seventeenth century. Ramón Goméz de la Serna lived for many years in a first-floor apartment at number 11, while the convent itself features in Galdós's *Miau* as the place where the exhausted Luisito sits down on one of its cold steps and experiences another of his visionary blackouts. From the convent the narrow Calle de Valverde sweeps southwards like a roller-coaster towards the tall silhouettes marking the Gran Vía. Emerging on the Gran Vía, you will see in front of you what must be Europe's most elegant McDonald's, situated in a former jeweller's lavishly adorned inside with marble and mirrors and fringed on the exterior with an ironwork canapy of the turn of the century. To your left, meanwhile, is the famous TELEFÓNICA skyscraper built by Ignacio Cárdenas in the 1920s to house Spain's National Telephone Company. Based on a design from the New York firm of Lewis S Weeks, but modified with ornamental elements of the Spanish baroque, this was the building which inspired Alfonso XIII to proclaim in 1929 that Spain had finally entered the modern world.

7

The Expanding City

....

THE CAFÉ GIJÓN *to* THE CAPRICHO DE OSUNA

The transformation of Madrid into the modern city of today, although symbolized for many by the creation of the Gran Vía, had begun in earnest with the laying out after 1860 of the vast and regular grid of streets extending north and east of the Paseo de Recoletos. From the muddle of mean, dark streets which characterizes much of the centre of the city you emerge into the spacious and elegant districts of Salamanca and Chamberí, where the distances become greater and the buildings taller. Grand residences of the turn of the century, spectacular modern blocks, and several outstanding museums are featured in this last itinerary, but the scale and monotony of the grid which you have to cross might deter all but the most hardened walkers from attempting to follow all the route on foot. The enormous size of the area which I am covering will become even more apparent as I continue hurtling north along the Paseo de la Castellana, passing from José María Castro's urban plan of 1860 to Bigador's of 1944. Logically I should have ended the book with some of the more recent and beautiful clusters of skyscrapers that punctuate the northern end of the Castellana, but, instead of finishing on this positive note of urban progress, I have left the reader amidst the waste-lands of the so-called Outer Belt, reserving for this final moment one of Madrid's greatest surprises.

The broad and shaded Paseo de Recoletos, with which I have begun this itinerary, serves as a last farewell to the Madrid of Charles III, the thoroughfare having been conceived in the 1770s as one of the series of *paseos* adorning the eastern border of the city. This avenue, which was not given a definitive form until the middle of the nineteenth century, contains also two monuments of particular relevance to the history of the city in modern times. One of these is the nineteenth-century palace of the marquis, banker and property speculator who gave his name to the district of Salamanca, while the other – on the opposite, western side of the road – is the CAFÉ GIJÓN, which is

OPPOSITE *The late nineteenth-century Columbus Monument rising over the waterfall marking the entrance to the cultural centre named after him.*

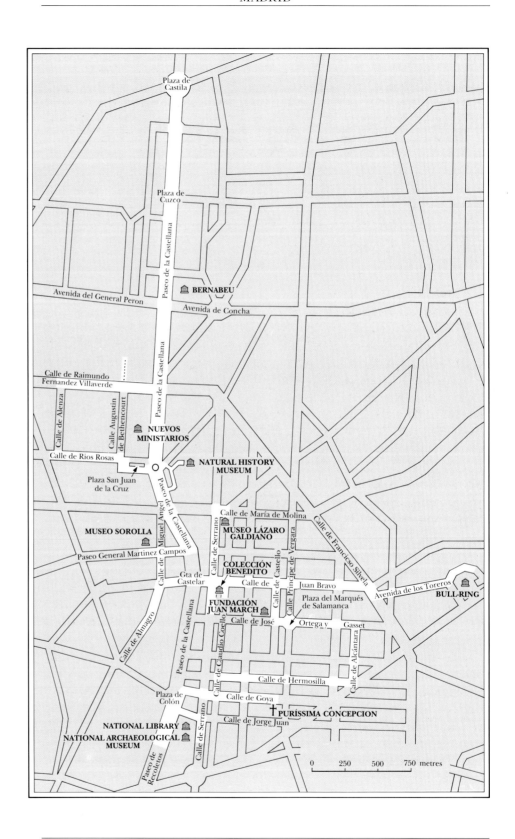

THE EXPANDING CITY

the last of the city's great literary cafés, and a place through which most of the recent protagonists of Spain's cultural and intellectual life have passed.

The Café Gijón, situated in between the calles de Prim and del Almirante, was founded in 1888 by Gumersindo Gómez, who came from the Asturian town of Gijón, but had accumulated his money while working as a young man in Cuba. His establishment soon attracted a distinguished clientele, among the earliest of whom were Pérez Galdós, José Canalejas and the pioneering neurologist Ramón y Cajal. The veiled Mata Hari entered the café in 1914 to ask for a *peppermint frappé* while in the 1920s the place was the scene of *tertulias* frequented by such poets as the brothers Antonio and Manuel Machado, Rubén Darío, García Lorca and Rafael Alberti, and by the painter of sultry Andalusian women Julio Romero de Torres, who had a studio off the nearby Calle de Fernando VI. But the café's heyday came after the Civil War, when, with the closure of El Pombo and other such celebrated institutions, it became the city's unrivalled literary café, rejected only by Hemingway, who once refused to go in on the grounds that he hated all literary *tertulias*, and that the people who attended them were just 'a load of show-offs'. The *tertulias* were not just literary ones, however, for there were daily discussion groups of every conceivable kind, from those attended by painters to others frequented by army officers, the café forming a neutral territory where political and intellectual differences could be absorbed. The playwright Buero Vallejo, one of the bright hopes of Spanish drama in the post-war years, recently talked to me of the Gijón in those years, and, while standing in the café itself, was able to point out the very tables where each of these various groupings had sat. The most significant of the various coteries was the group of young artists and writers known as *Juventud Creadora*, among whose members was the Nobel Prize-winning novelist Camilo José Cela. It was at the time of his daily visits to the Café Gijón that Cela wrote one of the most controversial and influential novels of the early Franco years, *The Hive* (1951), an episodic work centred on a Madrid café and dealing with the petty hopes and aspirations of the many who gravitated in its orbit.

The present decoration of the Café Gijón, a large and gilded mirrored space, with red-plush seating around the walls, and wooden chairs and tables in the middle, dates from the refurbishment of 1948, the main survival of the original institution being the elaborate clock under which Galdós is reputed to have sat. Under the management for many years of the white-haired men known as 'the two Pepes', and with an appropriately dignified and long-serving staff, the café is still haunted today by many of its habitués of the past, although the majority of those who came here now are either businessmen who enjoy the elegant setting or else tourists who have heard of the café's former reputation as a meeting-place for artists and writers. Gone forever are the days when aspiring writers from the provinces, such as Francisco Umbral, made the café the base from which – in the words of González Ruano – they set out 'to conquer the Puerta del Sol'.

The Marquis of Salamanca, whose grandiose palace is one of the main adornments of the eastern side of the Paseo de Recoletos, was one of the most flamboyant and successful of Madrid's conquerors from the provinces. 'He was', wrote his biographer and apologist the Count of Romanones, 'above all a conqueror of wealth. To conquer wealth, to create it, to amass a fortune, seems rather brutal and even prosaic, but this is not the case when the achievement is that of a genius ...' Born in Málaga in 1811, the son of a distinguished doctor, he became actively involved in liberal politics, and fell in love in Andalusia with the future herione Mariana Pineda, whose execution for having sewn a Liberal flag was to inspire in the 1920s a famous play by Lorca. He settled in Madrid in 1837, and through various financial ventures ranging from banking to speculating in the projected Aranjuez railway, soon became one of the wealthiest men in the city, as well as the first person in Spain to have a private bathroom. According to Romanones, his 'ostentatious life-style did much to break the monotony and miserliness which then reigned in Madrid', and he encouraged the hitherto easy-going Madrilenians to 'indulge furiously in speculation on the Stock Market', and to spend their money lavishly rather than to horde it. However, his use of inside knowledge to speculate in government securities led in 1845 to financial ruin and a brief period of exile in France. Returning to Madrid in 1849, he quickly remade his fortune, but was forced to flee Spain again in 1854, when, after a series of financial scandals associated with the liberals, Carlists sacked his house, and destroyed his gold-plated private railway coach. A remarkable survivor, Salamanca was soon back in Madrid and sufficiently wealthy again to bring to completion his palace on the Paseo de Recoletos, where he hung a remarkable art collection which included works by Goya, Breughel and Van Dyck, as well as some of the first paintings by El Greco to enter private hands. The revolutionary events of 1868 to 1874, combined with massive financial investment in what is now the 'Barrio de Salamanca', led to his third and final financial ruin, from which he never fully recovered. After what he described as 50 years 'without a single day of rest or for taking breath', he died in 1883 in a surburban retreat which has now become enveloped by the ugly sprawl of modern Carabanchel.

Salamanca's palace, an Italianate structure in a verdant enclosure at number 10 Paseo de Recoletos, was extended in the early years of this century, since when it has served, appropriately enough, as the headquarters of a bank. You are now on the edge of a district which bears Salamanca's name, but, before heading off into the heart of it, you should walk to the northern end of the Paseo de Recoletos, where you will find, to your right, an enormous neo-classical block dominated by a columned and pedimented frontispiece. The largest building conceived during the reign of Isabel II, it was begun in 1865 and completed in time for the celebrations in 1892 commemorating the fourth centenary of the discovery of America. The part of the building overlooking the Paseo de Recoletos houses the gloomy halls of Spain's national library, while its eastern wing, entered from the Calle de Serrano, is taken over by the MUSEO ARQUEOLÓGICO NACIONAL which was founded by Isabel II in 1867. The museum's extensive collections, worthily displayed in an old-fashioned but lacklustre setting, cover Spain's archaeology from prehistoric times up to the medieval period, and even include rooms devoted to ancient Egypt, Etruria, Greece, and the Middle East. Among the greatest treasures are the finds from Roman Spain, and, above all, such fascinating testimonies of ancient Iberian civilization as the three bejewelled and impassively staring female heads known as the *Damas* of Elche, Baza and Cerro de los Santos.

Immediately to the north of the building is the Plaza de Colón, the western side of which is dominated by a series of tall modern blocks, one of these housing the exceedingly tacky wax-works museum, where lovers of bad taste can enjoy – for a considerable fee – a wax tableau depicting Romero de Torres painting *La Piconera*, a crudely suggestive canvas featuring a young woman stirring the ashes of a brazier. The eastern side of the square is bordered by the large verdant space known as the Gardens of the Discovery, above which soars a neo-gothic monument of 1885 commemorating Columbus. Contained below the gardens are a car park, the airport bus terminal, and a cultural centre, the entrance to which is startlingly marked by a wide and powerful fall of water shooting out mysteriously from underneath Columbus's monument.

Heading east from here along the busy Calle de Goya, you enter the great grid of Salamanca, a succession of smart but interminable blocks where you could easily lose your sense of orientation. On the Calle de Goya itself, the one monument to break the monotony is the church of the PURÍSSIMA CONCEPCIÓN, a turn-of-the-century neo-gothic structure with art nouveau elements. A tall open-work spire, flanked by angels and garishly lit at night, gives consider-able drama to the building's exterior, but the interior is more theatrical still, thanks to the pierced star-shaped vault above the crossing, a work inspired by that of Burgos Cathedral. The building is a popular meeting-place for the conservative and elegantly dressed people who make up a large proportion of the Salamanca district's population, as is the ground-floor cafeteria of the American-style drugstore known as California, which stands on the other side of the street, at number 47, Recently revamped in a style which could be described as a cross between a Moroccan souk and a New York hamburger joint, California exposes itself to the street with a huge and outwardly sloping glass frontage, the upper half of which shields a high-tech bar eerily flooded with red light.

Madrid's high temple to modern design is to be found one block to the north, at the junction of the calles de Hermosilla and de Claudio Coello. Known as Teatriz, this is a bar, restaurant and night-club which has been created inside the former Teatro Beatriz by the Frenchman Philippe Starck, one of the most fashionable designers of today. The bar table, a free-standing transparent block lit from inside, has been placed at the centre of the stage,

One of the few neo-gothic monuments in Madrid: the interior of the church of the Purissimá Concepcion derives from Spanish medieval architecture.

which, apart from the addition of an enormous mirror, has otherwise been left largely untouched, complete with original stage mechanism and a back wall of unadorned brick. The restaurant tables cover the floor of the former auditorium, which is cut off at the back by a massive fall of drapery parted in the middle to reveal a glimpse of an upstairs bar, from which you can peer at those eating and drinking below. You are made conscious all the time of taking part in a spectacle, and you cannot even descend into the reddish-blue penumbra constituting the washrooms without escaping from onlookers, who marvel here at the curious marble slabs over which water pours as your foot

A shaded avenue in the wealthy residential district of Salamanca.

touches a button. The exorbitantly-priced Teatriz, with its crowds of *yuppís* and *pijos* (the spoilt young rich), is an institution more typical of Barcelona than it is of Madrid, and those in search of a cheaper, friendlier and more authentically Madrilenian experience should head towards the eastern end of the Calle de Hermosilla, where at number 99, you will find the old-fashioned night bar called El Avión. Comprising a dark, narrow, and smoke-filled room, it serves cheap beer accompanied always by bowls of *pipas* or sunflower seeds, the husks of which are spat out on to the ground. The main attraction of the place is the gaunt and pallid septuagenarian pianist known to everyone as

Don César. Although a winner at the age of fifteen of a national piano competition, he has devoted the greater part of his life to playing on the modest piano of El Avión, thumping out, with a cigarette constantly on his lips, the lively and heart-warming Madrilenian melodies of old.

Three blocks further north of the Calle de Hermosilla is the Salamanca district's central artery, the Calle de José Ortega y Gasset, which is usually referred to by its former and shorter name of the Calle Lista. At its exact centre is a round intersection named after the man whom Galdós considered the most fitting symbol of his age, the Marquis of Salamanca himself, a statue of whom crowns the traffic island in the middle. One block to the west, near the junction of the calles de Padilla and de Castelló, is the smoothly rounded marble and glass block forming the FUNDACIÓN JUAN MARCH, situated in a garden adorned with sculptures by Eduardo Chillida and other modern masters. March, a Catalan businessman who had spent time in prison for embezzlement, atoned for his past misdemeanours by presenting to the people of Madrid this remarkable cultural centre, where leading exhibitions of modern art can be seen free of charge, accompanied by excellent catalogues and posters at giveaway prices. Round the corner, at number 38 Calle de Padilla, rises a palatial residential block of the 1920s, with pedimented windows and coats of arms. This was the home of the poet and Nobel Prize-winner Juan Ramón Jímenez, who is commemorated here by a stone inscription carved with a copy of a lyrical homage of his to the expanding modern city of Madrid.

Continuing north along the Calle de Castelló you come to the broad, landscaped Calle de Juan Bravo. If you were to go to its eastern end and then continue east along the Avenida de los Toreros you will reach Madrid's splendid neo-Moorish BULL-RING, an enormous brick structure built between 1929 and 1932, and containing an excellent museum devoted to the sport. Madrilenians, like Hemingway, claim that this ring is the most beautiful in Spain, and that the best fights in the country are put on here, though the people from Seville would heavily dispute this. Ignoring this taurine distraction and heading instead west along the Calle de Juan Bravo, you will pass, at the junction of the Calle de Velázquez, the elaborate iron-work gates surrounding one of the grandest of this district's turn-of-the-century mansions, a lightly-coloured neo-baroque building originally the home of the marquises of Amboage, and now the Italian embassy. Further west you cross the Calle de Claudio Coello, where, just to the south, at number 91, you will find a plaque marking the site of the apartment block where the Galician-born Camilo José Cela lived immediately after the Civil War. The long plaque records that he wrote here his first collection of poetry, his first short story, and, more importantly, his first novel, *The Family of Pascual Duarte* (1942), a work of sensationalist realism which gave rise to the literary movement known as *Tremendismo*. Cela, who fought for Franco in the Civil War but was frequently in trouble with the authorities afterwards, is a man

The bull-ring of Las Ventas is the largest in the world after that of Mexico City.

who has always loved to shock and criticize. However, the poem of his quoted on the plaque shows him in one of his rare complimentary moods:

> *Madrid*
> *Gateway of Friendship*
> *Chamber of Wisdom and of Genius*
> *Granary of the most diverse situations*
> *And of the most extravagant adventures.*

It is difficult to know in which of these categories should be placed the COLECCIÓN BENEDITO, which is situated at number 4, Calle de Juan Bravo. One of the least known of Madrid's art galleries, it comprises an extensive series of canvases by the Valencian painter Manuel Benedito Vives (1875–1963), and can be visited by prior application. You will be greeted at the forbiddingly austere entrance portal by the diminutive Doña Vincenta Benedito, one of the artist's nieces and a woman who is convinced that her uncle's work deserves a position in the 'Chamber of Wisdom and of Genius'. The building itself was originally his home, though Doña Vicenta had to sell off most of it to create the enormous space constituting this museum, the walls of which are covered all over with a dark-green velvet such as you might find in a seedy night-club or on the lid of an extravagant box of chocolates. The artist himself, now almost entirely forgotten in Spain, enjoyed a considerable success in his day, as a landscapist, genre-painter, and above all, as a society portraitist. His works, ranging from the slick to the embarrassingly kitsch, have an undeniable nostalgic charm, though perhaps their primary value is to make you appreciate the more the genius of his teacher Joaquín Sorolla, whose museum is one of the forthcoming attractions of this itinerary.

Immediately to the west of the Colección Benedito the Calle de Juan Bravo intersects with the busy Calle de Serrano, which marks the western limits of the Salamanca district. If you were to head south down this street you would pass a crowded series of shops and banks, as well as the turn-of-the-century block at number 72 where the composer Manuel de Falla lived between 1901 and 1907. His fourth-floor flat here was the scene every Saturday night and Sunday afternoon of lively meetings with his piano-playing friends, but its principal claim to fame is for having been the place where Falla composed *La Vida Breve*. The northern end of the Calle de Serrano has a quieter and more spacious character, and you should make a detour along it to visit the MUSEO LÁZARO GALDIANO, which stands in a garden at number 122, occupying a tall classical-style building of the early years of this century. This was originally the private residence of Don José Lázaro Galdiano, who named it the Parque Florido in honour of his Argentine wife, Doña Paula Florido. The museum, inaugurated in 1954 following extensive remodelling, consists entirely of Lázaro's remarkably varied collections of the fine and applied arts, among the richest and most extensive amassed by a Spanish private collector. Arranged on four floors around an elaborate staircase well, this place is Madrid's answer to London's Wallace Collection, with sculptures and gold-framed paintings displayed in settings crammed with furniture, suits of armour, fans, medals and a plethora of other objects. The paintings include Flemish and Spanish primitives, works by El Greco, Goya and Murillo, and – reinforcing the snobbish eighteenth-century pretensions of the whole place – portraits by Reynolds, Gainsborough, Allan Ramsay, Raeburn and John Hoppner. Among the high points, if you can find them, is a self-portrait by Pedro Berruguete, a *St John on Patmos* by Bosch, a version of a well-known portrait by Velázquez of Góngora, and a *Portrait of Saskia* by Rembrandt. The great marvel of the applied arts collections is an exquisitely engraved goblet which belonged to Philip II's mad cousin, Rudolph II of Prague.

West of the Calle de Serrano the Calle de Juan Bravo merges into a broad overpass which spans the Paseo de la Castellana. In the squalid spaces below this construction is to be found what is euphemistically referred to as the Open-Air Sculpture Museum, an apparently haphazard collection of monumental sculptures by modern masters such as Joan Miró, Julio González and Josep María Subirachs. Next to one of the piers on the western side of the Castellana is a large bronze by Henry Moore, miserably sited and almost universally ignored. Continuing west on the Calle de Eduardo Dato, you enter the district of Chamberí, which was built at the same time as that of Salamanca, and has much the same character, if rather less of the latter's monumental uniformity. Almost immediately beyond the Castellana, you

Hieronymous Bosch's St John on Patmos. *Although relatively restrained by the artist's standards it is filled with enigmatic details.*

will see to your right the beautiful neo-Moorish palace of the Instituto de Valencio de Don Juan, while shortly afterwards comes the intersection commemorating the Nicaraguan poet and diplomat Rubén Darío, who worked in the nearby Nicaraguan embassy. This is the area of Madrid with the greatest number of embassies, a particularly large concentration being found around the Calle de Almagro, which runs south from the Glorieta de Rubén Darío. The Philippines embassy occupied until recently the magnificent French-style mansion built between 1899 and 1902 for the dukes of Santo Mauro (the main entrance is at number 36 Calle de Zurburán). In 1991 this building was transformed into Madrid's most luxurious hotel, the Hotel de Santo Mauro, the chandeliered and dazzlingly bright interior of which features a stylish restaurant built into a library which is still lined with leather-bound books.

The Calle de Miguel Angel runs north of the Glorieta de Rubén Darío, soon reaching the Paseo del General Martínez Campos, where you will find on turning left the much-altered building at number 8 which once housed the Institución Libre de Enseñanza. This experimental educational establishment, founded in 1876 by Francisco Gíner de los Ríos, came to be associated with most of the leading members of the Generation of 98, and paved the way for the Residencia de los Estudiantes, which we shall shortly be visiting. On the other side of the street, nearer the junction with the Calle Miguel Angel, is the MUSEO SOROLLA, a charming house at number 37 built after 1910 for the painter Joaquín Sorolla. Born in Valencia in 1863, Sorolla studied in Rome and Paris, and later received first prize in the Paris Universal Exhibition of 1900. By 1910 he was at the height of his fame, fêted not only throughout Europe but also in America, where he received the prestigious commission to decorate the library of the Hispanic Society of New York with a series of large canvases representing all the regions of Spain. The latter commission occupied him for over eight years, and he had only just finished it when he suffered a hemiplegia, dying soon afterwards, in 1923. Two years later his widow, who features in so many of his paintings, left the house and much of its contents to the nation.

As with the Danish artists Anders Zorn and P. S. Kroyer, with whom he can closely be compared, Sorolla was a painter who went very much out of fashion after his death, and it is only in recent years that he has begun to enjoy a revival in popularity, aided in his case by the bogus description of him as the 'Spanish Impressionist'. His art, which owed little if anything to that of the French Impressionists, evolved from the late nineteenth-century obsession with painting large-scale figure scenes in the open air, a tradition popularized by the French painter Bastien-Lepage. Sorolla shared the general concern of the time with vanishing rural traditions, but was at his best when painting member of his family in sunlit settings observed near his seaside home near San Sebastián. His virtuosity, even if degenerating on occasion into mere slickness, was also responsible for creating effects of invigorating freshness.

ABOVE *The garden of the painter Sorolla's former home, recalling exotic scenes of the south of Spain.*

OPPOSITE *The Glorieta de Emilio de Castelar, with the superimposed prisms of Rafael de la Hoz's Seguros Catalana Occidente building.*

Whatever your opinion of his works, however, you should make every effort to visit his house, if only to recover from the Madrid sun and traffic by sitting in the cool Moorish-style garden. The ground-floor rooms, where the studios are situated, have been left very much as they were in the artist's time, with Sorolla's paintings jumbled together amidst the ceramics, jewellery and other objects that he compulsively collected in the course of his extensive travels around Spain. A particular delight is the dining room, which Sorolla decorated with an illusionistic frieze of cornucopia and smiling members of his family. A gallery of his works from his student days onwards has been arranged in the upper rooms, while a changing selection of his vivid oil and other sketches can be seen in the tasteful modern extension outside.

From the Museo Sorolla you should head east back to the Paseo de la Castellana, rejoining this grand thoroughfare at the monumental Glorieta de Emilio Castelar, centred on Benlliure's stone and bronze memorial to the nineteenth-century politician. An especially striking group of modern blocks are to be found around this *glorieta*, the most recent of which, at the entrance to the Paseo del General Martínez Campos, is Federico Echevarría's BANCO DE EUROPA building, an irregularly shaped structure, with rounded corners and an overall dark-blue glow. An earlier building by Echevarría, with post-modernist elements such as a false upper arcade, houses the offices of the Compañía Hispánica on the opposite side of the Castellana. Next to this, and most impressive of all, is Rafael de la Hoz's headquarters of the Compañía de Seguros Catalana Occidente, a tall, suspended block of exceptional lightness, magically composed of two superimposed prisms. Heading north up the Paseo de la Castellana, you will shortly pass to your left, at number 61, the La Caixa building, another arresting structure, conceived in this case as an inverted chrome pyramid dripping with icicle-like formations. Further up, on the right-hand side, verdant slopes support a long, domed pavilion built as the centrepiece of the 1881 Exhibition of Industry and the Arts, and subsequently transformed into the city's natural history museum. The interior of this neo-renaissance building has recently been radically revamped, but in a way which gives prominence to the tall ironwork columns of the original structure, the whole providing an appealingly elegant post-modernist setting in which large elephants and other stuffed animals can happily roam.

The young Luis Buñuel spent a year working at the MUSEO DE CIENCIAS NATURALES under the guidance of a world-famous orthopterist, Ignacio Bolívar, thanks to whom he was able to boast in later life of a gift for identifying insects at a glance and giving their Latin names. Buñuel was living at the time in the RESIDENCIA DE LOS ESTUDIANTES, which lies immediately behind the museum, spread out over what Juan Ramón Jímenez referred to as 'the hill of poplars'. Owing to a line of dreary modern buildings in front of it, the Residencia is hidden today from the Castellana, and there are many Madrilenians who think that this legendary institution of the interwar years has long since disappeared.

Founded in 1910 by Alberto Jiménez Fraud, a visionary educationalist and anglophile, the Residencia was transferred to its specially built quarters on the 'hill of poplars' in 1915. Intended as a progressive cultural and scientific centre, it took as its model the campus of an English university, and had cheap residential quarters for students and teachers, as well as laboratories, lecture-halls, and a theatre. The Residencia played a vital role in the intellectual life of Spain, and acted as a point of contact between the Generation of 98 and the budding Generation of 27, a place where the likes of Juan Ramón Jímenez, Unamuno and the Machado brothers could exchange ideas with budding young talents such as Rafael Alberti and García Lorca. Buñuel described the Residencia as a place where 'you could study any subject you wanted, stay as long as you liked, and change your area of speciality in mid-stream.' Some idea of its intellectual range can be had from the list of distinguished foreigners who were invited to lecture here in the interwar years, among whom were such diverse talents as Albert Einstein, Walter Gropius, Marinetti, Le Corbusier, Louis Aragon, Bergson and Marie Curie. Moreover, thanks to the creation by Jiménez Fraud in 1923 of the Hispano-English Committee, this list included a particular large number of English speakers, such as G. K. Chesterton, J. M. Keynes, H. G. Wells, Lutyens and Howard Carter, the discoverer of Tutankhamen.

After the Civil War, the Residencia, with its strong Republican sympathies, was put to other uses. Its theatre was turned into a church, and the balconied laboratory building known as the '*Transatlántico*' was even converted into a home for an Egyptian sultan. In recent years, however, the place has been revived, and its tall but homely brick buildings – one of which was scaled by the athletic Buñuel – serve today for a wide range of cultural events, as well as a residence both for a select group of young artists, writers and scientists, and for visiting academics from abroad. Its present directorship is determined to bring back some of the institution's former intellectual character, and is also slowly restoring the buildings and surrounding gardens to their original state. The now ruined *Transatlántico* will be rebuilt to house a García Lorca foundation, and there is even talk of pulling down the modern structures that block the view towards the Castellana. In the meantime you can see the charming 'Garden of the Poets', laid out by Rámon Jímenez in the space between the wings of the main block, and also – inside this block – the room and piano used by Lorca and his friends for musical evenings. Not least you can read the lively account of the place featured in Buñuel's autobiography, which, apart from relating the antics of his friends Dalí and Lorca, includes a famous anecdote about Alfonso XIII suddenly appearing outside Buñuel's window to ask directions. Buñuel, taken by surprise, obsequiously addressed the king as '*Majestad*', and realized only afterwards that he had forgotten to remove his hat. Thus the honour of an anarchist was saved.

Across the Paseo de la Castellana from the Museo de Ciencias Naturales begins the stately Calle de Ríos Rosa, where, at number 54, you will find the

The Azca urbanization, with Yamasaki's Torre Picasso in the foreground.

austere apartment block where Camilo José Cela lived between 1949 and 1954, writing in those years his great novel of Madrilenian life, *The Hive*. Near the top of the street, at number 21, is another of the outstanding turn-of-the-century structures by Velázquez Bosco, this one the Academy of Industrial Engineers, and distinguished on the outside by huge ceramic murals by Daniel Zuloaga. Returning to the Paseo de la Castellana and continuing north along this thoroughfare you will skirt to your left the enormously long, de Chirico-like arcading guarding the forecourt of the NUEVOS MINISTERIOS. The deep recesses of this arcading provide today a convenient hiding-place for lovers, while the inhumanly sized complex behind it now houses three ministries. Conceived during the last years of Primo de Rivera's dictatorship, it was given its monstrous scale and bleak severity under Franco, whose equestrian statue stands on its southern side. The northern side of the complex overlooks the broad Calle de Raimundo Fernández Villaverde, the upper end of which is dominated by a characteristically fantastical structure by Antonio Palacios, the HOSPITAL DE MAUDES. Built in the second decade of the century as a hospital for the poor, it later fell into disuse, and has only recently been startlingly transformed inside for use as office and library space for the Comunidad de Madrid. Planned in the shape of a large cross, it presents a variegated profile of turrets and pinnacles, the whole being sometimes described as in a 'Windsor' style. The overall effect is in fact distinctly ghoulish, and the coarse detailing and textured stone give the building the look of something taken from either a zoo or a horror film. The chapel, on its northern side, is now a parish church, worth visiting for its lurid stained glass.

In terms of sheer numbers of skyscrapers, the Paseo de la Castellana reaches its architectural climax immediately to the north of the Calle Raimundo Fernández Villaverde, in the area to your left known unappealingly as the Azca Urbanization. Shopping arcades, teenage discothèques, cafeterias, restaurants and brash offices are centred here around a futuristic space called the JARDINES PICASSO, the dominant monument of which – the highest building in Madrid – is the TORRE PICASSO, a sleek white structure built in 1988 by the Japanese architect Minoru Yamasaki. The northern boundary of the Azca Urbanization is marked by the Avenida del General Perón, where you can admire, at the junction with the Paseo de la Castellana,

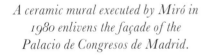

A ceramic mural executed by Miró in 1980 enlivens the façade of the Palacio de Congresos de Madrid.

PALACIO DE CONGRESOS DE MADRID

a colourful large mural by the Catalan artist Miró. On the other side of the Paseo de la Castellana is a monument of interest both to football and architectural enthusiasts, the Santiago Bernabeu Stadium, a building dating back to the late 1940s, but given a dramatic concrete casing in 1982, when this home ground for Real Madrid became the main stadium for the World Cup.

Beyond the Santiago Bernabeu Stadium the sense of architectural exhilaration which accompanies you for so much of the Castellana begins to diminish, the great thoroughfare planned by Bigador in 1944 reaching its uninspired conclusion in a large intersection dominated by an appropriately dreary monument to the right-wing politician Calvo Sotelo. From here, the Plaza de Castilla, it is a short walk to the modern railway station of Chamartín, which for many travellers represents their first and last glimpse of Madrid. Let me leave you instead near the international airport of Barajas, a journey involving a huge leap to the east, across the dual carriageway of the M30 and into what in Cela's day was one of the 'villages of the Outer Belt'. The concluding lines of Cela's novel, '*The Hive*' are those of an unfortunate young man laughing to himself as he reads the later expression in a newspaper. "'Ha, ha! The villages of the Outer Belt. What a funny expression! The villages of the Outer Belt!'". As you alight at the metro station of Canillejas, the last stop on line six, you might indeed feel that I am having a joke at the reader's expense as you find yourself confronted by a sad group of modern blocks facing a motorway junction and an apparently endless vista of wasteland. And now you must enter this wasteland, using the footbridge in front of you to cross the A-2, and head north-east from here along the narrow Paseo de la Alameda de Osuna. Small encampments of gypsies can be seen, and there are even flocks of sheep grazing in front of modern warehouses. However, the quiet shaded road which you are following is a vestige of an aristocratic past, for it leads to what was once one of the finest summer residences in the vicinity of Madrid.

This residence, known as EL CAPRICHO DE OSUNA, dates from 1783 and was the creation of one of the most powerful Spanish women of her age, the Duchess of Osuna. She built the place in a way which was clearly intended to impress her two main rivals at the Court, the Duchess of Alba and Queen María Cristina, both of whom she far outstripped in the range and depth of her cultural and intellectual interests. A francophile who preferred speaking French to Spanish, she invited to El Capricho numerous musicians, actors and academicians from Paris, and assembled here a renowned library of works in French translation. It is for its park, however, that El Capricho is best remembered today, and for this the Duchess secured the services of the designer of the Petit Trianon gardens at Versailles, Pierre Mulot, who was contracted to the Duchess on the understanding that he would work for no one else in Spain. The laying out of the park continued into the nineteenth century, the work being taken over by a Spanish theatre designer called Tadey. El Capricho experienced its Indian summer under the 10th Duke of

Osuna, who inherited the property in 1844 and died heirless and bankrupt in 1882, after a lifetime given almost wholly to the pursuit of pleasure.

After numerous changes of ownership, El Capricho was acquired by the Municipality of Madrid in 1974, which is attempting at present to restore the palace and its park back to their former glory. The elegant neo-classical palace, with traces inside of Pompeian-style frescoes, was commandeered during the Civil War as the headquarters of the Republican defence of Madrid led by General Miaja. The large underground bunker which Miaja built next to it still survives, and there is talk of turning this evocative labyrinth into a Republican Civil War monument to counteract the gruesome office of General Moscardó in Toledo. Beyond '*El Bunker*' extends a classical French parterre, offering views to the south of a recently replanted maze. A large 'English garden' lies further on, its undulating verdant slopes covered with a wonderful range of follies, including a miniature citadel from which an automaton dressed as a soldier once fired gun salutes, accidentally killing a gardener on one occasion. A winding river, spanned by the first iron bridge in Spain leads from the citadel to a boating lake, where you will find a charming boat-house built in wicker and painted inside with illusionistic landscapes. From here boating parties of costumed guests once set off on their journey to a neo-classical ballroom, passing on their way an island adorned with a monument to the 3rd Duke of Osuna. The culminating folly is a half-timbered and quaintly rustic cottage, through the windows of which could formerly be seen automatons of peasants at work. Though the mechanical peasants have gone, the days when aristocrats pursued dreams of rural simplicity spring back to life as you enter the cottage's magical interior, with its balustrade made from the branches of a tree, and its delightful illusionistic decoration of kitchen utensils, dangling pimentoes, rows of washing, and old prints pinned to the walls.

Madrid is the gateway to the skies. This is the gist of a much quoted saying which has been reduced in the language of bumper stickers to the enigmatic words, '*De Madrid al Cielo*'. The saying takes on a particular appropriateness as you stand in the grounds of El Capricho, brought back to reality by the constant sounds of planes from Barajas airport, barely a mile away. 'From Madrid to the Skies, and from the Skies a telescope to look back at Madrid'. Sometimes, on leaving Madrid from Barajas airport, I have tried to catch a glimpse of El Capricho from the ascending plane, but the site, like so many of this city's attractions, remains obstinately hidden, lost in an urban sprawl which in turn disappears, absorbed by a crumpled arid landscape of intimidating proportions.

OPPOSITE *The formal French gardens at the entrance to the park of El Capricho de Osuna.*

Appendices

....

CHRONOLOGY OF EVENTS • RULERS
ARTISTS • OPENING TIMES

CHRONOLOGY OF EVENTS

939 First documented reference to Madrid, at the time a Moorish fortress called Magerit.

1083 Madrid captured from the Moors by Alfonso VI of Castile and Leon.

1309 Madrid chosen for the first time as a meeting place of the Cortes (parliament) by Ferdinand IV.

1469 The marriage of Isabella of Aragon to the future Ferdinand V of Castile paves the way for a unified Spain.

1492 Granada, the last Moorish stronghold is captured, and Ferdinand and Isabella are rulers of the whole of Spain.

1516 Charles I, son of Joanna the Mad, who is unfit to rule, succeeds to the throne on the death of the regent, his grandfather Ferdinand V; Charles, founder of the Hapsburg dynasty in Spain, the ruling house until 1700, becomes Holy Roman Emperor (as Charles V) in 1519.

1556 Charles abdicates in favour of his son Philip II.

1561 Philip II declares Madrid to be his 'only court'.

1563 Escorial begun.

1605 Cervantes publishes the first part of Don Quixote.

1607 Philip III declares Madrid the capital of Spain, making official the position it has enjoyed since 1561.

1700 Charles II dies without an heir, bequeathing throne of Spain to Philip Duke of Anjou (a grandson of Louis XIV of France), who becomes King as Philip V; discontented at this extension of French power results in the War of the Spanish Succession, which lasts until 1713 and in which many European powers, including England, are involved.

1759–88 Reign of Charles III, one of Spain's most prosperous periods; he does much to beautify and improve Madrid.

1808 Charles IV abdicates in favour of his son Ferdinand VII, but Ferdinand is forced by Napoleon to return the crown to Charles, who grants it to Napoleon, who in turn installs his brother Joseph Bonaparte as King; an uprising in Madrid against the French is bloodily suppressed.

1808–14 The Peninsular War fought by Britain, Portugal and Spanish guerillas against the French, who are decisively beaten by the Duke of Wellington at the Battle of Vitoria in 1813.

1813 Ferdinand VII restored to the throne.

1819 Prado opened to the public.

1868 Isabella II abdicates and a constitutional monarchy is proclaimed.

1873 Amadeus of Savoy, chosen king in 1870, abdicates and a republic is formed but is unsuccessful.

1874 Alfonso XII becomes King and restores Bourbon line.

1902 Alfonso XIII assumes full authority on his 16th birthday (he had been King since birth, having been born after his father's death).

1914–18 Spain stays neutral during First World War.

1931 Alfonso XIII abdicates and the Second Republic is established.

1936–39 Spanish Civil War, in which the Second Republic was overthrown and the right-wing Nationalists, led by Franco, defeated the left-wing Loyalists (Republicans); the war ended with the capture of Madrid, a siege of 29 months.

1939 Franco becomes dictator.

1939–45 Spain remains technically neutral during Second World War but supports Germany.

1969 Franco names Juan Carlos, grandson of Alfonso XIII, as his successor.

1975 Franco dies; Juan Carlos becomes King.

1981 An attempted right-wing military coup collapses after the personal intervention of Juan Carlos.

1982 Socialist party wins national elections, giving Spain its first left-wing government since before the Civil War.

1992 500th anniversary of the completion of the Christian reconquest of Spain and of Columbus's discovery of America.

RULERS

Rulers of Castile from 1035, when it gained independence from Navarre, until 1516, when Charles V established the Habsburg dynasty. Several of the early kings also ruled Léon for all or part of their reigns before the two kingdoms were permanently united in 1230 under Ferdinand III.

Ferdinand I	1035–65	Philip IV	1621–65
Sancho II	1065–72	Charles II	1665–1700
Alfonso VI	1072–1109	Philip V	1700–46
Urraca	1109–26	Ferdinand VI	1746–49
Alfonso VII	1126–57	Charles III	1759–88
Sancho II	1157–58	Charles IV	1788–1808
Alfonso VIII	1158–1214	Ferdinand VII	1808
Henry I	1214–17	Joseph	
Ferdinand III	1217–52	Bonaparte	1808–13
Alfonso X	1252–84	Ferdinand VII	1813–33
Sancho IV	1284–95	Isabel II	1833–68
Ferdinand IV	1295–1312	Francisco	
Alfonso XI	1312–50	Serrano y	
Peter the Cruel	1350–66	Dominquez	
Henry II	1366–67	(regent)	1869–70
Peter the Cruel	1367–69	Amadeus	1870–73
Henry II	1369–79	Estanislao	
Juan I	1379–90	Figueras	
Henry III	1390–1406	(president)	1873
Juan II	1406–54	Nicolás Salmerón	
Henry IV	1454–74	y Alonso	
Isabel I and		(president)	1873
Ferdinand V of		Emilio Castelar y	
Aragón	1474–1504	Ripoll (prime	
Joanna the Mad		minister)	1873–74
(with co-ruler		Alfonso XII	1874–85
Philip I)	1504–16	Alfonso XII	1886–1931
(then regent		Niceta Alcalá	
Ferdinand V)	1506–16	Zamera	
Charles I (Holy		(president)	1931–36
Roman		Manuel Azaña	
Emperor		(pesident)	1936–39
Charles V)	1516–56	Francisco Franco	
Philip II	1556–98	(chief of state)	1939–75
Philip III	1598–1621	Juan Carlos I	1975–

ARTISTS

Bayeu, Francisco (1734–95) Spanish painter, the teacher and brother-in-law of Goya: Casita del Príncipe; Pardo Palace; Royal Palace.

Benlliure, Mariano (1862–1947) Spanish sculptor, responsible for many of Madrid's monuments: Alfonso XII monument; Alvara de Bazán monument; Goya monument; María Cristina monument; Pantheon of Illustrious Men.

Bosch, Hieronymus (c. 1450–1516) Netherlandish painter, admired and collected by Philip II: Museo Lázaro Galdiano; Prado.

Chillida, Eduardo (b.1924) Spanish abstract sculptor: Buen Retiro Park; Fundación Juan March.

Churriguera, family of Spanish architects and sculptors, of whom the most important was José Benito de Churriguera (1665–1725): former convent church of Las Calatravas; Royal Academy of San Fernando; San Cayetano.

Coello, Claudio (1642–93) Spanish painter, the leading painter in Madrid in the late seventeenth century: Convent of the Descalzas Reales: Convent of San Placido.

Fernandez, Gregório (c. 1576–1636) Spanish sculptor, one of the greatest masters of the painted wooden figure: Convento de la Encarnación; Convent of San Placido.

Giaquinto, Corrado (1702–65) Neapolitan decorative painter, active in Spain 1753–62: Convent of Las Salesas; Royal Palace.

Giordano, Luca (1639–1705) extremely prolific Neapolitan decorative painter, active in Spain 1692–1702: Casón del Buen Retiro; Church of Las Comendadoras; El Pardo.

Gómez de Mora, Juan (1586–1646/8) Spanish architect, the most prolific in Madrid in the early 17th century: Capitanía General; Casa de la Villa (Town Hall); Casita del Príncipe; Convento de la Encarnación; Court Prison; Plaza Mayor; Retiro Palace; San Antonio de los Portugueses.

Gonzalez Velázquez, Isidro neoclassical Spanish architect: 2nd May Obelisk; Teatro Real (Opera House).

Goya, Francisco de (1746–1828) Spanish painter and engraver, one of the greatest European artists of his era: College of Escolapian Fathers; Museo Lázaro Galdiano; Museo Municipal; Museo Romántico; Prado, Royal Academy of San Fernando; San Antonio de Florida; San Francisco el Grande.

Greco, El (1541–1614) Cretan-born artist (his real name was Domenikos Theotocopoulos and his nickname means 'the Greek') who settled in Toledo in 1577 and became the first great painter of the Spanish School: Museo Lázaro Galdiano; Prado, San Ginés.

Gutiérrez Soto, Luis (1900–) Spanish architect: Air Ministry; Museo Chicote.

Herrera, Juan de (1530–97) Spanish architect, whose strong, solemn, severe style won official approval during Philip II's reign: Casa de las Siete Chineneas; Royal Palace.

Madrazo, Federico (1815–94) Spanish painter, mainly of portraits, a member of a distinguished family of artists: Museo Romántico; Palacio de Liria.

Mengs, Anton Raffael (1728–79) German painter, active in Spain 1761–9 and 1773–7, an artist important as one of the pioneers of Neoclassicism: Casita del Principe; Palacio de Liria; Royal Palace.

Murillo, Bartolomé Estebán (1617/18–82) Spanish painter mainly of religious subjects appealing to popular piety; his work was enormously popular in the 18th and early 19th centuries and endlessly copied and imitated: Museo Lázaro Galdiano; Prado.

Palacios, Antonio (1876–1945) the outstanding Spanish architect of the early 20th century: Bellas Artes Building; Hospital de Maudes; Post Office Building.

Picasso, Pablo (1881–1973) Spanish painter, sculptor, graphic artist and designer, the most illustrious artist of the 20th century: Casón del Buen Retiro, Royal Academy of San Fernando.

Ribera, José de (1591–1652) Spanish painter, active in Naples (a Spanish possession at the time): Convento de la Encarnación; Prado.

Ribera, Pedro (c. 1683–1742) the most prolific architect of the early 18th century in Madrid, working in a lavishly ornamented Baroque style: Barracks of the Conde Duque; Fuente de la Fama; Hospicio of San Fernando; Mariblanca Fountain; Palace in Calle de Las Huertas; palace in Carrera de San Jerónimo; portal in Calle de La Magdalena; promenade and hermitage, Paseo Virgen del Puerto; San Cayetano; San José; Toledo Bridge.

Rodriguez, Ventura (1717–85) the leading Spanish architect of the late 18th century: Convento de la Encarnación; fountains in Paseo del Prado; Palacio de Liria, San Isidro, San Marcos.

Rubens, Sir Peter Paul (1577–1640) Flemish painter and designer, one of the greatest and most influential artists of the 17th century; he twice visited Spain – in 1603–4 and 1628–9 – and became friendly with Velázquez: Convent of the Descalzas Reales; Palacio de Liria; Prado.

Sabatini, Francesco (1722–97) Italian architect, active in Spain from 1760, the favourite architect of Charles III: Centro Cultural Reina Sofia; church of Las Comendadoras; Customs House; Palacio de Liria; Puerta de Alcala; San Francisco el Grande; tombs of Ferdinand VI and Barbara of Braganza, Convent of Las Salesas.

Sacchetti, Giovanni Battista (1700–64) Italian architect who was called to Madrid in 1736 to continue work on the Royal Palace, for which his master Filippo Juvarra (1678–1736) had made designs: Royal Palace.

Tacca, Pietro (1577–1640) Florentine sculptor: statues of Philip III (completion of work by his master Giambologna) (1529–1608) and Philip IV.

Tiepolo, Giambattista (1696–1770) the greatest Italian painter of the 18th century: he settled in Madrid in 1762 at the invitation of Charles III: Royal Palace.

Titian (c. 1485–1576) Venetian painter, one of the supreme artists of the 16th century; Charles V and Philip II were among his most important patrons: Palacio de Liria; Prado.

Toledo, Juan Buatista de (d. 1576) Spanish architect: Casa de las Siete Chimeneas; Convent of the Descalzas Reales.

Velázquez, Diego (1599–1660) the greatest of all Spanish painters, one of the supreme geniuses in the history of art: Museo Lázaro Galdiano; Prado.

Velázquez Bosco, Ricardo (b.1843) Spanish architect: Academy of Mining Engineers; Casón del Buen Retiro; Ministry of Agriculture.

Villaneuva, Juan de (1739–1811) Spain's outstanding Neoclassical architect, brother of the architect Diego de Villeneuva (1715–74), who published a book attacking the Churrigueresque style in 1766: Casa de la Villa (Town Hall); Casita del Príncipe; Observatory; Oratory in Caballero de Gracia; Plaza Mayor; Prado; Royal Academy of History; Teatro Espanol.

Zuluoga, Daniel late 19th-century Spanish ceramicist, noteworthy for his decoration of the buildings of Ricardo Velázquez Bosco: Academy of Mining Engineers; Ministry of Agriculture.

Zurbarán, Francisco de (1598–1644) Spanish painter, mainly of powerful, sombre, religious works: Prado; Royal Academy of San Fernando; San Francisco el Grande.

OPENING TIMES

Most of the principal churches are open at standard hours, but depending on the times of services when they are closed to tourists. All hours of opening, including some of those given in the following list, are periodically liable to alteration (winter hours, too, often differ from summer), and it is always advisable, therefore, to check before planning a visit.

Armería, see Palacio Real.

Casa de Lope de Vega, Calle de Cervantes 11: daily 11.00 a.m. to 6.00 p.m.; public holidays 10.00 a.m. to 2.00 p.m.; closed 1 August to 15 September.

Cason del Buen Retiro, Calle Felipe IV: Monday–Saturday 1.00 a.m. to 2.00 p.m. and 5.00 p.m. to 9.00 p.m.; Sunday 1.00 a.m. to 2.00 p.m.

Convento de las Descalzas Reales, Plaza de las Descalzas Reales: guided tours only: Monday to Thursday 10.30 a.m. to 1.30 p.m. and 4.00 p.m. to 6.00 p.m.; Friday to Sunday 10.30 a.m. to 1.30 p.m.

Convento de la Encarnación, Plaza de la Encarnación: daily 10.00 a.m. to 1.00 p.m. and 4.00 p.m. to 6.00 p.m.

Museo Arquelógico Nacional, Calle Serrano 13: daily 9..30 a.m. to 1.30 p.m.; closed 1 January, Maundy Thursday, Good Friday, 1 May, 24 June and 25 December.

Museo Cerralbo, Calle Ventura Rodríguez 17: daily except Tuesday 9.00 a.m. to 2.00 p.m.; closed August.

Museo del Ejército, Calle Méndez Núñez 1: daily except Monday, 10.00 a.m. to 2.00 p.m.

Museo Español de Arte Contemparáneo, Avienda Juan de Herrera: Tuesday to Saturday 10.00 a.m. to 6.00 p.m.; Sunday 10.00 a.m. to 2.00 p.m.

Museo Lázaro Galdiano, Calle de Serrano 122: daily 9.15 a.m. to 1.45 p.m.

Museo Municipal (Hospicio de San Fernando), Calle de Fuencarral 78: daily except Monday 10.30 a.m. to 1.30 p.m.

Museo del Prado, Paseo del Prado: summer Tuesday to Saturday 10.00 a.m. to 6.00 p.m.; Sunday and public holidays 10.00 a.m.to 2.00 p.m.; winter Tuesday to Saturday 10.00 a.m. to 3.00 p.m.; Sundays and public holidays as summer; closed 1 January, Good Friday, 1 November and 25 December.

Museo Romántico, Calle San Mateo 13: daily 11.00 a.m. to 6.00 p.m.; public holidays 10.00 a.m. to 2.00 p.m.; closed from 1 August to 15 September

Palacio Real, Plaza de Oriente: summer 10.00 a.m. to 1.30 p.m. and 4.00 p.m. to 6.15 p.m.; Sunday and public holidays 10.00 a.m. to 1.30 p.m.; winter 10.00 a.m. to 12.45 p.m. and 3.30 p.m. to 5.45 p.m.; Sunday and public holidays as above. Because of its use for royal and official functions, parts or all of the Palacio Real are liable to be closed to the public at short notice, so check before planning a visit.

Real Academia de Bellas Artes de San Fernando, Calle de Alcalá 13: daily 10.00 a.m. to 2.00 p.m.

Real Oficina de Farmacia, see Palacio Real.

San Antonio de la Florida, Paseo de la Florida: summer: Monday, Tuesday and Thursday to Saturday 10.00 a.m. to 1.00 p.m. and 4.00 p.m. to 7.00 p.m.; Sunday 10.00 a.m. to 1.00 p.m.; closed Wednesday; winter: Monday, Tuesday and Thursday to Saturday 11.00 a.m.to 1.30 p.m. and 3.00 p.m. to 6.00 p.m.; Sunday 11.00 a.m. to 1.30 p.m.; closed Wednesdays.

Glossary of Terms

....

Alcázar A Moorish word for a palace or fortress.

Art Deco A fashionable style of architecture and design in the 1920s and 1930s, characterized by geometrical shapes and stylized natural forms.

Art Nouveau Style of architecture and decoration flourishing from about 1890 to the First World War; it was characterized by sinuous, asymmetrical lines, reminiscent of twining plant tendrils.

Attic Storey In classical architecture, a low subsidiary storey above the main entablature of a building.

Baldacchino A canopy (often highly elaborate) over an altar or other hallowed object.

Balustrade An ornamental railing supported by balusters (decorative posts).

Baroque A style of art and architecture prevalent in the 17th and 18th centuries, characterized by emotional rhetoric and a dynamic sense of movement; in Spain, Baroque art is often notable for its extremely lavish decoration.

Barrel vault A vault shaped like the roof of a tunnel (it is indeed sometimes called a tunnel vault). A cross vault (or groin vault) is produced when two barrel vaults intersect at right angles.

Basilica A term applied to churches built on the same plan as Roman basilicas (meeting halls) – rectangular with long internal colonnades – and also, in a different sense, to certain churches that enjoy special papal privileges; more loosely, the word can be applied to any church that is especially large, important or venerable.

Bay A major, repeated vertical division of a building (exterior or interior); a church NAVE, for example, is said to have four bays when there is a series of four arches and four windows on each side.

Blind arcade A range of arches (arcade) attached to a wall as a decorative motif.

Chapter house A building attached to a cathedral or abbey in which the administrative body (chapter) of the church holds its meetings.

Chinoiserie The evocation or imitation of Chinese styles in European art, particularly popular in decoration in the 18th century.

Choir stalls Sets of seats, in major churches often magnificently ornamented, for the choir and officiating clergy.

Churrigueresque A lavish style of architecture and ornament named after the Churriguera family and highly popular in Spain in the 18th century.

Classical architecture A very general term covering all styles of architecture that use the forms and decorative treatments established in ancient Greece and Rome; it is subdivided into more specific styles such as Baroque and Neoclassicism.

Classicism Aesthetic attitudes and principles based on the art of Greece and Rome.

Cloister A covered walkway around the walls of buildings opening onto a quadrangle; cloisters are particularly associated with monasteries.

Console A decorative bracket, used to support an architectural or sculptural feature, such as a bust.

Corinthian see Order.

Cornice A decorative horizontal projection running along a wall or other surface, in particular the top element of an entablature.

Costumbrista A writer of novels with a strong local flavour.

Cross vault see Barrel Vault.
Cupola A dome, particularly a small decorative dome.
Custodia A receptacle for holy objects, specifically for the consecrated bread or water of the Eucharist.

Doric see Order.
Dormer window A window projecting from the slope of a roof.

Eclecticism The selection and combination of artistic ideas from varied sources.
Entablature In classical architecture, a group of three horizontal decorative bands (architrave, frieze and cornice) surmounting a column or group of columns.

Falange Spanish Fascist movement founded in 1933; it was the only legal political party in Spain under the Franco regime but was abolished in 1977.
Fictive A word meaning 'false' or 'assumed' applied typically to painted decoration that is intended to deceive the spectator into thinking it is of some expensive material such as marble.
Flamboyant A style of late Gothic architecture, originating in France and characterized by flamelike ('flamboyant') decorative forms.
Frontispiece A large, highly ornamented or otherwise striking entrance feature on the façade of a building.
Functionalism A doctrine that design (particularly of buildings) should be determined solely by function, rather than by decorative considerations, and that anything perfectly designed for its purpose will be inherently aesthetically pleasing; it has been an influential (but often arid) creed in 20th-century art.

Giant column or order see Order.
Gothic The style of architecture predominant in the late Middle Ages (very roughly 1200–1500); its most obvious characteristic is the use of pointed arches.
Greek cross A cross in which the four 'arms' are of equal length (as opposed to a Latin cross, in which one arm is appreciably longer than the others); the term is often used in referring to church plans with four equal arms meeting in a central area.

Maja A Spanish belle of the lower class, a popular type in art and literature.
Majo A Spanish dandy of the lower class, a popular type in art and literature.
Mannerism A movement in art that originated in Italy in about 1520 and spread throughout Europe in the 16th century; it was characterized by exaggerated elegance and flourished particularly at sophisticated courts.

Manolo An alternative term for majo – a lower-class dandy.
Minaret A tall slender tower of a mosque, with a balcony from which a crier called a muezzin summons the faithful to prayer.
Mudéjar A term applied to Moors who were allowed to remain in Spain after the Christian reconquest and to the style of architecture they practised.

Nave The western (and usually longest) 'arm' of a typical cross-shaped church, leading from the enclosure to the crossing, where the four arms meet: more specifically, the term can be applied to the central part of the arm when it is flanked by aisles.
Neo A prefix meaning 'new' used in art and particularly architectural writing to describe styles (especially those of the 19th century) that consciously revive features of earlier periods as in neo-Baroque, neo-Churrigueresque, neo-Gothic (an alternative name is Gothic Revival), neo-Rococo, neo-Romanesque.
Neoclassicism A major movement in European art and architecture in the late 18th and early 19th centuries in which the farms and spirit of Greek and Roman art were revived.
Netsuke A small toggle, often elaborately carved in ivory, used in Japan to fasten articles to the sash of a man's kimono (traditionally this garment had no pockets).

Oratory A place for prayer, particularly a small private chapel.
Order In classical architecture, a unit or system of design based on the type of column used. Each order consists of the column plus the entablature it supports and its pedestal (if any). The three main types – becoming progressively slimmer and more decorative – are called Doric, Ionic and Corinthian. The orders were regarded as the heart of classical architecture and their proportions and detailing were studied and codified with great care. A giant (or colossal) order (or giant column) is one that rises through two or more storeys.

Pier An architectural term for any masonry support that is more substantial than a column or pillar.
Pilaster A flat pillar projecting only slightly from a wall; pilasters are usually decorative rather than structural.
Plateresque A style of Spanish arhitecture of the early 16th century characterized by a medley of extremely lavish applied ornament (the word means 'silversmith-like' and suggsts that the delicacy of the ornament seems more typical of metalwork than of stone).
Polychrome A term meaning 'many-coloured', applied particularly to statues that have been painted in more or less naturalistic colours. Spain has an extremely rich tradition of polychromed wooden sculpture.

Portico A porch with a roof supported by columns.
Presbytery The part of a church in which the high altar is situated.
Proscenium arch In a traditional theatre, the arch that frames the stage and separates it from the auditorium.

Relief Sculpture that projects from a background surface.
Reliquary A receptacle for keeping or displaying holy relics.
Renaissance An intellectual and artistic movement based on the revival ('Renaissance' means 'rebirth')of the values of ancient Greece and Rome; it began in Italy in the 14th century and spread throughout Europe.
Romanticism A movement in European art, literature and music characterized by an emphasis on the free expression of personal feelings.
Rotunda A circular building, particularly one with a dome.
Rustication Stonework with a roughly textured surface or cut with deep channels between the blocks, often used on lower storeys of a building to convey a feeling of massive strength.

Sacristy A room in or attached to a church housing sacred vessels and vestments.
Salmonica A column with a twisted shaft, like a stick of barley sugar, a common feature in Spanish Baroque art.

Saloon A large room in a palace or other grand building for receptions, entertainment and so on.
Stucco A kind of light, easily moulded plaster used for sculpture and architectural decoration (both external and internal).
Surrealism A movement in art and literature, flourishing mainly in the 1920s and 1930s, marked by a fascination with the bizarre, the irrational and the workings of the subconscious mind.

Transepts In a cross-shaped church, the two short 'arms' that run across and at right angles to the main arms; occasionally a church has more than one pair of transepts.
Trompe l'œil A painting (or part of a painting) that is intended to deceive the spectator into thinking (if only momentarily) that it is a real object rather than a two-dimensional portrayal of it; the term is French for 'deceives the eye'.

Vault An arched roof or ceiling, particularly one built of stone or brick.

Zarzuela A Spanish traditional form of opera or musical comedy with spoken dialogue.

Further Reading

....

Barea, Arturo, *The Forging of a Rebel*, London, 1972.

Borrow, George, *The Bible in Spain*, London, 1842.

Boyd, Alastair, *The Companion Guide to Madrid and Central Spain*, London, 1986.

Brown, Jonathan, and Elliot, J. H., *A Palace for a King: the Buen Retiro and the Court of Philip IV*, London, 1980.

Cela, Camilo José, *The Hive*, London.

Chanon Berkowitz, *Perez Galdós, Spanish Liberal Crusader*, 1948.

Chueca Goitia, Fernando, *Madrid and Toledo*, London, 1972.

Epton, Nina, *Madrid*, London, 1964.

Erskine, Steuart, *Madrid, Past and Present*, London, 1922.

Kany, C. E., *Life and Manners in Madrid, 1750–1800*, 1932.

Lyall, Archibald, *Well Met in Madrid*, London, 1960.

Perez Galdós, *The Spendthrifts* (transl. Gamel Wolsey), London, 1951.
—— *Miau* (transl. J. M. Cohen), London, 1963.
—— *Fortunata and Jacinta* (transl. Agnes Moncy Gullón), London, 1987.

Thomas, Hugh (ed), *Madrid: A Travellers' Companion*, London, 1988.

Index

....

References to illustrations appear in italics, after the text references